*The Cambridge Introduction to the*
## Nineteenth-Century American Novel

Stowe, Hawthorne, Melville, and Twain: these are just a few of the
world-class novelists of nineteenth-century America. The
nineteenth-century American novel was a highly fluid form, constantly
evolving in response to the turbulent events of the period and emerging
as a key component in American identity, growth, expansion, and the
Civil War. Gregg Crane tells the story of the American novel from its
beginnings in the early republic to the end of the nineteenth century.
Treating the famous and many less well-known works, Crane discusses
the genre's major figures, themes, and developments. He analyzes the
different types of American fiction – romance, sentimental fiction, and
the realist novel – in detail, while the historical context is explained in
relation to how novelists explored the changing world around them.
This comprehensive and stimulating introduction will enhance students'
experience of reading and studying the whole canon of American fiction.

Gregg Crane is Associate Professor of English at the University of
Michigan.

# Cambridge Introductions to Literature

This series is designed to introduce students to key topics and authors. Accessible and lively, these introductions will also appeal to readers who want to broaden their understanding of the books and authors they enjoy.

- Ideal for students, teachers, and lecturers
- Concise, yet packed with essential information
- Key suggestions for further reading

The Cambridge Introduction to the
# Nineteenth-Century
# American Novel

GREGG CRANE

CAMBRIDGE
UNIVERSITY PRESS

CAMBRIDGE UNIVERSITY PRESS
Cambridge, New York, Melbourne, Madrid, Cape Town, Singapore, São Paulo

Cambridge University Press
The Edinburgh Building, Cambridge CB2 8RU, UK

Published in the United States of America by Cambridge University Press, New York

www.cambridge.org
Information on this title: www.cambridge.org/9780521603997

First published 2007

Printed in the United Kingdom at the University Press, Cambridge

A catalogue record for this publication is available from the British Library

Library of Congress Cataloguing in Publication data
Crane, Gregg D. (Gregg David)
The Cambridge Introduction to the Nineteenth-Century American Novel / Gregg Crane.
    p.   cm. – (Cambridge introductions to literature)
Includes bibliographical references and index.
ISBN-13: 978-0-521-84325-6 (hardback)
ISBN-10: 0-521-84325-1 (hardback)
ISBN-13: 978-0-521-60399-7 (pbk.)
ISBN-10: 0-521-60399-4 (pbk.)
1. American fiction – 19th century – History and criticism.   2. Literary form – History –
19th century.   3. Literature and history – United States.   4. Popular literature – United
States – History and criticism.   5. National characteristics, American, in literature.
I. Title.   II. Series.
PS377.C73   2007
813'.409 – dc22
2007014638

ISBN 978-0-521-84325-6 hardback
ISBN 978-0-521-60399-7 paperback

*For Robert David Crane and Barbara Gregg Crane*

# Contents

## Acknowledgments

For their counsel and encouragement, I am indebted to Sara Blair, George Bornstein, Jonathan Freedman, John Kucich, Kerry Larson, Robert Levine, Dianne Sadoff, and Eric Sundquist. I also wish to express my gratitude for the many thoughtful revision suggestions made by John Whittier-Ferguson and Samuel Otter. From the book proposal through to final revisions, Ross Posnock and Cindy Weinstein have generously helped me with indispensable advice and critique. Leslie Ford deserves special thanks for her meticulous and insightful appraisal of the manuscript. And I want to acknowledge and thank my daughter, Zoe, for our ongoing conversation about the ingredients of a good story.

While writing this book, I have frequently found myself thinking about pedagogy and the alchemy of excitement and knowledge that characterizes good teaching. This train of thought always seems to conclude with some memory of my parents. Over the years, I have been in many classrooms but none more inspiring than those of my mother and father. I know of no better teachers.

# Introduction

Defining the novel is easy: it is a fictional prose narrative of substantial length. While one may question the distinction between fact and fiction or the requirement that the novel be written in prose, this simple definition seems generally apt, describing the books we commonly label as novels. It does not, however, say anything about why we read novels. A few key features accounting for the genre's appeal seem fairly plain. First, the novel lives and dies by its ability to create the fictional illusion of a complete world. This world may be highly realistic in the sense that it conforms closely to a recognizable historical moment, or it may be utterly fantastic. In either case, we must be able to see ourselves in it, imagine breathing its atmosphere and encountering its creatures and landscapes. Second, the reader must be driven to know what happens next, or, in all likelihood, he or she will put the book down. The other pleasures of the prose will probably not be sufficient to hold the reader in the absence of a compelling storyline and/or characters. Third, even if it is only to suggest the impossibility of finding meaning in art and experience, the narrative will have some significance beyond a mere recitation of characters and events. Stories of all types tempt us to connect them with explanations of larger meanings, values, and phenomena. Indeed, it is often impossible to explain such things without resort to stories (as any parent, lawyer, cleric, or scientist giving a public lecture can attest).

Having glanced at features shared by all novels, we should briefly consider a couple of traits apparently dividing the genre. First, while some novels are easily consumed, others obstruct our progress through the narrative. These "slower reads" are characterized by a density of description and/or complexity of plot and/or opacity of language resisting translation or paraphrase. Balking the reader's progress through a book of some length would seem to be a considerable risk. Why take that chance? Answers would probably vary, but it seems likely that the authors of these more taxing stories generally hope that their readers will feel that the extra work was rewarded by some deeper,

1

broader, or richer experience or some significance not otherwise available. Second, some novels overtly seek to push society in a particular direction. All artifacts, even those posing as pure entertainments, have some economic, material, psychological effect on society, but certain works of art are manifestly designed to advance social change, such as Harriet Beecher Stowe's *Uncle Tom's Cabin* (1852) or Upton Sinclair's *The Jungle* (1906). As a result of these differences, novels can be arrayed on a sliding scale of complexity or a gradient of social engagement, and, for some critics, complexity and social efficacy represent competing principles of literary appreciation (though we might well demur that this opposition of values is neither inevitable nor particularly coherent).

When compared to the elaborate structural and metrical requirements of certain poetic forms, such as the sestina or villanelle, the novel seems remarkably flexible. Open-ended and amorphous, it is capable of taking any number of particular shapes and drawing on a wide variety of formal elements. It is "plasticity itself," in Mikhail M. Bakhtin's words, "a genre that is ever questing, ever examining itself and subjecting its established forms to review" (39). As a highly plastic form, the novel readily receives the impress of historical change, and many scholars and theorists focus on historical change to define and locate the genre. In a well-known essay, Walter Benjamin distinguishes the novel from the earlier narrative form of storytelling. The term "storytelling" conjures the image of people sitting around a fire, listening to tales that have been told and retold over the ages. It is a communal occasion, a practice not a product. The novel, by contrast, is purchased or borrowed by the individual and consumed individually. The storyteller's oral tale invisibly weaves new or discrepant facts into a seamless and apparently unchanging web of tradition. Once such a tale is in print, however, discrepancies between different versions become apparent, and continuity is replaced by a sense of change (Benjamin 87).

In a similar vein, Northrop Frye, Claude Lévi-Strauss, Georg Lukács, Ian Watt, and Michael McKeon describe the novel as a modern replacement for the epic. Unlike the epic recounting the larger-than-life actions of heroic characters caught up in an archetypal and timeless drama, the novel resembles a newspaper or a history. Its dramas are time bound, and its characters are particular individuals rather than mythic types. The epic addresses universal issues and eternal conflicts, but the novel (even in its more fantastic formulations) describes specific causes and effects. Emphasizing social change, particular individuals rather than mythic types, and the concrete particularities of the world it describes, the novel is, as Georg Lukács says, "the epic of an age in which the extensive totality of life is no longer directly given, in which the immanence of meaning in life has become a problem, yet which still thinks in terms of totality" (56). The novel may be epic in scope (e.g., Tolstoy's *War and Peace* (1863–69) or Hugo's *Les Misérables* (1862)), but it uses grand conflicts, such as war and revolution, as a backdrop for its main concern – the smaller, more particular triumphs and defeats of specific and flawed individuals.

This account of the "rise of the novel" is propelled by a particular historical narrative. In this story, Western societies were once unchanging, primarily rural affairs in which the people shared bloodlines, religion, language, and culture, but things have changed. Modern society is highly volatile, primarily urban and industrial, and largely held together by either various forms of economic and political coercion or voluntary agreements. With the splintering of traditional society comes the alienation of the individual from society and the fracturing of the individual's identity (Lukács 66; Todorov 103). For Lukács, Watt, McKeon, and others, the novel is plainly marked by such momentous changes as the Reformation, the emergence of print culture, and the advent of mechanical reproduction, empiricism, and capitalism, as well as the rise of the middle class. The stream-like linear narrative of what happens to a character becomes a vital element of continuity in the novel's always-changing world. Whatever else changes, including the characters themselves, a measure of coherence and unity is furnished by the mere fact that the events of the narrative happen to or are observed by a particular set of individuals.

This intertwined narrative of Western history and the emergence of the novel can be easily extended into the American context. What Ian Watt describes as the novel's Protestant focus on the interior landscape of the individual's mind and its empiricist emphasis on a perspective in which the individual is responsible for his own scale of moral and social values can also serve as a sweeping description of the perspective of the American novelist (Watt 78–80, 12–22). Looking at the rise of the American novel, critics find an emphasis on notions of independence and beginnings. As Terence Martin puts it, the American novel seeks "to wipe the slate clean of European history and institutions (sometimes with festival energy) and thus establish the conditions for a national identity" (x). For William C. Spengeman, an appetite for discontinuity helps to define the national character of the American novel. The British novel, Spengeman contends, centers on the domestic scene as a source of social repose and continuity. Home "represents the unconditioned ground of man's being; the eternal unchanging place from which he has fallen into the world of time and change; the native land to which the exiled pilgrim longs to return so that he may be blessed" (71). American fiction, by contrast, is characterized by a competition between the poetics of adventure and the longing for domestic equilibrium (3, 69). Romances by Twain, Hawthorne, and Melville, he argues, embody both dreams, and "they prove just how irreconcilable the two visions are. For it is the failure of these abortive romances to recover the sheltering assurances of a home long since abandoned which confirms, finally and ironically, the lesson of the Romantic American adventure: we have made ourselves and our world and cannot go home again" (117).

Given the scale of the transformations characterizing the nation in the nineteenth century, it is not surprising to find critics focusing on change as a central theme in the era's fiction. By conquest, purchase, and treaty, the nation's land mass quadrupled. Its population grew from approximately 4 million to 76 million by 1900. It endured the bloodiest war in its history (at least 620,000 soldiers were killed in the Civil War, almost as many as in all other US wars combined) and the assassination of two presidents, Lincoln and Garfield (McKinley was assassinated in 1901). Bloody conflicts were waged with Native Americans, Britain, Mexico, and Spain. At its inception, the nation's economy was predominantly agrarian, and its society was chiefly rural. Barter and trade were still prevalent modes of economic exchange. By 1900, after undergoing an industrial revolution of its own, the United States produced 35 percent of the world's manufactured goods, more than the combined output of Germany, France, and Great Britain. The nation's population had relocated to urban centers. The slower agrarian economy had been replaced by heavy industry, the stock market, currency controversies, and boom and bust economic cycles, producing an astonishing number of bankruptcies, panics, and depressions as well as a staggering record of economic growth. As Melville put it in *Pierre* (1852), the fortunes of nineteenth-century "families rise and burst like bubbles in a vat" (13).

The book trade exemplified the rapid pace and thoroughgoing nature of the era's transformation. In the early republic, publishing was a small and primarily local affair. From these relatively rudimentary beginnings, the production and sale of printed material underwent a technological and commercial revolution in the first half of the nineteenth century. The advent of mechanized printing and improvements in papermaking, book binding, and improved means of shipping books (by new roadways, turnpikes, canals, and railroads) lowered the cost and greatly facilitated book production on an unprecedented scale. During the same period, the audience of literate readers grew. These and other factors resulted in the emergence of a mass market for printed materials of all kinds and the novel in particular. As Cathy Davidson and others have shown, novels attracted wide readership among both genders and across other social divisions (Davidson vii, 9–10). Where sales of a few thousand copies of a novel in the early republic would have been a dramatic success, by 1860 sales of hundreds of thousands of copies of a novel were not uncommon (Davidson 16–37; Gilmore 46–54).

Never homogeneous and always stratified by differences in wealth, religion, race, ethnicity, and gender, in 1790 the nation's populace included free and enslaved African Americans, different Native American tribes or nations, and people of English, Irish, Scottish, Welsh, German, Dutch, and French backgrounds. There were Anglicans, Congregationalists, Quakers, Presbyterians, Dutch and German Reformed, Lutherans, Mennonites, Catholics, Jews, and Baptists. This social picture would become considerably more diverse in the course of the nineteenth century, as the nation expanded into Texas, California, and the Southwest, and as wave upon wave of immigrants came to the US from England, Ireland, Wales, Germany, Scandinavia, China, Austria-Hungary, Poland, Russia, Romania, Italy, and Greece.

This growing, increasingly diverse, and often fractious society was characterized by a considerable degree of ferment, much of it violent, such as Shay's Rebellion of 1786–87, the Whiskey Rebellion of 1794, Nat Turner's Slave Rebellion of 1831, the Anti-Rent War of 1839, John Brown's raid on Harper's Ferry in 1859, the Draft Riots of 1863, the Haymarket Affair in 1886, the Homestead Strike in 1892, the Pullman Strike in 1894, as well as race riots and the rise of lynching following Reconstruction. Even a simple list of such incidents gives one a sense of the significant social divisions running through nineteenth-century American society. Reform movements, such as abolitionism, suffragism, the temperance movement, and the labor union, played a role in inspiring some of the period's tumult, and such arguments for reform did not go unopposed. Newspapers and politicians inveighed against the abolitionists and the nascent women's movement. Organized labor had to contend with increasingly powerful corporations, the Pinkerton Detective Agency (which played a central role in repressing the Homestead Strike and in infiltrating the Molly Maguires in 1875), hostile courts, and elected officials. Some Americans were convinced that the unlimited immigration of certain groups posed a threat to the nation (the antebellum Know-Nothing party and the Chinese Exclusion Act of 1882 were products of such xenophobia). But reformers also had victories, such as Reconstruction, the Civil War Amendments, Married Women's Property Acts, statutory regulations protecting the health and safety of workers, and the Sherman Antitrust Act. In the early part of the twentieth century, reformers succeeded in pushing through the federal Income Tax and the Nineteenth Amendment entitling women to vote. Reforms of a different sort included the Johnson-Reed Immigration Act of 1924 and eugenic sterilization laws.

American fiction could not help reflecting something of the turbulence of nineteenth-century life. The ups and downs were simply too dramatic to overlook or ignore. "In this republican country," Nathaniel Hawthorne wrote, "amid the fluctuating waves of our social life, somebody is always at the drowning point" (*Seven Gables* 35). Some novels directly engage in a cultural tug of war over whether or how to transform American society. For example, some vehemently call for the end of slavery; others stridently support the South's peculiar institution and reject the very notion of reform as contrary to the design of God and nature. Often the conflict is internal to the individual novel. Many nineteenth-century fictions simultaneously embrace and reject various forms of social mobility, such as the greater autonomy and freedom of women or the crossing of class, racial, or ethnic boundaries. At times, the era's fiction seems to desire a rational compromise or balance between change and stasis, freedom and order, being able to create or revise the society one inhabits and having to yield to certain traditional, natural, or divinely prescribed values and forms of association. At other times, it seems intent on plunging into the tides of change, come what may.

## The early American novel

The nation's earliest novels express considerable uncertainty about the coherence and stability of American society. How far would the ideal of self-rule be extended? What happens to the social order when each member of society is authorized to judge for him (or her?) self what is proper? The Revolution ostensibly represented a powerful endorsement of such autonomy. Ordinary people, according to republican political theory, are "the best Judges, whether things go ill or well with the Publick," for they are "the Publick," and "Every ploughman knows a good government from a bad one" (Wood 235). State a moral case to a ploughman and a professor, said Thomas Jefferson, echoing this line of thought, "the former will decide it as well, and often better than the latter, because he has not been led astray by artificial rules" (Wood 240). But this belief in the agency of the common folk to decide for themselves how to live licenses a considerable degree of social innovation. Is one really comfortable with the resultant movement and change? If not, what does the feeling of discomfort say about one's egalitarianism, one's faith in democratic principles such as self-rule? And how would one regulate or curb such revolutionary enthusiasm without betraying the principles authorizing the new republic?

For the person recalling the ringing endorsements of self-rule justifying the American Revolution, it is perhaps surprising to find that the very first American novels were seduction tales. In novels such as William Hill Brown's *The Power of Sympathy* (1789), Susanna Rowson's *Charlotte Temple* (1791), and Hannah Foster's *The Coquette* (1797), the exercise of independent judgment and the flouting of convention are criticized and dutiful obedience to established authorities is recommended.[1] The storyline of these tales is fairly straightforward – a young man seeks to conquer the virtue of a particular maiden. The young woman resists but ultimately succumbs to her own desire and/or to her beau's fraud or coercive measures. In each case, the romantic connection violates some norm of social and sexual propriety, and the affair results in disaster for both parties. In Rowson's *Charlotte Temple*, the eponymous heroine deviates from accepted social norms (instead of waiting for her parents' approval and patiently enduring a proper courtship, she elopes) only to be deceived and abandoned, dying pitifully after being briefly reunited with her father. Her lover Montraville lives but is tortured by the memory of the evil his cavalier disregard for social custom and sexual morality has wrought. Foster's independent and freedom-loving heroine, Eliza Wharton, dies with her illegitimate baby unattended by family and friends in a remote inn. Losing everything – his wife, his estate, and his good name – Eliza's lover, Peter Sanford, cautions, "Let it warn you, my friend, to shun the dangerous paths which I have trodden, that you may never be involved in the hopeless ignominy and wretchedness of Peter Sanford" (Foster 255). In Brown's *The Power of Sympathy*, Harriot and Harrington's love affair is doomed by the fact that she is the offspring of her mother's prior seduction by Harrington's father. When faced with the choice between incest and living apart, the lovers commit suicide. It is hard not to feel some retrenchment of revolutionary ardor in the fact that these first American novels feature disasters brought on by various breaches of convention.

But these tales do not simply recommend deferring to parental authority and the imperatives of tradition. They also voice many of the overt themes of the American Revolution: independence, freedom, and equality.[2] For example, Rowson plainly endorses the decision of Charlotte Temple's father to marry a poor but worthy girl in defiance of paternal instruction (18–21). And despite the fact that Brown's would-be rake, Harrington, pays lip service to social class, deeming Harriot too lowborn for marriage, he also expresses disgust at the spectacle of class prejudice: "INEQUALITY among mankind is a foe to our happiness . . . and were I a Lycurgus no distinction of rank should be found in my commonwealth" (11, 34). Hannah Foster condemns her heroine's coquetry, but she also appreciates Eliza's independence of spirit. When one female character defers to male authority in all things political, another responds, "'Miss Wharton and I,' said Mrs. Richman, 'must beg leave to differ from you, madam. We think ourselves interested in the welfare and prosperity of our country; and, consequently, claim the right of inquiring into those affairs, which may conduce to, or interfere with the common weal'" (139).

The founders' notion of an indwelling moral sense shared by the ploughman as well as the professor is the central theme of *The Power of Sympathy*. The epistolary form of Brown's novel, in effect, allows us to overhear Harrington planning his seduction of Harriot. He tells a friend that he intends to use the venerable lover's gambit of arguing that the lovers' natural passion should take precedence over mere social conventions: "Shall we not . . . obey the dictates of nature, rather than confine ourselves to the forced, unnatural rules of – and – and shall the halcyon days of youth slip through our fingers unenjoyed?" (14). Harrington's invocation of nature is a familiar one (recalling Andrew Marvell's "To His Coy Mistress"), but, in the revolutionary context, one is also reminded of the rebellious colonists' claim that their natural rights trump the hollow traditions of royal preeminence and authority. When Harrington's own innate feelings of sympathy prevent him from pursuing his illicit sexual ends, the connection between the seduction tale and the founding fathers' political philosophy comes to the fore. Faced with Harriot's implicit question, "because I am a poor, unfortunate girl, must the little I have be taken from me?," Harrington finds himself incapable of pursuing her seduction (14–15). His native compassion stops him from ruining Harriot. The founders' claims for the legitimacy of the Revolution and the propriety of self-government depended in part on the assumption of an inherent human ability to discern right from wrong by means of such feelings of sympathy.

The seduction novelists' belief in the capacity of the common man and woman for virtuous self-rule is manifest in the overt didacticism of their tales. If ordinary people were not capable of learning and using their own judgment, there would be no point in tutoring them by fictional or other means. Primarily justifying their fiction on the basis that it educates young women about the dangers of seduction, Brown, Rowson, and Foster also hope that their tales model the kind of fellow feeling that should animate and knit the commonwealth together. Because fiction can speak "the language of the heart," the novel's combination of educational material and gripping entertainment makes it uniquely useful to the education of a virtuous citizenry (Brown *Sympathy* 53). To advance this goal, these novelists are quite willing to sacrifice complexity, ambiguity, and irony. Thus, Rowson embraces the novel as a lesser art, which is redeemed by its potential moral instruction rather than its artistry:

> If the following tale should save one hapless fair one from the error
> which ruined poor Charlotte, or rescue from impending misery the
> heart of one anxious parent, I shall feel a much higher gratification in
> reflecting on this trifling performance, than could possibly result from
> the applause which might attend the most elegant finished piece of
> literature whose tendency might deprave the heart or mislead the
> understanding.  (L)

Given the presence of both more and less socially conservative views in these novels, we may well doubt that these tales are quite as simple and clear as Rowson and others claim, but it is nonetheless telling that these authors expressly conceived of their fictions as unvarnished moral lessons (Brown *Sympathy* 7, Foster 241).

For Brown, Rowson, and Foster, the educative function of fiction requires that characters, events, and emblems should be relatively transparent in their significance. For instance, when Charlotte's father meets the young woman who will become his bride, he sees that "a pellucid drop had stolen from her eyes, and fallen upon a rose she was painting. It blotted and discoloured the flower. 'Tis emblematic,' said he mentally, 'the rose of youth and health soon fades when watered by the tear of affliction'" (8). Emblems, for Rowson, should be pellucid, transparently communicating a clear and single meaning. The tears staining the painting cannot be permitted to improve it in some curious fashion, for that would obscure the meaning of the comparison of the painted rose and the young girl. If the painting became subtly more beautiful by the accident of the tears, the unforeseeable or the unknowable would be introduced into Rowson's consideration of suffering. Suffering might become something to be appreciated, even courted, and Rowson's depiction of Charlotte's suffering might be rendered ambiguous. Instead, the seduction tale wants to insist that the interpretive task before its characters and its readers (especially the young female reader) is to recognize the signs of moral character and reach correct conclusions about people and their intents. Thus, in *The Coquette*, Eliza is warned that Sanford is "a second Lovelace" and that she may wind up a second Clarissa if she is not careful (134).[3] Foster's equation of fiction and life assumes that real people as well as fictional characters are highly legible.[4]

However, the sheer frequency of the insistence that moral character is legible (e.g., that blushes offer indisputable evidence of Harriot's feeling for Harrington and Charlotte's feeling for Montraville or that Charlotte's features convey her unmistakable goodness) hints at a fear that some people will not be readable (Brown *Sympathy* 9, Rowson 3, 66, Foster 130, Ziff 17). This fear is plainly manifest in the figure of the rake, who uses fraud and disguise to deceive the young maiden and her friends. The prominence of anonymous or mysterious characters in these novels suggests a general apprehension that, as society becomes more fluid, it becomes increasingly obscure and undecipherable. The absence of a well-established and clear social context and well-known family histories creates the possibility of some rather nasty surprises: Harriot turns out to be Harrington's sister, Mademoiselle La Rue is not a proper young lady of impeccable virtue, and Sanford is not wealthy. Seduction novels hold up the value of legibility but acknowledge its frequent absence; as a consequence, their endorsement of independent judgment is hedged. Because she is incapable of reading Montraville, her suitor, or La Rue and Belcour, Montraville's confederates, Charlotte Temple must not rely on her own reason but must submit to parental authority and clear-cut traditional prohibitions.

Even if Charlotte were more experienced and skilled, interpreting such characters as Mademoiselle La Rue would be a considerable challenge given their mutability. La Rue approaches human connection as an entrepreneur speculating about the desirability of a particular asset and, consequently, her relations are entirely fungible (Rowson 60–1). Appalled by the shifting affections of La Rue and Belcour, Charlotte questions Montraville about Belcour's decision not to keep his word and marry La Rue. "Well, but I suppose he has changed his mind," Montraville says, "and then you know the case is altered" (65). Charlotte is horrified to realize that her romantic relation with Montraville is secured only by their continuing mutual affection and their ongoing consent to be with each other. Everything could change, and she could be replaced by another (of course, the stakes of this fungibility for Charlotte as a woman without other practical means of support are much greater than they are for Montraville [65]). What Charlotte wants and expects is a romantic relation that will be as pure and fixed as her relation to her parents. Instead of the frightening specter of an endlessly changing society held together only by temporary agreements based on shifting notions of self-interest, Charlotte wants what is freely chosen to ascend to the level of the given or ordained, which is what the founding fathers wanted the American Revolution to seem like – a choice made inevitable by certain fixed and inalienable principles and rights.[5] La Rue and Belcour, as their French names suggest, represent the excesses of the French Revolution, the pursuit of self-interest without restraint of divine norms or social traditions, which results ineluctably in a "vortex of folly and dissipation" (55). In *The Power of Sympathy*, the monstrous potential of consensual relations severed from the restraint of moral tradition can be felt in Harriot and Harrington's temptation to commit incest (Brown 86–7). Unalloyed with some other principle of regulation or restraint, consent will permit any form of human relation, including incest.

In Foster's novel, Major Sanford represents both the allure and the danger of this more volatile manner of existence. Unlike Eliza's "good" suitor, the Rev. Boyer, Sanford is, as he puts it, "a mere Proteus, and can assume any shape that will best answer my purpose" (121). This is part of Sanford's appeal to Eliza. The Rev. Boyer offers Eliza a calm and sedate life as a minister's wife; by contrast, Sanford represents the excitement and pleasure of variety, invention, and excess (118, 126, 135). And, despite the fact that such a response is not overtly sanctioned by the novel's sad outcome, contemporary readers are justifiably tempted to endorse the appetite for transformation and excitement manifest in Eliza's attraction to Sanford. Eliza's desire for moments of hilarity which engross every faculty and swamp reason can be seen as intimations that not all of experience can be neatly divided into either the good category of knowable and unchanging things or the bad category of unknowable and mutable things. Something of value may yet exist outside the bounds of rationality and balance. Permanence may turn out to be a prison, such as a marriage to the Rev. Boyer would surely have been for the spirited Eliza Wharton. In the seduction novels and other early American fiction, one ever feels a tension between the divergent attractions of stasis and metamorphosis. The image of a stable society operating by immemorial traditions and commonly held beliefs has its appeal, but so does the vision of a highly mutable society, constantly in motion, offering new opportunities and new conceptions of life.

For early Americans, the social transformation unleashed by the Revolution held great promise but it also raised important questions.[6] What would the nature of that change be? Would it go far enough? Would it go too far? Would it work in a genuinely positive direction? Or would it pervert society? Some feared that the old hierarchical social system would simply be replaced with another: "There are some among us who call themselves persons of quality," an early republican ranted, but these were really a sort of "mushroom gentry" – fakes aping a displaced aristocracy (Wood 241). The use of the phrase "mushroom gentry" strikes a curious note in a republican diatribe. Literary precedents, such as Ben Jonson's *Every Man Out of his Humour* (1599) and Henry Mackenzie's *The Man of Feeling* (1771), use the figure of "mushroom gentlemen" to express a fear that social hierarchy will be undermined by upstarts and impostors infiltrating the upper class, not a concern that such distinctions will be erected. In *Kelroy* (1817), Rebecca Rush (niece of Benjamin Rush, a signer of the Declaration of Independence) worries, in this more conservative vein, that the social mobility authorized by the Revolution will substantially erode the quality of American society. She describes a disreputable character named Marney as a gentleman "of the mushroom sort" who "can pop up in a night's time out of the dirt nobody can tell how." He is the antithesis of the gentleman who has "come of a decent old stock, that has been growing some time" (149). In *Modern Chivalry* (1792–1815), Hugh Henry Brackenridge uses the figure of the gourd to similar effect:

> In the natural world there is a gradation in all things. Animals grow to their size in a course of years; trees and plants have their progress; Jonah's gourd might spring up in a night by a miracle; but in general all productions of nature have a regular period of increase. The attainments of men are made to depend upon their industry. As ye sow, so shall ye reap. (222)

In the context of the new republic, the sudden, insubstantial, and unwholesome growth of the mushroom or gourd represents the threat of swift and unmerited change. Brackenridge would permit upward movement but only at a slow pace warranting the genuineness of the social improvement. To elect the ignorant Irish servant, Teague O'Regan (*Modern Chivalry*'s version of Sancho Panza), to the legislature without the incremental progress of education would be a monstrous perversion of democracy, and, by requiring education, Brackenridge can respect the egalitarian ideals of the Revolution and retain the meritocratic ideal of awarding leadership roles to those best able to lead: "Genius and virtue are independent of rank and fortune; and it is neither the opulent, nor the indigent, but the man of ability and integrity that ought to be called forth to serve his country" (21). For Brackenridge, gradualism offers a way to marry egalitarianism and a hierarchical social structure.

The novelistic form Brackenridge uses in *Modern Chivalry*, the picaresque, is particularly well suited to a consideration of the pros and cons of social mobility. The hero of the picaresque is usually in constant motion, traveling geographically and socially and crossing boundaries of both kinds. Propelled by coincidence, the string of adventures making up the narrative are connected only by the fact that they happen to the protagonists rather than by any notion or requirement that one scene build or necessarily lead to the next, and this episodic freedom allows the author to explore the widest array of social milieus and settings. The genre's appeal derives in large part from the reader's taste for a series of reversals in which the main characters are alternatively raised up and brought low by the hand of fate. For example, in *Fortune's Foot-Ball* (1797), James Butler tells of the ups and downs of Mercutio, who escapes one catastrophe only to be threatened by another. Involving a series of romantic adventures and such perils as sea battles, the Algerian slave trade, and the British impressment of sailors, the novel moves forward by a series of adverse accidents – "the kicks of fortune" – but also by the kindnesses of strangers and friends. Charles helps Mercutio, Mercutio and Charles help George, George helps Mercutio and Lenora, George and Mercutio help Eugenio escape with his beloved Terentia, and so on. The net effect of these compassionate gestures is to valorize sympathy as the proper foundation of community and to emphasize the importance of community to the individual's well-being. Butler's wild tale ends in a series of happy marriages, and this felicitous conclusion removes some of the metaphysical significance of the reversals and turmoil Mercutio and the other main characters have endured. Despite his many reversals of fortune and his experiences of different cultures, Mercutio remains highly conventional, so conventional in fact that he and his beloved Isabella do not share a bed after their Roman Catholic marriage because Mercutio is aware that that ceremony would not satisfy the Church of England (II, 186). They happily renew their nuptial vows in an Anglican ceremony at the end of the novel, signifying the enduring force and stability of social traditions in the face of even radical changes in circumstance.

In his narration of the comic adventures of the patrician Captain Farrago and Teague O'Regan, Brackenridge takes social mobility a bit more seriously, wondering whether or how society might genuinely be changed by individual reversals of fortune. Unflinchingly bold in his ignorance and relentlessly opportunistic, Teague has a series of brief successes as a fashionable man about town, a popular actor, a tax collector, the King of the Kickapoo Indians, and a scientific exhibit at the American Philosophical Society. Part of the comedy of Teague's career derives from the fact that he never really changes. He is always the same ill-educated "bog-trotter." Yet, while Teague's assumption of fitness for any and all positions and roles is ludicrous, even potentially dangerous, as Farrago points out, there is something appealing in the energy and sheer tenacity of the Irishman. His irrepressibility is charismatic. As Christopher Looby points out, Brackenridge is drawn to Teague's ability to "maneuver socially between contexts, to imagine himself crossing boundaries and transgressing hierarchies, and to express himself intelligibly in social contexts for which his upbringing and education did not fit him" (255).

Beneath Brackenridge's laughing and satiric depictions lie both a genuine concern about unchecked social mobility and an appreciation of the vitality and insight contributed to the new republic by common people striving to better their condition.[7] At one point, the good Captain urges that each member of society ought to keep to his/her place, declaring "Every thing in its element is good, and in their proper sphere all natures and capacities are excellent . . . Let the cobbler stick to his last" and "There is nothing makes a man so ridiculous as to attempt what is above his sphere" (11, 14). But Farrago also speaks out against the notion that birth and breeding determine who should have power and hold sway in society:

> Do we not find that sages have had blockheads for their sons; and that blockheads have had sages? It is remarkable, that as estates have seldom lasted three generations, so understanding and ability have seldom been transmitted to the second . . . I will venture to say, that when the present John Adamses, and Lees, and Jeffersons, and Jays, and Henrys, and other great men, who figure upon the stage at this time, have gone to sleep with their fathers, it is an hundred to one if there is any of their descendants who can fill their places. Was I to lay a bet for a great man, I would sooner pick up the brat of a tinker, than go into the great houses to chuse a piece of stuff for a man of genius. (7–8)

In Teague's ambitious antics and Farrago's kindly but critical responses, Brackenridge creates a synecdoche for the dual pressures shaping and informing American democracy – the upward force of those seeking to advance and the downward exertions of those seeking to regulate the lower orders. At times, Brackenridge agrees with Duncan, a Scotsman, who observes, "Every thing seems to be orsa versa here: the wrang side uppermost" (267). But he also appreciates the nutritive potential of the conflict between the "multitude" and the "patrician" class:

> There is in every government a patrician class, against whom the spirit
> of the multitude naturally militates: And hence a perpetual war; the
> aristocrats endeavoring to detrude the people, and the people
> contending to obtrude themselves. And it is right it should be so; for by
> this fermentation, the spirit of democracy is kept alive.   (19)

The push and pull of this democratic confrontation of different sectors of society leads to hybrid conclusions, new compromises, and unforeseen solutions to political and social problems (21).

The targets of Brackenridge's satire are the "errors" and "excesses" of democracy not the thing itself (507). Carried to an excess, democracy can create oppression and tyranny as horrible as any enacted by monarchs. "[T]he rules of justice," as James Madison observes in the *Federalist Papers,* can be supplanted in a democracy by "the superior force of an interested and overbearing majority" (123). As a protection of discrete political minorities, Brackenridge endorses the Federalists' constitutional division of powers, checking direct democratic power: "It is the balancing with stays and braces of distributed powers that gives safety" (740). Of course, the minority Madison and Brackenridge are worried about is comprised of wealthy landowners, who may be dispossessed by a democratic majority bent on using political power to redistribute wealth, but we should note that their reasoning contains nothing logically preventing it from being extended to other minorities. Mocking democracy's excesses, *Modern Chivalry* recommends not an unqualified deference to tradition and social hierarchy but a balance between forces for and those resistant to social transformation.

Tabitha Gilman Tenney's picaresque, *Female Quixotism* (1801), and Rebecca Rush's novel of manners, *Kelroy* (1817), skeptically examine the effect of social mobility on the drama of courtship and marriage and the domestic foundation of American society. *Female Quixotism* recounts the amorous adventures of Dorcas "Dorcasina" Sheldon and her maid, Betty. The narrative is propelled by Dorcasina's desire for a romantic passion that will transport her to a romantic Elysium beyond reason and social convention. In pursuit of this ideal, she embarks on a series of romances. Each time, disaster is narrowly averted, sometimes by a fortuitous accident (e.g., a sleigh accident that results in the revelation of an impostor), sometimes thanks to the efforts of her father or friends. The only alternative offered to this string of increasingly painful and ridiculous fantasies is Dorcasina's first and only genuine suitor, Lysander, who courts her in an honest but plain style. Lysander, to his credit, offers reasonable friendship rather than overwhelming passion, the kind of friendship which promises to ripen into a stable and wholesome marital partnership. Dorcasina rejects what she sees as Lysander's pale and tepid imitation of romance. Betty, like Sancho Panza, brings a common-sense perspective to Dorcasina's misadventures (though, over time, Betty is susceptible of being influenced by Dorcasina, just as Panza is swayed by Don Quixote; late in the narrative, Betty has a romantic delusion of being courted by a man who is her social superior). Unlike Charlotte Lennox's *Female Quixote or The Adventures of Arabella* (1752), a precedent for Tenney's novel, *Female Quixotism* does not end well for its heroine. Dorcasina's foolish romanticism is mocked with increasing bluntness, and her end is pathetic. Much of the blame for her fall is attributed to the romantic novels she loves. Novel reading is dangerous for young women because it fills their heads with flights of fancy rather than spurring them to develop a rational and pragmatic plan for life (4–5).

Tenney's satiric vision is squarely focused on the status of women in the new republic. Unmarried women could hold property but could not vote, and they had very few economic alternatives to marriage as a means of support. Once married, they could not possess property separate from their husbands, could not enter into contracts, or make wills. Divorce was very hard to obtain, and divorce laws in this period were unfavorable to women. These circumstances raised the stakes of the marriage decision. It was not merely one of many important decisions a young woman in the early republic would make, but the sole and absolutely determinative choice she would make (assuming she was allowed to make it at all). Dorcasina's romantic pratfalls are shadowed by very serious potential consequences. She could marry badly and be saddled with an unscrupulous and cruel husband who would deplete her inheritance and doom her to a life of poverty and abuse. Even if her marriage proved to be a happy one, like that of General and Mrs. Richland in *The Coquette* or that of Harriot Stanly and Captain Barry in Tenney's novel, it would not be romantic. In the best of circumstances, marriage includes a steady round of severe trials and challenges, including childbirth, the sickness and death of children, and economic or other material misfortunes (Tenney 321).

Though it warns of the dangers of novel reading, *Female Quixotism* endorses the education of women, reproaching those "enemies to female improvement" who "thought a woman had no business with any book but the bible" (14). The target of Tenney's criticism is not Dorcasina's independent judgment as such; rather, Tenney's criticism is leveled at Dorcasina's preference of emotional excess over rationality. Lysander's courtship is doomed to fail because Dorcasina insists on being overwhelmed by rapture and love at first sight. Lysander represents the rational choice of mate based on established and plausible companionability. His careful and balanced approach is bound to disappoint Dorcasina, who "never considered that the purest and most lasting affection is founded upon esteem and amiable qualities of the mind, rather than upon transitory personal attractions" (11). Instead, Dorcasina falls for Patrick O'Connor, who proves to be a more sinister version of Teague O'Regan (19). Having been lead by her devotion to romantic novels to mistake fiction for life, she is easy prey to his fake passion (28). She devours his fable about a noble birth, a fine family fortune, and disobeying his father's injunction to marry a cousin whom he does not love (30–31). Though played for farce, the courtship between Dorcasina and O'Connor represents a serious social problem. In a changing and anonymous society of immigrants and strangers, identities are as easily put on and off as clothing (72). The stakes of the marital game, particularly for a woman, are considerably raised by the presence of such impostors.

As Dorcasina's series of courtship fantasies continues, the comedy becomes bleaker. As she ages, the implausibility of her romantic delusions reaches a level of grotesque exaggeration. Mistaken by Dorcasina for a gentleman in disguise, her servant John Brown fails not only to save her from an unruly horse, as a romantic hero should, but he cannot even save her fallen wig from being devoured by a hog (227). Presumably, this harsh, even cruel humor was justified, for Tenney, by the threat posed to the social order by Dorcasina's romantic exploits. Betty expresses the conservative social view of the novel when she urges John Brown to "stick to [his] kind" (233). Betty and her fellow servants are just as unhappy as Dorcasina's genteel friends are at the spectacle of John's sudden elevation. Eventually, brought very low by her desire for a grand passion, Dorcasina gives up her assumed, romantic name, signing the letter closing the book with her given name – the more prosaic "Dorcas." In *Female Quixotism*, Tenney mocks not only the romantic fantasy of an all-consuming passion but also the notion of attempting to create a substantially different or idealized vision for one's life instead of humbly accepting one's inherited station and role in life. Apparently willing to tolerate certain social innovations, Tenney seems to approve of Dorcasina's father's liberal views on slavery and religion, but she carefully surrounds Mr. Sheldon's new-fashioned notions with his otherwise impeccable conventionality, his respect for the opinion of others, and his balanced and rational approach to life.

In Rebecca Rush's *Kelroy* (1812), economic and social instability make the kind of rational balance and social equilibrium recommended by Tenney seem impracticable. People of various sorts and backgrounds are continually rising and descending the social scale, including the family at the center of Rush's novel, the Hammonds. As the novel begins, Mr. Hammond has died, leaving his family comfortable but not flush. Mrs. Hammond wants a more luxurious life than her husband's modest estate will provide, so she undertakes to prepare and market her marriageable daughters to wealthy men. Under the pretext of grief, she removes her family from Philadelphia to the countryside where she can make the most of her limited financial resources. There she trains her daughters in the social skills and fashions necessary to make them attractive to the highest class of suitor. Then in a bold and risky venture, she gambles her remaining money on a return to Philadelphia society in a grand manner, showcasing her beautiful and talented daughters in opulent attire and costly parties. Unknown to her daughters, Mrs. Hammond will soon go broke if they do not quickly marry to economic advantage. The young Miss Hammonds, Lucy and Emily, are very marriageable. In addition to being beautiful and accomplished, their lavish home and fashionable dress promise substantial dowries.

The eldest daughter, Lucy, succeeds brilliantly, attracting and marrying a wealthy English lord, the good-hearted Walsingham. The younger daughter, Emily, falls for Kelroy, a handsome and romantic young man whose father has died leaving his estate mired in a legal dispute. In Mrs. Hammond's view, Kelroy's problematic financial situation utterly disqualifies him as a suitor, but, because she has not been frank regarding her own dire financial circumstances, Emily and others cannot understand her objection. Later, when Walsingham, who is friendly toward Kelroy, discovers Mrs. Hammond's motives, he attempts to compel her to permit the engagement, giving Kelroy a chance to improve his monetary situation. Superficially assenting to the engagement, Mrs. Hammond works behind the scenes to thwart Kelroy's suit by means of fraudulent correspondence. As a result, Emily marries Mr. Dunlevy, who is likely to inherit a vast estate from his uncle. Mrs. Hammond does not, however, live to enjoy the fruits of her deception. After her mother's death, Emily discovers the ruse and dies of shock. Revelation of the fraud drives Kelroy to the brink of insanity.

Rush's divided feelings about social mobility are evident in her depiction of the Gurnets, a nouveau riche family living in the neighborhood of the Hammond's country home. Mr. Gurnet is a peddler, who metamorphoses first into a "wholesale huckster" and then into a "monstrously" rich salt merchant (153). Rich enough to send their children to school, the Gurnets attempt the project of social uplift, but remain decidedly vulgar. Old Mr. Gurnet's habits are described as "inveterately low," and their new "style of living" is "so little congenial to their natures, that they [are] perpetually committing blunders which [subject] them to unavoidable ridicule" (154–55). When Emily Hammond and her friends visit this "set of originals," the ensuing comedy's cutting edge comes from the apparent contrast between the genteel visitors' easy elegance, good manners, and sympathy and their hosts' uncouth, blunt, and potentially brutal qualities. Replete with the distinctive pronunciations, grammatical errors, and the colloquialisms of her class, Mrs. Gurnet describes the travails of their move from the city to the country:

> I packed up every morsel of glass and chany my own self, and an ugly job it was for a lusty body like me to go through! – I saw every thing put into the wagons too, safe enough as I thought; yet for all that, the careless creeters of gals out here, broke four blue chany plates, and I don't know how many of my very best ankeen cups and saucers . . . And Gurnet, he always gets so made when any thing's broke.   (156–57)

The Gurnets' earthy dialect is accompanied by a straightforwardness that strikes Emily and company as comic. Unlike the highly restrained and complex social decorum characterizing the courtship rituals of the upper class, the Gurnet girls are blunt and open in their appraisals of the male visitors. Miss Eleanor unblushingly tells Helen that her brother, Charles, is "a very pretty man" (157).

The Gurnets' raucous energy and directness clearly offers some comic relief to the story's romantic intrigues, and, on a superficial reading, one might be tempted to dismiss them as clowns. But such an interpretation would flatten the scene into simple snobbery and ignore the signs of an appreciation of the Gurnets' uncontainable energy. The guests are engaged by the Gurnet girls' pranks, and they enjoy the meal prepared by Mrs. Gurnet. There is humor and industry in these people. They embody the democratic and sometimes explosive energy from below that Rush, like Brackenridge, finds appealing. When Mr. Gurnet's black servant Ben breaks a punch bowl, spilling the wine, Gurnet sallies forth to give him "a good licking" (161). An explosion worthy of George Washington Harris's Sut Lovingood follows. The entire company goes out, "impelled by curiosity," to behold

> old Gurnet, furious with rage, chasing Ben, who had escaped from his grasp, and taken refuge among the cows, where he dodged about, until his master in the heat of the pursuit, happening to tread on the edge of a puddle, slipped and fell sprawling at full length, with his face in the mire. The negro then jumped over the fence, and ran out of sight. The Miss Gurnets, the maid who was milking, and the man who was feeding the horses on the other side of the yard, burst into a roar of laughter in which Helen, Charles and Emily joined.   (162)

This "roar of laughter" shared by both sides of the class divide represents a contagious form of emotional and psychic energy that runs through the crowd at the sight of this pratfall. To be sure, this is fairly broad comedy (not without serious implications as regards Ben's racial status), but it is also a scene in which the surge of slapstick energy temporarily demolishes the class divide. Instead of being embarrassed as members of the genteel class would have been, the Gurnets share in the laughter. In this lack of self-consciousness, this freedom from shame and constraint, there is a measure of power (163). The Gurnets' social pretensions may be absurd, but their energy, honesty, and material success is not. Rush leaves open the question of what the Gurnets and their descendants will become. It is, as yet, too soon to say, but some development seems unavoidable, and the Gurnets' upward trajectory would seem to be a bellwether for American society.

Part of what keeps the reader from becoming too alarmed by the Gurnets' ascendance is that they are what they seem to be. Whether in marriage or in business, no potential partner will suffer an unpleasant surprise as to the real character of the Gurnet family. The essential qualities defining all of Rush's characters, for good or ill, do not shift or undergo any metamorphosis. At the novel's conclusion, Emily Hammond and her mother are as good and bad as they are, respectively, at the beginning. Trouble comes in *Kelroy* when people disguise their real natures, as when Lucy Hammond successfully deceives Walsingham as to her character. Mrs. Hammond, in particular, is singled out as the tale's chief villain by virtue of her steadfast unwillingness to allow anyone to see her real nature. As Walsingham observes, Mrs. Hammond is a veritable "Proteus" – "Last night she was all gaiety and animation! – This morning, the emblem of despondency: – next, raving like a fury! – then immoveable as marble: – and now, she is weeping like a fountain to disarm me of my purpose" (88). Even when she is facing bankruptcy and the loss of her house to fire, Mrs. Hammond exercises considerable restraint to prevent anyone from registering how happy she is at winning the lottery: "exerting every particle of energy that nature had gifted her with to remove the civil impressions which might remain from her having fainted, [Mrs. Hammond] received [Kelroy's] congratulations with considerable apparent composure, whilst her heart throbbed with convulsive joy" (129). While inwardly she can be shaken by "convulsive joy," her appearance remains under her control. The tragedy of *Kelroy* is the triumph of artifice and control over sincerity. Bad social mobility takes the form of disguise and deception. Good social movement, such as that embodied in the Gurnets, is transparent and legible. But in neither case is the change substantive.

In the stability of her characters' moral natures and even in the prodigious ability of her prime villain to control her appearance, Rush sidesteps a more disturbing prospect. While the completeness of her disguise is troubling,

Mrs. Hammond's rational self-possession is reassuring. Once discovered, her motives and means are understandable and predictable. However, what if the Proteus-like metamorphoses associated with Mrs. Hammond were more than mere changes of clothes and expression? What if her convulsive feelings overwhelmed her self-discipline, resulting in a substantial transformation of her character in some unforeseeable fashion? This is the type of question posed by Charles Brockden Brown's Gothic novels. Dispensing with notions of rational equilibrium and taking mutability seriously as something more than a matter of mere appearances, Brown plunges the reader into a doubtful realm where meaning and character are perpetually in flux. Centrally addressing transformation and identity and embracing the strange and fantastic, Brown's Gothic novels are a subspecies of the romance and precursor of many nineteenth-century examples of that genre of fiction (the subject of the next chapter).

Beginning with Horace Walpole's *The Castle of Otranto* (1765), the Gothic novel uses spectral apparitions, dark and labyrinthine settings, the figure of the vulnerable woman, and the sudden appearance of moral peril to arouse, intensify, and prolong the reader's emotional reaction. Brown described the desired effect of his Gothic tales as "wind[ing] up the reader's passions to the highest pitch" and overwhelming reason with "catastrophe" of the most "unexpected and momentous" nature (Pattee xxvii). Often, the hero and the villain of the Gothic novel resemble each other in some fundamental aspect (to the hero's consternation as he or she comes to recognize the similarity), and the novel's setting is marked by decay – the mansion, castle, or abbey in a state of ruin, the overgrown and corrupted garden, the monstrous wilderness (e.g., the caves of Brown's *Edgar Huntly*).[8] Strange and mysterious events, such as the disembodied voice in *Wieland* (1798) or sleepwalking in *Edgar Huntly* (1799), are used to suggest realities or perceptions which defy cool analysis and exceed human understanding. For many, the Gothic novel's terrifyingly fluid world warns of the nightmare society heralded by the French Revolution, a society driven by unregulated desire and open to monstrous forms of social and political experimentation.[9] While apt, such associations do not account for the genre's continuing appeal. Since its first appearance, the Gothic novel has continued to prove useful as a means of expressing skepticism about the sufficiency of reason and logic as guides to the meaning of existence and the order of society.

While other types of early American fiction consider how social mobility may threaten the coherence and stability of society, Brown pushes notions of individual and social mutability to a philosophical extreme (Ringe 49–50). Brown's fiction generates a kind of philosophical terror by dissolving boundaries. Is Edgar Huntly a savage beast or a civilized man? Is Clithero Edny mad or sane? Is Wieland listening to a voice in his head or to Carwin's ventriloquism? The fact that we can answer "both" to each of these questions signals Brown's intent to cast doubt on our rationalist efforts to separate reason and imagination, progress and regress, growth and decay, life and death, the corporeal and the non-corporeal (Cameron *Corporeal Self* 8).[10] Like these distinct categories, discrete beings in Brown's Gothic novels tend to merge into or transfigure each other. The sleepwalking and murderous Clithero Edny's very state of being proves to be contagious, and, after close contact with Edny, Huntly becomes a sleepwalker and a killer.

Brown shifts back and forth in *Edgar Huntly* between settlement and wilderness as though the geographical movement signified a distinction between the rational world of civilized people and the irrational world of savage people.[11] However, by the end of the tale, the distinction between civilization and wilderness has come to seem doubtful, even delusional.[12] The event generating Brown's convoluted narrative is an act of vengeance by a small group of Delaware Indians under the influence of an ancient squaw-sachem known as Old Deb. Huntly's comparison of Old Deb and "Queen Mab," the Celtic fairy of Shakespeare's *Romeo and Juliet*, suggests the interpenetration of dream and waking worlds characterizing Brown's novel (200). At the outset, the novel seems as though it is going to be a murder mystery. Huntly seeks to discover the identity of the person who has murdered his friend Waldegrave. But the tale soon departs from this relatively straightforward project. Almost as an afterthought, it is revealed near the novel's conclusion that Waldegrave has been the random victim of marauding Indians. Early in his investigation, Huntly comes into contact with Clithero Edny, an Irish servant of mysterious background. At night, Clithero wanders about in an apparently somnambulant state, regretting his hard fate and bad deeds. When Huntly confronts him, Clithero confesses not to Waldegrave's murder but to the killing of another man.

Clithero recalls his humble Irish family and how a great lady, Mrs. Euphemia Lorimer, took him in and raised him like a son. Obsessively grateful to her, Clithero becomes her loyal steward. Like boxes within boxes, Mrs. Lorimer's story is contained within Clithero's. Arthur Wiatte, Euphemia's twin brother, thwarts her courtship with Sarsefield (who later turns up as Edgar Huntly's tutor) and manages to have a rich but immoral suitor imposed on her. Fortunately, Euphemia's husband soon dies, leaving her the master of her own fate and fortune with Clithero's able assistance. Wiatte turns to crime and is deported, and Euphemia raises Clarice, Wiatte's abandoned illegitimate daughter, as her own child. Clithero and Clarice fall in love, and Sarsefield reappears. For a moment, a happy ending seems imminent, but Wiatte returns and is killed by Clithero in self-defense. When his mistress swoons on hearing that her brother is dead, Clithero flees, turning up in rural Pennsylvania. Edgar's desire to bring Clithero some psychic relief leads to nighttime searches for the tortured Irishman. Thus, Huntly's story mutates from detective story to mission of mercy, eventually becoming a nightmare of human metamorphosis when he enters the wilderness.

The novel repeatedly questions whether various antitheses may not prove to be somehow mistaken, whether the opposed terms are not in fact either intertwined or merely different words for the same thing. We might assume that the earth under Huntly's foot is solid, stable, and unchanging, but it is not. It is riddled with caves and constantly undergoing a process of erosion and decay (22). The sleepwalking Clithero is both like and unlike a wakeful man. Though asleep, he labors, speaks, weeps, and looks about him when called (10–12). When urged by Edgar to act like a man, Clithero shudders (31). Like his somnambulism, Clithero's shuddering reminds us of the many actions and reflexes that are not subject to our control, raising a question about the degree to which human existence is made up of involuntary acts and reflexive impulses. Edgar's apparently rational inquiry into the murder of his friend ("Curiosity, like virtue, is its own reward") merges with "the most complex and fiery sentiment in [his] bosom," making it hard to separate the quest for knowledge from the desire for vengeance (16).

The evil Arthur Wiatte and his noble sister, Euphemia Lorimer, are uncannily similar: "Nature had impressed the same image upon them, and had modeled them after the same pattern. The resemblance between them was exact to a degree almost incredible. In infancy and childhood they were perpetually liable to be mistaken for each other." While the original mental and physical similarity of the twins is offered as a sign that the choices people make in life are more important than their origins, the narrative's insistence on the twins' identical "intellectual character" and "form" is disconcerting (43). The fact that such different people can come from identical materials makes reading the outward signs of inner character difficult and renders the confident prediction of an individual's career in life impossible. At moments, the novel seems to endorse the kind of personal transformation and upward social mobility represented by Clithero, who is raised from peasant to educated gentleman, but this positive appraisal is shadowed by the fact of his descent into a homicidal insanity. Was Clithero's madness engendered by the effort to lift him out of his original place in life? The obsessive nature of his earliest devotion to Mrs. Lorimer hints that his mind may have begun to deteriorate when she adopted him.

Not stopping with the destabilization of the categories we use to organize experience and knowledge (e.g., blurring the boundary between cool reason ["curiosity"] and hot imagination ["fiery passion"]), Brown further disrupts our mental equipoise by suggesting that things and people are constantly mutating, often becoming their opposites. Human metamorphosis is most dramatically instanced in the transformation of the peace-loving Huntly into a wild animal or savage being. Having become a sleepwalker himself, Huntly falls into a pitch-black pit. On awakening, he is overwhelmed by sensations of hunger and thirst:

> I tore the linen of my shirt between my teeth and swallowed the fragments. I felt a strong propensity to bite the flesh from my arm. My heart overflowed with cruelty, and I pondered on the delight I should experience in rending some living animal to pieces, and drinking its blood and grinding its quivering fibres between my teeth. (156–57)

He kills a panther with his "Tom-hawk" and feasts on its still warm blood and twitching flesh (159–60). Finding his way to the cave where a group of Indians hold a young woman captive, he kills the Indian sentry with the same spontaneous predatory skill he displayed when killing the panther (172). Though repeatedly claiming that he is averse to violence and bloodshed, Huntly becomes a ferocious killer, creeping about on all fours and not hesitating to take life (191). He is quickly "inured to spectacles of horror . . . grown callous and immoveable," thinking only of his physical survival (222). The rapidity and extent of Huntly's metamorphosis would seem to be intended to shake the reader's confidence in the immutability of human personality.

Brown uses the human mind's capacity for delusion and madness to make facile invocations of the human capacity for self-rule and the progress of civilization seem distinctly ridiculous. His prefatory comment in *Wieland* that he wants to offer the reader the "most instructive and memorable" examples of the human psychology suggests that we read the portrait of Theodore Wieland's horrible descent into madness as representative of a general human propensity to self-destructive fantasy (3). From this perspective, it becomes hard to trust the independent judgment or the moral compass of the average citizen. And without this confidence, the idea of a society cut loose from the moorings of hierarchical authority and time-honored tradition becomes frightening. In *Wieland*, the disembodied voice that moves the characters to various misapprehensions and delusional acts allegorically represents the chaos potential in choosing one's inner lights over well-established social customs and roles.

The events of *Wieland* are contemporaneous with the debates and ferment leading to the American Revolution.[13] Clara and Theodore Wieland, sister and brother, live on an estate outside of Philadelphia. Their lives in this idyllic setting are disturbed by the apparition of a voice (later turning out to belong to

Carwin, a ventriloquist). In the novel's climactic catastrophe, Theodore Wieland murders his wife and four children and attempts to murder his sister, Clara, under the delusion that he is obeying a divine commandment. Clara narrates the tale. This tragedy is foreshadowed by the career of Wieland Sr. An isolated individual following his own unique faith, Wieland Sr. withdraws from the mundane realities of everyday social intercourse to pursue a radically individualistic religious vision. But his isolation increases the chance that what he sees as divine inspiration could be madness. There is no community or tradition to warrant that his faith is not delusional. By not making his family comply with his religious beliefs, Wieland Sr. does not even have the benefit of the dissent that such a requirement might produce, inspiring some modification or qualification of his faith (13). The absence of religious instruction and democratic dedication to freedom of conscience leaves the Wieland children open to choose their own faiths, fatally as it turns out in the case of Theodore (whose given name ironically means "gift of God").

The monstrous potential of this freethinking position is manifest in the evolution of Theodore's absolutist faith. What begins as a credulous openness to supernatural explanations of such events as his father's death and the disembodied voice becomes an unshakeable conviction that God is directly speaking to and acting through him. Wieland is driven by the desire to know divine will with "certainty," and this is the essence of his murderous impulses – the desire for and belief in certainty (186). If he could tolerate doubt, he would have been unable to commit his heinous acts. When he sets his sights on knowing the will of God, Wieland abandons both doubt and judgment. He does not know or care whether his act in killing his wife and children is good or evil, depending solely on his certainty that it has been commanded by the supreme power: "Thou, Omnipotent and Holy! Thou knowest that my actions were conformable to thy will. I know not what is crime; what actions are evil in their ultimate and comprehensive tendency or what are good. Thy knowledge, as thy power, is unlimited. I have taken thee for my guide, and cannot err" (199). Paradoxically, Wieland's complete submission produces the exultation of a rush of God-like feeling:

> I lifted the corpse in my arms and laid it on the bed. I gazed upon it with delight. Such was the elation of my thoughts, that I even broke into laughter. I clapped my hand and exclaimed, "It is done! My sacred duty is fulfilled! To that I have sacrificed, O my God! Thy last and best gift, my wife!" For a while I thus soared above frailty. (194)

To defy conventional notions of morality and sentiment in obedience to one's sense of the dictates of a higher power is to become God-like, exceeding the limitations of human vision and behavior. When he testifies at his trial for murder, Wieland is said to have a "significance of gesture, and a tranquil majesty, which denoted less of humanity than godhead" (184).

Like the caves Edgar Huntly falls into, Brown's Gothic fiction is a catacomb of doubts and questions. When is Wieland responding to Carwin's voice and when is he acting on some internal revelation? Huntly's intuitively sympathetic response to Clithero Edny initially seems plausible but proves to be horribly misguided. Edny is beyond sympathy and reason. How do we separate the sound from the unsound in Theodore Wieland's convictions, which include his ardent rejection of primogeniture, an important theme in the Revolution?[14] Brown's depictions of delusion and error cast doubt on individual assertions of the kind of higher-law intuition urged by the founders as justification for the American Revolution, and these doubts would seem to require the testing of moral and political presentiments in the court of public opinion. However, doesn't such deference to public opinion and tradition risk that meritorious though novel or unconventional insights and inspirations will routinely be swept aside as delusional? In addition, after reading Brown's fiction, readers may find it difficult to have much confidence in the possibility of a lucid public consensus. Communication in these novels is no less distorted than the individual's impulses and perceptions. The monstrous potential of private inspiration and the grim failures of communication depicted by Brown challenge the reader to accept uncertainty and doubt as concomitants of the democratic experiment. As we shall see in the next chapter, some nineteenth-century novelists could not accept an ambiguous or experimental approach to the national narrative, turning, instead, to the mysteries of racial identity for signs of the nation's destiny. Others more open to change urged that we consider the nation's always evolving and fractious process of establishing moral consensus as the only worthy principle of national cohesion and destiny.

# Chapter 1

# The romance

## What is the romance?

As the term is used here, "romance" does not mean love story. The fictions taken up in this chapter may or may not include love stories. Labeling these novels "romances" has more to do with certain formal and thematic character-istics than with notions of courtship, sexual attraction, and marriage. Romance designates a wide variety of novels featuring out-of-the-ordinary adventures, mysterious or supernatural circumstances, difficult quests, and miraculous tri-umphs. These novels often have an epic or mythic cast and display a marked lack of concern for questions of plausibility.[1] Together with the sentimental novel, the romance predominates in the first two-thirds of the nineteenth century.

The story of the novel's emergence told by Walter Benjamin, Georg Lukács, Ian Watt, and others helps to situate the subgenre of romance. According to these theorists of the genre, the novel, as we know it, is a relatively late literary invention, coming into being roughly coincident with the Reformation and the emergence of bourgeois capitalism.[2] A modern form for modern times, the novel, observes Benjamin, marks a substantial departure from the storyteller's legends, fairy tales, and epics (87). Benjamin describes the storyteller as an artisan and his/her oral tales as akin to handicrafts, such as pottery. These tales incorporate the shared wisdom and experience of the community and change subtly over time as the community changes. By contrast, the novel is more like a newspaper, a vehicle of bits of information rather than a living record of communal insight. The literary forms of the storyteller, such as the legend or epic, feature heroic or archetypal characters and miraculous events occurring in a timeless realm of universal truths (Benjamin 89, Lukács 66). This account of the novel tends to identify the genre with an empirical approach to experience. Ian Watt characterizes the novel's emphasis on plausibility as part of a general philosophical shift away from a priori ideas toward the particulars of experience (12, 18). Defined in part by its choice of believable fact over the improbable or extraordinary, the novel rejects the literary conventions of the legend, epic, or fairy tale, which, in their very conventionality, seem implausible (such as the traditional plot and the archetypal hero).

When compared with the type of novel described by Benjamin, Lukács, and Watt, the romance seems to be something of a throwback to the earlier forms of the storyteller. The romance employs supernatural elements or characters with extraordinary capabilities as well as archetypal heroes and traditional plots. Though grounded in a specific historical context, the romance often has a timeless quality (for example, Alymer's attempt to rid his bride of her one visible defect in Nathaniel Hawthorne's story "The Birthmark" is set in a specific time, but, like the story of Pygmalion, its main action could easily be staged in any period). The romance reaches out beyond the fate of its particular characters toward some larger issue or theme, such as the foundation of an American race in the union of Duncan Heyward and Alice Munro at the end of James Fenimore Cooper's *The Last of the Mohicans* (1826) or Ahab's quest to penetrate the mask of material reality and grasp the ultimate meaning of existence by hunting down Moby-Dick. Rather than focusing on a heterogeneous society of isolated individuals, romances describe (or lament the passing of) a world in which communities still seem to have cohesive identities. Like the fables and myths of a previous era and the sentimental novels of its own era, the nineteenth-century romance is not reluctant to indulge in allegory. A small but revealing sign of the novel's emergence, according to Watt, is the shift away from type names, such as Mr. Badman, to the use of realistic names, such as Tom Sawyer (19). The romance, however, is not averse to including names with allegorical significance, such as Cooper's Hawkeye (*The Last of the Mohicans*), Hawthorne's Faith ("Young Goodman Brown"), and George Lippard's Devil Bug (*The Quaker City*).

Authors of nineteenth-century romances understood well that their productions represented an anomalous continuation of the epic or mythic impulse. In prefatory material he appended to his romance *The Yemassee* (1835), William Gilmore Simms expressly connects the romance with the epic and distinguishes it from the kind of fiction described by Watt, Benjamin, and Lukács:

> Modern romance is the substitute which the people of to-day offer for
> the ancient epic. Its standards are the same. The reader, who, reading
> Ivanhoe, keeps Fielding and Richardson beside him, will be at fault in

every step of his progress. The domestic novel of those writers, confined to the felicitous narration of common and daily occurring events, is altogether a different sort of composition.   (I, vi)

Famously, Nathaniel Hawthorne appreciated the romance's "latitude" in regard to the novel's requirement of a "minute fidelity . . . to the probable and ordinary course of man's experience" (*Seven Gables* 3). The romance, Hawthorne says, furnishes a theater "a little removed from the highway of ordinary travel, where the creatures of [the author's] brain may play their phantasmagorical antics, without exposing them to too close a comparison with the actual events of real lives" (*Blithesdale* 1–2). In a similar vein, Simms characterizes the romance as "seek[ing] for its adventures among the wild and wonderful. It does not insist upon what is known, or even what is probable" (I, vi–vii).

Ostensibly, romancers, such as Hawthorne and Simms, merely desire not to be too constrained by the requirement that fiction believably mirror life as we know it. In writing prefaces announcing that their tales are romances and not novels, they seek to preclude the reader's complaint that such and such a character or event is not believable. But to what end do they seek such latitude? The answer is, I think, that they find in the romance's more overtly imaginative and inventive features, in its mingling of the marvelous and the plausible, a superior route to certain important truths – a route that is not available to the mere fact-gatherer and reporter. Borrowing a phrase from Henry James's description of the romantic, we might say that the romancer is after things "we never *can* directly know; the things that can reach us only through the beautiful circuit and subterfuge of our thought and our desire" (qtd. Carton 6). Taking us into "a neutral territory, somewhere between the real world and fairyland, where the Actual and the Imaginary may meet, and each imbues itself with the nature of the other," the romance reveals the power of the imagination to shape or transform the raw data of experience, giving it meaning rather than merely recording it (*Scarlet Letter* 111). As Joel Porte suggests in *The Romance in America*, the romancer turns to fantasy, magic, archetypal heroes, traditional storylines, parable, and allegory as a means of uncovering otherwise inaccessible realities, such as the nature of human motivation, the destiny of a people, and the meaning of existence (ix–x). Believing in the existence of truths or realities that exceed or elude empirical approaches, the romancer sets aside the requirements of plausibility in the interest of making a stronger claim on a deeper, more imaginative form of veracity.

We can get a feel for the formal devices and themes characteristic of the nineteenth-century romance by looking briefly at two famous stories by Washington Irving, "Rip Van Winkle" and "The Legend of Sleepy Hollow," both from *The Sketch Book* (1819–20). Both stories blend everyday facts with the marvelous or strange. For instance, after beginning with a matter-of-fact description of Rip Van Winkle's life, his village, his clothes, personality, habits, and home life, Irving's story takes a romantic turn with the appearance of the English explorer Henry Hudson and his crew of men playing nine-pins. Rip drinks some of their liquor and falls asleep for twenty years, during which time the Revolutionary War takes place. Similarly, in "Sleepy Hollow," Irving's detailed description of a rural community of Dutch folk in the Hudson River Valley is interrupted by the appearance of the headless horseman. Wanting the reader "to grow imaginative – to dream dreams, and see apparitions," the romancer insinuates the extraordinary into the ordinary or shows how the prosaic or unremarkable detail can cast a supernatural shadow in our minds (994). In "My Kinsman, Major Molineux," Hawthorne describes this state of mind as an oscillation "between fancy and reality; by turns, the pillars of the balcony lengthened into the tall, bare stems of pines, dwindled down to human figures, settled again in their true shape and size, and then commenced a new succession of changes" (1259). Whether or not the "legend" is believed as literally true is, I think, less important to the romancer than the reader's sense of its imaginative and emotional power. Whether or not the headless horseman is in fact Brom Bones is less important to Irving than the creation of some measure of terror in the reader, pointing to the power of the imagination to transform the bucolic countryside into a haunted and alien terrain and otherwise rationally explainable events into a supernatural pursuit.

Both tales are supposedly "found" in the papers of one Diedrich Knickerbocker. Superficially a gesture toward plausibility and historical accuracy, this device is not uncommon in American romances. For instance, Edgar Allen Poe's *The Narrative of Arthur Gordon Pym* (1838) and Hawthorne's *The Scarlet Letter* (1850) purport to be documentary narratives based on historical papers. Given the overtly fantastic nature of these fictions, such claims or allusions to historical accuracy are plainly provocative, calling our attention to the different kinds of truth claim made by fiction and history. Just because certain events cannot have happened – there is no headless horseman and Rip cannot have slept for twenty years – does not mean that such flights of imagination do not reveal what Hawthorne termed "the truth of the human heart" (*Seven Gables* 3). Irving describes his tales' "strange sights," "voices in the air," "marvelous beliefs," and "trances and visions" as the beliefs of a past era, but his success in resurrecting these old legends, their grip on readers from his own era to the present, suggests a truth about his audience's continuing desire for the experience of imaginative reverie ("Sleepy Hollow" 993). The retrospective nature of these fantasies makes it tempting to describe the imaginative effect of Irving's romances as escapist nostalgia. Taking this line, we might conclude that Irving and his audience want to shut out the forces of historical change. Tales such as "Rip Van Winkle" and "Sleepy Hollow" comfort the reader with images of a seemingly static and timeless moment in the nation's past before the nation's population exploded, before the national economy was shifted from agriculture and handicrafts to heavy industry and capitalist speculation, and before the substantial relocation of the nation's population to urban centers. This escapist interpretive line, however, is too narrow to capture Irving's approach to social transformation.

When Rip awakes from his twenty-year sleep, no one recognizes him. The village is larger and more populous. Yankee names, such as Jonathan Doolittle, have replaced the Dutch ones, such as Nicholas Vedder. Rip's home and wife are gone. The portrait of King George the Third on the village inn's sign has been changed to a picture of George Washington. Rip is no longer a subject of the king but a citizen of a republic. In "Sleepy Hollow," the "drowsy, dreamy" little Dutch community is threatened with similar changes by the arrival of Ichabod Crane (993). By marrying Katrina Van Tassel, Ichabod hopes to be able to use her father's considerable farm lands as a basis for future real estate speculation: "his heart yearned after the damsel who was to inherit these domains, and his imagination expanded with the idea, how they might be readily turned into cash, and the money invested in immense tracts of wild land, and shingle places in the wilderness" (999). The Yankee schoolmaster heralds the coming wave of development in the east and expansion to the west. Irving contrasts him with Katrina's father, "Old Baltus Van Tassel," who is "a perfect picture of a thriving, contented, liberal-hearted farmer," who "seldom . . . sent either his eyes or his thoughts beyond the boundaries of his own farm; but within those every thing was snug, happy, and well-conditioned" (998). Yet, despite these signs of change, much remains constant. Rip remains the same. His appetites and inclinations have not been altered in the slightest, and he resumes "his old walks and habits." Ichabod is expelled from Sleepy Hollow by the apparition of the headless horseman. Katrina marries Brom Bones, and life goes on as before Ichabod's arrival. The manners and customs of Sleepy Hollow's inhabitants "remain fixed, while the great torrent of emigration and improvement, which is making such incessant changes in other parts of this restless country, sweeps by them unobserved" (994). The greater and more revealing magic of these tales lies in their compelling portraits of continuity in the face of change. The changes are real and visible but there are also continuities of the human heart that wondrously withstand change and give an enduring, if not permanent, identity to places and peoples. As we shall see in this chapter, transformation and identity are central themes in all formulations of the nineteenth-century romance.

As Richard Chase, Joel Porte, George Dekker, and many others have shown, the romance is a particularly capacious category of nineteenth-century fiction. It includes the historical romances of James Fenimore Cooper, Robert Montgomery Bird, Lydia Maria Child, William Wells Brown, and others, the philosophical romances of Edgar Allan Poe, Nathaniel Hawthorne, and Herman Melville, and such sensational or popular romances as George Lippard's *The Quaker City* (1845), E. D. E. N. Southworth's *The Hidden Hand* (1859), or Edward Wheeler's *Deadwood Dick* (1877). Before the advent of realism in the latter decades of the century, the romance and the sentimental novel are, in effect, the default categories of nineteenth-century fiction. With notable exceptions, such as Rebecca Rush's *Kelroy* (1812), Caroline Kirkland's *A New Home* (1839), and Elizabeth Stoddard's *The Morgesons* (1862), most of the American fiction before 1870 takes the form of either the sentimental novel or the romance. Not only were these two novelistic forms predominant for most of the nineteenth century, they overlap substantially. Novels such as Catharine Maria Sedgwick's *Hope Leslie* (1827) and William Wells Brown's *Clotel* (1853), or Lydia Maria Child's *Romance of the Republic* (1867), could be convincingly classed as either romances or sentimental fiction. Historical romances, such as Cooper's *The Last of the Mohicans*, draw on the affective devices of the sentimental novel (e.g., scenes of tearful reunion between family members and sorrow at the death of a child), and sentimental novels, such as Harriet Beecher Stowe's *Uncle Tom's Cabin* (1852), share many of the traits of the romance (e.g., supernatural apparitions and incredible escapes from danger). Indeed, the ubiquity of the romance was such that, as Nina Baym has pointed out, the terms "novel" and "romance" were used interchangeably in the antebellum era ("Concepts of Romance").

All three types of romance – historical, philosophical, and sensational – feature the extraordinary in the form of astonishing or supernatural events, amazing escapes, unbelievably fortuitous coincidences, characters with almost superhuman abilities, shocking acts of violence, and/or otherworldly apparitions (even when they do not qualify as the Gothic version of the romance, these novels often employ Gothic elements). And all three types claim to illustrate some theme of epic significance, such as the fate of the nation, the malign or benign forces animating nature, or the monstrous deformation of humanity in the modern city. While making various claims to authenticity and accuracy, such as the device of the found papers and the inclusion of historical events and realistic details, the nineteenth-century romance recounts larger-than-life tales filled with strange or astonishing events having some apparent mythic significance. In effect, the romancer makes a novel of the stuff of fairy tale, myth, and legend.

Each variety of romance will be delineated at greater length below, but here we can use the idea of a legend, a myth-like tale containing some fundamental human truth, to introduce briefly the key differences. The historical romance takes some bit of history (e.g., an episode of espionage in the Revolutionary War) and elevates it to the level of myth. The philosophical romance mines a larger-than-life tale (e.g., the story told by sailors of a great white whale) for its metaphysical or psychological import. And the sensational romance seeks to create a popular legend (e.g., the tale of a notorious outlaw), which will alternatively thrill, horrify, and excite the reader. Like the historical romance and the philosophical romance, the sensational romance often includes Gothic elements, and the Gothic novel could, as I have mentioned, be treated as a subgenre of the romance. I have not focused on the Gothic as a category of romance, because I find it not to be as capacious a category of nineteenth-century American romances as those I have chosen. As one might expect, any given example of one of these types of romance may well do all of these things. Nineteenth-century novelists often produced more than one type of romance. George Lippard, for instance, wrote both sensational romances, such as *The Quaker City*, and historical romances, such as *Blanche of Brandywine* (1846). These different types of romance are neither fixed nor static, and each borrows liberally from the others. While they are not impermeable taxonomic barriers walling one type of romance off from the others, nonetheless, such distinctions, like many we use to classify the changing and hybrid productions of the human imagination, help us to clarify points of emphasis in these novels.

## The historical romance

As the two parts of the label "historical romance" suggest, this subgenre of the novel blends bits of history with the strange or extraordinary. The idea conjured by this label may well strike us as odd. The term "historical" would seem to point in the direction of verifiable facts and empirically persuasive demonstrations of cause and effect, but the term "romance" suggests legendary heroes and marvelous events – stories starkly incompatible with notions of historical accuracy (Dekker 26, 58–59). Yet this is precisely what the historical romancer has in mind – a merger of verifiable history and the extraordinary. William Gilmore Simms claims both the historical accuracy of his Indian characters and his right as a romancer to indulge in the "wild and wonderful." In his various prefaces to *The Last of the Mohicans*, James Fenimore Cooper asserts both the authenticity of his fictional portrait of the French and Indian War and the poetic license he has taken in rendering it.

Using the extraordinary and marvelous to invest otherwise prosaic events with mythic significance, the historical romancer transforms known history into legend. "Legend" is an apt word to associate with this type of fiction, for, as Hawthorne understood, it suggests the heroic or timeless luster that can be given to history when we "attempt to connect a bygone time with the very present that is flitting away from us" (*Seven Gables* 4). Many Hawthorne tales and novels contain particular "legends" within the overarching legend of the romance (e.g., "The Legend of Zenobia" chapter of *The Blithesdale Romance*). By recasting history as legend or myth, the romancer attempts to give the past an archetypal or universal significance. To this end, the romancer invents characters plausible to the historical context, such as a backwoods scout or a colonial era peddler, and endows them with larger-than-life qualities, such as astonishing skill in battle, unswerving courage, or a miraculous ability to appear when most needed. While they may begin as relatively believable individuals from the period and place being described, over the course of the narrative they become epic figures engaged in a struggle for the fate of a nation or people. Not only do these characters have plain allegorical significance (e.g., the noble Indian who must retreat before the advance of [white] civilization or the heroic pioneer woman who, in her self-sufficiency, bravery, and skill, seems a veritable mother of the republic), but also the events described (e.g., a brutal and chaotic battle) have a comparatively straightforward emotional impact and unambiguous moral implication (e.g., the phoenix-like emergence of a noble American people from their bloody conflict with a corrupt force of French and Indians). In the romancer's hands, a motley group of bored, weary, and frightened revolutionary-era troops becomes a brotherhood of valiant men united by their eagerness for battle and glory, and a common peddler risking his life to spy for General Washington becomes an archetype of the selfless patriot (Cooper's *The Spy* [1821]).

Mark Twain's famous critique of James Fenimore Cooper provides a revealing perspective on the historical romancer's transformation of history into legend. By jettisoning concerns for credibility, the romancer's attempts to give history heroic significance become, in Twain's view, far-fetched and absurd ("Cooper's Literary Offenses"). Cooper's heroic Hawkeye speaks in a floridly noble style one moment and a laughably vulgar mode the next, and his skills, such as being able to drive a nail fifty yards distant with a bullet from his rifle, are ridiculously exaggerated. Twain similarly criticized the patent artificiality of the characters and plots of Cooper's literary forerunner, Sir Walter Scott. In effect, Twain's objection to the romancer's alloy of extraordinary events and historical facts reflects the realists' desire to replace the grandiose and melodramatic with a close and accurate observation of the everyday details of life and to substitute the complexity of moral and social dilemmas as they are actually experienced by highly believable characters for the allegorical clarity of the romance's heroes and villains and their symbolically transparent conflicts.

Twain's criticisms of the historical romance were anticipated by a variety of authors. Southern humorists, such as Johnson Jones Hooper, Augustus Baldwin Longstreet, and George Washington Harris, were particularly blunt in poking fun at romantic visions of frontier life.[3] Instead of the heroic, self-sacrificing frontiersman, the eponymous hero of Hooper's *Some Adventures of Captain Simon Suggs* (1845) is an unscrupulous rascal whose motto is "It is good to be shifty in a new country," and the romance's depiction of fierce battles between Indians and whites is replaced with a game of lacrosse and gambling – victory belonging not to the bravest but to the craftiest (114–17). In her first-hand experience of carving out a settlement in Michigan, Caroline Kirkland found a reality far different from that she had been led to expect by romances of the West. Her novel, *A New Home, Who'll Follow?* (1839), depicts many of the hard and unromantic realities of life in the wild. Instead of the sublime spectacle of a group of intrepid settlers making their way around a wilderness waterfall, Kirkland describes a wagon stuck in a forest mud hole (6–7). The only "warwhoop" her heroine hears is the sound of drunken Indians wanting more liquor (29). Hardly a valiant clan bonded and ennobled by their experiences in planting civilization in the wild, her community of settlers is prone to drunkenness, indolence, greed, and dishonesty. For these writers, the dream inspired by the romance inevitably runs aground on the more humble and base aspects of reality, an outcome brilliantly imaged in *Huckleberry Finn* as the wreck of a steamboat named the *Walter Scott.*

Despite such criticisms, the historical romance, with its larger-than-life characters, often ornate dialogue, melodramatic love triangles, miraculous escapes, astonishing coincidences, and relatively transparent symbolism, has proven to be one of the most durable of fictional genres. Even after the rise of realism, historical romances, such as *Ben-Hur* (1880) by Lew Wallace and *When Knighthood was in Flower* (1898) by Charles Major, were tremendously successful. As George Dekker has pointed out, "No other genre has even come close to the consistent popularity enjoyed by historical romances from *The Spy* in 1821 down to . . . *Roots* in recent times" (1, 4–5). This sustained popularity would seem to be due in part to the sheer variety of the genre's subjects, which are drawn from every historical period from classical antiquity to the recent past. Consider, for instance, *Gone with the Wind, The Hunchback of Notre Dame, The Last of the Mohicans,* and *Ivanhoe.*

By comparison, however, when one looks at American examples of the genre taken from the first three-quarters of the nineteenth century, the historical romance seems considerably less varied. At least initially, the American historical romance is fixated on the theme of national identity, repeatedly attempting to imagine the formation or transformation of an American people. Many of these tales use the image of the frontier and violent conflicts between European Americans and Native Americans to stage the birth of an American identity.[4] In Cooper's *The Last of the Mohicans* and Simms's *The Yemassee*, the Indians, a "once mighty nation," are displaced by an emergent "American" people. Additional conflicts between Anglo-American colonists and France, Spain, or Britain work to separate the emergent "American" people from their "Old World" heritage. The natural environment is often a character in its own right, playing an important role in forging the character and testing the mettle of the emerging people. Some romances focus on the crucial part played by strong and independent women in the drama of national identity, such as Child's *Hobomok* (1824) and Sedgwick's *Hope Leslie* (1827). The plantation idyll of the Old South, as exemplified by John Pendleton Kennedy's *Swallow Barn* (1832) and Simms's *Woodcraft* (1852), recasts the question of identity from a distinctly regional perspective. And other romances, such as William Wells Brown's *Clotel* and Child's *A Romance of the Republic*, attempt to imagine a national identity defined by democratic principles rather than race and blood. When one juxtaposes Robert Montgomery Bird's *Nick of the Woods* (1837) with *The Last of the Mohicans* or Lydia Maria Child's *Romance of the Republic* with John Kennedy Pendleton's *Swallow Barn*, the genre of the historical romance begins to resemble a heated debate, with each romancer arguing for a different conception of the national character and a different myth of the national genesis.

The historical romance's passion for the subject of national identity is best understood in light of a few important historical facts. Perhaps the most basic and obvious consideration is the fact that the two constitutive elements defining the concept of nation, territory and people, were in a state of radical flux during the nineteenth century. By conquest, treaty, and purchase, the nation's territory quadrupled, and its population grew at an exponential rate. The sheer diversity of religions, nations of origin, races, ethnicities, and cultures represented by the nation's populace by the end of the nineteenth century would seem to complicate if not preclude the possibility of a unitary national identity. To allay concerns aroused by this rapid and extensive change in the nation's populace, the historical romance attempts to imagine a shared or core national identity impervious to or able to withstand such transformations. It also seems likely that certain ambiguities in the identity of the nation's citizenry invited the genre's repeated attempt to imagine the quintessential American character.

At least from one perspective, American citizenship is defined by political and ethical abstractions rather than a particular bloodline. The nation's seminal document, the Declaration of Independence, speaks of universal political principles, not a shared genealogy, and, while it contains provisions permitting slavery, the Constitution does not set forth any religious, racial, or ethnic traits as identifying the national body politic. The men authoring the open-ended abstractions of the Declaration and the Bill of Rights, however, tended to conceive of their republican political philosophy as the inheritance of a particular people. As they invoked self-evident and apparently universal truths, such as "all men are created equal," the founders assumed the existence of an organic community whose interests and outlook were generally homogeneous. Thomas Jefferson suspected, as Garry Wills puts it, that "a certain homogeneity was necessary" for a democratic society (301). The Declaration's figure of "one people" implicitly drew on a myth of Anglo-Saxon liberty deeming the Americans' capacity for self-rule to be a shared racial heritage. In asserting their constitutional liberties, British colonists, in the view of James Otis (a Boston lawyer and pamphleteer whose arguments on behalf of the colonists' natural rights influenced the course of revolutionary thinking) were simply recovering a family tradition: "liberty was better understood and more fully enjoyed by our ancestors before the coming in of the first Norman tyrants than ever after" (47). This tendency to ascribe the ostensibly universal political and ethical principles of the American nation to a particular group is well captured by Jefferson's proposal for the Great Seal of the United States. John Adams told his wife that Jefferson's seal had on one side "the children of Israel in the wilderness, led by a cloud by day and pillar of fire by night; and on the other side, Hengist and Horsa, the Saxon chiefs from whom we claim the honor of being descended, and whose political principles and form of government we have assumed" (Horsman 22). Adopting the Exodus story, the seal's first side embodies the moral universal of freedom in a symbol that superficially, at least, cuts across lines of ethnic, racial, or cultural difference, but the seal's flip side reverses the thrust of the symbolism to represent the ethos animating the new American nation as the racial legacy of a certain tribe.

At a minimum, the ambiguity of whether the foundational documents express universal values or the birthrights of a particular clan created a gap in the notion of a national identity, which the historical romancers attempted to fill with compelling narrative descriptions of the emergence of the American people. The ostensibly universal principles of the Declaration suggest the contours of one such narrative, and Jefferson's reference to Hengist and Horsa on his proposed seal suggests those of another.

The historical romance's fixation on national identity was also a product of the romanticism which gave birth to the form itself. The romanticism we associate with figures such as Johann Gottfried von Herder, James Macpherson, and Sir Walter Scott tended to privilege the particular genius and identity of each culture as the natural basis for national identity. In the late eighteenth and early nineteenth centuries, intellectuals and artists began to turn their attention to the vernacular culture of their countries' natives, their crafts and folk arts. Previously derided as ignorant and uncouth, the peasant class seemed a veritable gold mine of authentic culture. The folk came to be associated with certain particularly authentic aspects of national identity. While Cooper and Simms and other romancers do not replace the genteel classes with the peasantry, they invoke the notion that humble everyday people embody values and experiences critically important to the emerging national identity. The genteel hero of *The Last of the Mohicans*, Duncan Heyward, must learn from and bond with the somewhat coarse Hawkeye to become a real American. Hawkeye's closeness to nature, his canny understanding of the wild and its natives, as well as his rough but honest nature make him an apt tutor of the young officer in the ways of the land he will one day govern.

In giving both the common folk and the genteel class important roles to play in the national drama, Cooper, Simms, and other historical romancers follow the pattern established by Sir Walter Scott (1771–1832). Scott's historical romances, such as *Waverly* (1814), *Rob Roy* (1817), and *Ivanhoe* (1819), use heroic characters, grand action, and clear historical significance to create an appealing replacement for the epic. Frequently, the drama of Scott's novels is generated by the conflict between cultures and peoples, such as the clashes between Christians and Moslems in *The Talisman* (1825), the Scottish and English in *Rob Roy*, or the Saxons and Normans in *Ivanhoe*. While taking a nostalgic tone in addressing the lost or threatened cultural identity of particular groups, such as the highland Scots, Scott's romances also exhibit a general optimism about the progressive evolution of society, a feeling shared by American historical romancers, who tend to describe progress as a kind of *force majeure*, an inexorable tendency in all things to move in an upward direction. Though they are frequently noble and brave, the less-advanced Indians of Cooper's and Simms's novels are doomed by the tide of progress to obsolescence and extinction. The American historical romance also echoes Scott's romanticizing of the connection between the natural environment and the national character. In *The Lay of the Last Minstrel* (1805), Scott famously celebrated a reverence for one's native land, despising the man who "never to himself hath said, / 'This is my own, my native land!'"

Scott's influence was widespread and varied. It could be felt, as Mark Twain lamented, in the cavalier pretensions of the Old South, its cult of honor, and the valorization of clan or family membership. (Twain went so far as to hold Scott's influence accountable for the Civil War.) However, while we can find Scott's influence in such proslavery romances as William Gilmore Simms's *Woodcraft* (1852), we can also find it in the choice of Frederick Douglass's surname, which was drawn from Scott's poem *The Lady of the Lake* (1810). The name was aptly chosen. Frederick Douglass escaped the slave catchers much as Scott's "black Douglas," a courageous outlaw and member of an "exiled race," escapes his pursuers. Recounting a slave revolt aboard the *Creole*, an American slave ship, Douglass's romance, *The Heroic Slave* (1853), features the heroic Madison Washington, a man with "a giant's strength" and a noble heart. Standing for the "principles of 1776," Douglass's Byronic black rebel subverts the racially homogeneous version of the national identity, implicitly laying claim to the symbolic role of archetypal patriot. Pioneered and made popular by Scott, the historical romance offered a useful template for a variety of idealized scripts of national identity. In the following discussion, I track the course of the nineteenth-century historical romance's preoccupation with national identity through what seem to me to be its most important formulations: the frontier romance, the plantation idyll, and the romance of race and republicanism.

## The frontier romance

As noted above, the historical romance is a capacious form, and nineteenth-century American examples include depictions of the time of Christ (*Ben-Hur*) and the reign of King Henry VIII (*When Knighthood was in Flower*) as well as topics closer to home. A notable line of historical romances takes up the theme of the American Revolution. In Cooper's *The Spy* and Lippard's *Blanche of Brandywine*, common revolutionary soldiers as well as the Founding Fathers become epic heroes in the courageous struggle for a new national identity (though the political implications of this revolutionary moment differ for the conservative Cooper and the radical Lippard). Romances of the Revolution, however, are eclipsed by the frontier tale and its cousins (the plantation romance and the western), which predominate the form of the historical romance in the nineteenth century.

For writers concerned with the theme of national identity, the frontier tale is a natural choice because it prominently features both the territory and the people constituting the nation. In the frontier romance, both of these elements are in a state of flux, becoming "American" through, as Robert Montgomery Bird puts it, the "sanguinary struggle by which alone the desert was to be wrung from the wandering barbarian," a struggle which unites the frontiersmen and settlers in "a common sense of danger" (42, 43). Despite certain variations (consider the contrast between Cooper's noble Indian characters and Bird's utterly brutal savages), frontier tales share an emphasis on the British-American frontiersman or pioneer as representative (with occasional modifications) of important aspects of the national character, and they describe the fight to survive in the land as formative of this identity. Even when protesting the violent oppression of Indians, as Helen Hunt Jackson does in *Ramona* (1884), the frontier romance identifies the American people as Anglo-American in origin and culture.

One of the important precursors to the nineteenth-century frontier romance is John Filson's history *The Discovery, Settlement, and Present State of Kentucky* (1784), particularly the pages purporting to be a first-hand account of "The Adventures of Col. Daniel Boon" [sic]. Gilbert Imlay, James Fenimore Cooper, and Robert Montgomery Bird prominently feature scenes resembling the rescue of Boone's daughter described in Filson's book, and Boone is the forerunner of a long line of intrepid wilderness heroes, such as Cooper's Natty Bumppo (*Leatherstocking Tales*) and Bird's Nathan Slaughter (*Nick of the Woods*) (Smith *Virgin Land* 55–60). For Filson, Cooper, Bird, and others, the iconic frontiersman seemed a figure of tremendous national importance. As Richard Slotkin points out,

> Boone undergoes a series of initiations which give him progressively
> greater insights into the life of the Indians, the peculiar necessities
> imposed by the wilderness, and the natural laws which govern
> life. Through his attempts to interpret these initiations, Boone
> attains a higher degree of self-knowledge and self-discipline and an
> ability to impose his own order on both the wilderness and the
> settlement. (*Regeneration* 274)

While different versions of the Boone narrative have emphasized different aspects of the hero (Filson's book gives more play to Boone, the settler, and later versions of the story emphasize Boone, the backwoodsman), he is always a transitional figure – someone who marks the beginning of the end of the wild and the emergence of a people indelibly marked by their struggles to survive in and domesticate the wilderness (Kolodny 29–31). Time and again, the nineteenth-century historical romances turned back to the Boone narrative for its key elements: casting its melodramatic battles, love stories, and rescues in the wild and featuring skilled Boone-like woodsmen, settlers, and other newcomers to this beautiful but dangerous environment, and beautiful women who repeatedly fall into peril, some of whom prove extremely capable. A highly conventional form, the frontier romance's dense forests are often tunnel- or cave-like. The gentleman newcomer and good Indian share graceful and manly features indicating their noble characters, while the ignoble savage's character is denoted by his swarthy features. And the beautiful women are either "fair" or "dark," a color code indicating which one will wind up with the handsome gentlemen heroes of these tales.

The landscape forming the backdrop for these heroic adventures is perhaps the frontier romance's most defining feature. These romances spend a considerable amount of time detailing the natural environment in which the novel's action takes place. The environment plays a central role, often coming to seem a character in its own right. The descriptions range from Robert Montgomery Bird's appreciation of the wild as an economic resource (the "unexampled fertility" of Kentucky which irresistibly lures the frontiersmen and settlers to brave its dangers) to Lydia Maria Child's romantic response to it as a site of poetic and imaginative wonder where a would-be bride is able to conjure an ideal mate in the moonlight (*Nick* 39–40, *Hobomok* 13). These narratives habitually contrast the more and less benign aspects of life in the wild. In *Hope Leslie*, Catharine Maria Sedgwick describes the wild as a form of divine utterance and as a "savage howling wilderness" continually threatening the fragile outposts of civilization established by white settlers (83, 18). In Ann Stephens's popular romance *Malaeska* (1860), a hunter ravished by his "sense of the glorious handiwork of the Almighty" almost falls victim to an Indian ambush. The uplifting feeling inspired by a "little body of water, curling and foaming downward like a wreath of snow sifted from the clouds, breaking in a shower of spray over the shelf of rocks which stayed its progress, then leaping a second foaming mass, down, down, like a deluge of flowing light, another hundred feet to the shadowy depths of the ravine" is accompanied by the horror of a "half-naked" and murderous "savage" lurking at the base of the falls (65–66). Among other effects, this contrast enables the reader both to appreciate the wilderness and to sanction its domestication or containment. Despite its great beauties, the unfettered and always-present danger presented by the wild cannot be tolerated. The land must be settled, and the Indian must be vanquished.

As such sharp juxtapositions in feeling suggest, the wild is associated with tremendous transformative energy. Lulled into a peaceful state of mind by the harmonious beauty of nature, Stephens's hunter is suddenly changed by the Indian attack into a kind of white savage:

His knees trembled, his cheek burned, and, with an impulse of fierce excitement, he leaped over the intervening rocks and stood by the slain savage. He was lying with his face to the earth, quite dead; Jones drew forth his knife, and lifting the long black hair, cut it away from the crown. With the trophy in his hand, he sprang across the ravine. The fearless spirit of a madness seemed upon him, for he rushed up the steep ascent, and plunged into the forest, apparently careless of what direction he took.   (65)

The wilderness described by Stephens and others conjures different kinds of emotional or psychic transport, making one dizzy with its vertiginous beauties or driving one mad with its dark cruelties. Like the "neutral ground" of Cooper's Revolutionary-War era romance *The Spy* (1821), the dangerous and uncertain territory between British and American forces, and like Hawthorne's "neutral territory . . . where the Actual and the Imaginary may meet," the wild is a place where odd or amazing things can happen, where human beings can take on animal qualities or display superhuman abilities (*Scarlet Letter* 111). On a rescue mission in *The Last of the Mohicans*, Cooper's tale of the French and Indian War of 1757, Hawkeye, Uncas, and Chingachgook appear out of nowhere, a "sudden visitation of death," leaping into the midst of their adversaries, striking with uncanny accuracy, gliding and bounding among their enemies like their animal namesakes – "Le Cerf Agile" and "Le Gros Serpent" (111). Later in the novel, Hawkeye's incredibly lifelike imitation of a bear enables him to seize the evil Magua (256–57, 262). The Ovidian tendency of people and things to metamorphose in the wild disrupts normal perception. Each "waving bush" or "fragment of some fallen tree" seems a human form, and a collection of beaver dens around a pond becomes a village of hostile Indians (*Mohicans* 45, 218–19).

In exploring the intersection of imagination and perception and tracing the distortion of the latter under great stress, the romance comes close to psychological realism. However, our recognition of the role played by fear and horror in transforming what is perceived does not relieve the wild of its mystery and otherworldly quality – it is a place where such visions seem to be inevitable, even natural, and where some ability to transform seems to be a prerequisite for survival. Fortunately for the people he saves, Bird's frontiersman Nathan Slaughter can morph from nonviolent Quaker into Nick of the Woods, a fearsome Indian killer. Cooper's Duncan Heyward cannot persist in his stiff gentlemanly manner and survive. He must become more pliable and chameleon-like, a feat he attempts when he impersonates a madman (228–29). Borrowing Edwin Fussell's description of the West, we might say that certain romancers suspected that the wild might better "be defined as a condition of the soul than as a physiographical region" – a place where the soul goes through some kind of transformative experience redefining the person (9).

The "neutral ground" of the wild is a territory between the imaginary and the actual where extraordinary things can and do happen. Though it is not a frontier tale, one can see the potential political and social ramifications of this transformative, even revolutionary energy in Douglass's romance *The Heroic Slave*, where the wild setting of the ocean facilitates and inspires a revolt that would be far less possible on land: "It is one thing to manage a company of slaves on a Virginia plantation, and quite another thing to quell an insurrection on the lonely billows of the Atlantic, where every breeze speaks of courage and liberty" (228). As this passage suggests, in the wild, outside the bounds of the law and social convention, identity becomes malleable and whatever social order is present may be refashioned or transformed. Madison Washington, the slave, becomes Madison Washington the captain. Duncan Heyward, the Major, learns to take orders from the uneducated Hawkeye and his Indian friends. Eventually, the "imbecility" of British leadership will be replaced by a "Virginia boy" whose deeds in the French and Indian War are the one bright spot in an otherwise dismal effort. While frontier romances vary considerably in their political outlook, they all imagine some degree of social fluidity as essential to wilderness experience, and even the more conservative of these tales recognize some benefit in this increased malleability. In part, it is the mutable nature of society and identity in the wild that recommends it to the romancer wanting to envision the formation of a new national identity. The confrontation or clash of rigid manners and social expectations associated with the Old World and the liberating yet threatening formlessness of the wild become generative of new forms, new attitudes, and new social patterns in the frontier romance (Fussell 16).

The wild also appeals to the nineteenth-century historical romancer for its ability to connect historical time to a kind of mythic timelessness. The wild environs described in these novels are caught in a historical process of settlement and domestication, but these primordial forests and unmarked wildernesses also paradoxically appear to be places where the passage of time has made no apparent difference. For instance, the genteel hero and heroine of Bird's *Nick of the Woods*, Edith and Roland, make their way into a vast, powerful, and unchanging wilderness:

> The forest, into which they had plunged, was of the grand and gloomy
> character which the fertility of the soil and the absence of the axe for a
> thousand years imprint on the western woodlands, especially in the
> vicinity of rivers. Oaks, elms, and walnuts, tulip-trees and beeches, with

other monarchs of the wilderness, lifted their trunks like so many pillars, green with mosses and ivies, and swung their majestic arms, tufted with mistletoe, far over head, supporting a canopy, – a series of domes and arches without end, – that had for ages overshadowed the soil. Their roots, often concealed by a billowy undergrowth of shrubs and bushes, oftener by brakes of the gigantic and evergreen cane, forming fences as singular as they were, for the most part, impenetrable, were yet at times visible, where open glades stretched through the woods, broken only by buttressed trunks, and by the stems of colossal vines, hanging from the boughs like cables, or the arms of an oriental banyan; while their luxuriant tops rolled in union with the leafy roofs that supported them. (95)

The monumentality of the wilderness and its apparent stillness is useful to the historical romancer who would turn prosaic events of the past into something larger and more mythic. The heroic qualities of the actors in the frontier drama, their bravery and fortitude, are magnified by the contrast between their relative puniness and the vastness of untrammeled nature, as when Cooper describes a sizable force of reinforcements marching off to Fort William Henry and "the forest at length appeared to swallow up the living mass which had slowly entered its bosom" (*Mohicans* 15). The romancer's appreciative description of the majesty of the wild simultaneously applauds the intrepid backwoodsmen and settlers who tamed this vast and apparently impervious realm and registers some bittersweet nostalgia for the vanquished primeval forests and the obsolete frontiersmen and pioneers who conquered the wild.

Such nostalgia reflects, in part, the ambivalence nineteenth-century audiences felt toward the massive changes overtaking their world, making it smaller, domesticating it, such as the advent of the steamship, telegraph, and railroad. Writers in the nineteenth century were fond, as Leo Marx has noted, of using the phrase "The annihilation of time and space" to indicate the remarkable pace of technological progress during their era (194). The romancer's image of the wild, in its vastness and apparent immutability, appealingly resists such "annihilation" and stands for something more basic and permanent in life than advances in transportation and communication. Unlike the "overcivilized," "effeminate," and relatively luxurious world produced by technological progress and increasingly enjoyed by the middle and upper classes in the nineteenth century, the frontier romance's representation of a primeval and unchanging wild stands for a kind of "authentic" experience, appealing to its audience's desire, in Jackson Lears's words, "to smash the glass and breathe freely – to experience 'real life' in all its intensity" (xiv, 4–5). Yet the view offered by the historical romance is retrospective – the frontier it examines has passed away and been replaced by civilization and progress. If the frontier appeals because it represents some more authentic, essential, or permanent conception of life, then what happens to those values as we acknowledge the frontier's passing? For the romancers and their audience, the answer would seem to be that what is authentic and valuable in the wild has been imbibed by the American people. They have absorbed the wild and the formative experiences of those exploring and domesticating it and have become the repository of the land's essential, pre-domesticated character. Actual frontier figures, such as Boone or Kit Carson, are made into symbols of a certain kind of pre-modern, authentic experience by Cooper, Bird, James Kirke Paulding, Emerson Bennett, Charles Averill, and many others, and the figure of the frontiersman survives the end of the frontier famously announced by Frederick Jackson Turner, continuing to reside in the national imaginary as definitional of the national character.

In addition to sharing plots centered on the conflict between white settlers and Indians, frontier romances prominently feature love triangles. In Lydia Maria Child's *Hobomok*, the valiant Indian Hobomok and genteel Charles Brown both fall in love with Mary Conant. Mary initially marries the Indian, but, thanks to Hobomok's self-sacrifice, she is eventually able to become the bride of the Englishman. Decades later reprising many of the elements of Child's tale, Helen Hunt Jackson's *Ramona* describes the love of two men, the noble Indian Alessandro Assis and the aristocratic Californio Felipe Moreno, for Ramona. Ramona runs away to become Alessandro's wife, but after his murder she is rescued by Felipe, becoming a part of the genteel, landowning class of Spanish descent. The harrowing and violent events of the French and Indian War fail to obstruct the romantic intrigue connecting Heyward, Cora, and Alice in *The Last of the Mohicans*. Heyward, the reader recognizes straightaway, is not destined for the dark beauty Cora who has black blood on her mother's side. His bride must be Cora's fair half-sister, Alice. In *Nick of the Woods*, Rolland (the Duncan Heyward figure) is caught between Esther, a fair (Alice-like) beauty, and Telie Doe, the dark beauty. Of course, like Heyward, Roland is destined for the former, while the latter is better suited for marriage to the humble woodsman, Richard Bruce. In Cooper's revolutionary-era romance *The Spy*, the turbulence of the relations of Frances Wharton, Isabella Singleton, and Major Dunwoodie can reach a kind of stasis with the death of Isabella. Culminating in happy unions, the stories of Mary Conant and Charles Brown, Ramona Ortegna and Felipe Moreno, Duncan Heyward and Alice Munro, Roland and Esther Forrester not only give a comic or providential gloss to the chaos and terror of the tale's wilderness violence but also suggest in the figure of marriage the ordering of a new national family.

Perhaps the most revealing line of inquiry to take with these romances lies in tracing their ostensibly positive and negative characterizations of Indians. This topic is, of course, central to figures and themes of national identity. As many have observed, even as they were engaged in a campaign to appropriate Indian lands and decimate tribal populations, nineteenth-century white Americans often looked to Indian life and culture for attributes distinguishing the American character, such as a rugged self-sufficiency and an indomitable spirit enabling survival even in the most trying of circumstances. Without exception, as far as I am aware, all of the nineteenth-century frontier romances assume the inevitability of the conflict between whites and Indians as well as the eventual dominance of white Americans, but they approach this conflict and its result from somewhat different perspectives. Some see it as tragic if inevitable (e.g., Cooper and Simms). Others see it as a subject of some degree of national disgrace (e.g., Child, Sedgwick, and Jackson). And still others view the first two positions as absurd, even dangerous, given the threat posed by this savage race to the forces of civilization (Bird, Edward Ellis, and Edward Wheeler).

The more positive renderings of Indian character often stress the physical signs of an essential nobility which seems to flow from the grandeur of the landscape into the children of the wild. Hobomok has a "tall, athletic form" and a natural dignity that marks him as a kind of gentleman of the forest (16). Cooper's Uncas has a form and features worthy of a "Grecian chisel," and his inherent nobility of character is intuitively recognized by the wilderness neophyte, Duncan Heyward, who shares some of his fundamental traits, such as valor and self-sacrifice, "Shaking hands, the two young men exchanged looks of intelligence, which caused Duncan to forget the character of his wild associate" (73). The nobility of Chief Sanutee in Simms's romance *The Yemassee* is apparent in his handsome and athletic lineaments, just as the degraded character of the pirate Richard Chorley is apparent in his "daring insolence of look and gesture," his "red, full face, and the watery eye" which speak of his profligate indulgences (I, 30). When the villainous Chorley kills (with apparent relish) Sanutee's dog, the reader sides completely with the noble Sanutee (there is no clearer marker of wickedness in American culture than the wanton killing of a pet, especially a dog), a neat reversal of character type Simms uses to align our initial vision of the conflict with that of the noble Indian in opposition to the savage European (I, 32). The degradation suffered by the Indian people is, Simms suggests, the colonists' fault (I, vii). While he does not see their fate as avoidable, Simms has considerable sympathy for the Indians as a once great nation now overcome by the tide of history. More than once he compares them to the Romans and Sanutee to Cassius, who was mourned by Brutus as the last of the Romans (I, 18).

The more sympathetic portraits of Indians in this fiction arise from the romantic belief that, as Catharine Maria Sedgwick puts it in *Hope Leslie*, "there is a chord, even in the heart of a savage man, that responds to the voice of nature" (83). For these writers, untamed nature is occasionally capable of producing superbly noble characters. Sedgwick's Indian heroine Magawisca is a perfect example of this natural valor. She unflinchingly sacrifices her arm to save young Everell Fletcher from death, and, in the novel's climactic trial scene, she appears to be a kind of Indian Patrick Henry demanding that the colonists give her "death or liberty" (293). Cooper's Uncas and Chingachgook, Sedgwick's Magawisca, Child's Hobomok, and Helen Hunt Jackson's Alessandro Assis all derive some sense of the divine spirit animating all things directly from the wild (e.g., Hobomok "imbibed his faith from the lights of nature," and Assis "had never read of God, but he had heard his chariot wheels in the distant thunder, and seen his drapery in the clouds" [*Hobomok* 117, *Ramona* 34]).

While, as Richard Drinnon rightly reminds us, even relatively sympathetic writers such as Cooper frequently portray Indians as "stock merciless savages," the fact that these romances contain a few spectacularly heroic Indians raises the possibility that history might have taken a different course, that there might have been something akin to a partnership between these peoples and cultures (160). Ann Stephens, for example, describes her eponymous heroine Malaeska as combining "all that was strong, picturesque, and imaginative in savage life, with the delicacy, sweetness, and refinement which follows in the train of civilization, had trod with her the wild beautiful scenery of the neighborhood" (124). Malaeska's very incarnation of the best of both worlds would seem to recommend the project of integrating Euro-American and American Indian societies and cultures. When Hawkeye, Uncas, Chingachgook, Heyward, and Colonel Munro attempt to pursue the villainous Magua who has captured Cora and Alice during an ambush, Hawkeye and his Indian friends argue about whether they should proceed by land or cross Lake George in canoes. The disagreement is in earnest and respectful, and when Hawkeye musters the better argument, Chingachgook and Uncas "became converts to his way of thinking" with "liberality and candour" (Cooper *Mohicans* 199). Despite the fact that the white man has made the better argument, the debate and subsequent agreement is striking for the mutual respect displayed by all three. Each participates in the discussion and the informed consent of each is critically important to the success of their dangerous venture. The cooperation between Chingachgook, Uncas, and Hawkeye is a striking example of a kind of natural republicanism and consensual process that cuts across racial lines. However, such hopeful visions are repeatedly conjured in the more sympathetic examples of this genre only to be dismissed, signaling the limits to these romances' appreciations of the Indians' natural nobility. As Sankar Muthu points out, valorizations of the Indian's *natural* or *primitive* virtue come at the cost of seeing them as incapable of cultural and moral development, a thesis that unintentionally offers further grounds for the imperialist project (23). The savage may be noble, but he isn't civilized. And when push comes to shove, it's the latter that matters most.

Child's *Hobomok*, which goes further than most of these romances in the direction of envisioning a white/Indian partnership in the form of Mary Conant's marriage to the noble Hobomok, ends with Hobomok voluntarily sacrificing himself and his marriage so that Mary can unite with her first love Charles Brown. While Hobomok and Mary's child has Indian blood, he will be raised as white and educated in England. Hobomok himself will go west to die (139). Little Charles Hobomok Conant's father

> was seldom spoken of; and by degrees his Indian appellation was silently omitted. But the devoted, romantic love of Hobomok was never forgotten by its object [i.e., Mary]; and his faithful services to the "Yengees" are still remembered with gratitude; though the tender slip which he protected, has since become a mighty tree, and the nations of the earth seek refuge beneath its branches. (150)

This final passage of Child's novel portrays Hobomok's protection and sacrifice as key factors in the nation's birth and survival. His blood mingles with the family tree of white America, and his sacrifice facilitates a resolution to the family crisis, Mary's alienation from her father in a divisive split over religion (Charles Brown is a High Church Anglican to which Mr. Conant as a Puritan objects). But having helped heal this breach, Hobomok must depart. There is no room for Hobomok himself in the figure of the unified people who will proceed to develop the nation and its cultural identity.

Hope Leslie rescues the noble Indian maid Magawisca, and is briefly reunited with her lost sister Faith, who was taken and held captive by the Indians, but Magawisca must return to the forest as will Faith who, now married to Oneco, Magawisca's brother (to Hope's reflexive and "natural" revulsion), has been transformed into an Indian (188, 331). There is no possibility of an interracial community including all three sisters: Hope, Faith, and Magawisca. Even Helen Hunt Jackson's 1884 novel *Ramona*, which is the most ardent of these romances in protesting the fate of the Indian at the hands of white Americans, ultimately despairs of any better possibility. Whites relentlessly prey upon the Indians, taking their lands and diminishing their numbers by violence and economic exploitation. At the novel's end, Alessandro Assis, the handsome and strong son of an Indian chief and husband of Jackson's half-Indian heroine, Ramona, has been driven mad by this endless persecution before he is murdered, and

Ramona's fate is not to live with the Indians but to be rescued by the aristocratic Felipe Moreno who gives her a very different life as the wife of a wealthy Californio. Of course, we should hasten to point out that, as sympathetic as Child, Sedgwick, and Jackson were to the Indians' plight, history allowed their romances little latitude to envision a happier ending.

The pathos of these unhappy endings is enhanced, in the more sympathetic romances, by the fact that it is the heroic Indian characters who most clearly foresee the dire fate of their people, such as Hobomok, who has a "melancholy presentiment of the destruction of his race," and Chingachgook, who yields to the inevitable tide of history: "all of my family departed, each in his turn, to the land of spirits. I am on the hill-top, and must go down into the valley; and when Uncas follows in my footsteps, there will no longer be any of the blood of the Sagamores, for my boy is the last of the Mohicans" (*Hobomok* 33, *Mohicans* 33). At the end of Cooper's novel, the great prophet and chief of the Delawares, Tamenund, concludes that "The pale-faces are masters of the earth, and the time of the red-men has not yet come again" (350). Similarly, Simms's Sanutee sees "the destiny which awaits his people" (*Yemassee* I, 23). His campaign against the British is a valiant but ultimately futile effort to stave off the inevitable. Contemporary readers, however, may well be struck in these moments by the feeling that having these dignified and resolute Indians acknowledge the inevitability of white dominance converts the conscious decision of one people to undertake the violent conquest of another into something like cosmic destiny or fate – events for which no one is responsible.

The fate of the Indian provokes different explanations or responses in these romances. One line of reasoning that crops up in several of them seems to be an early version of what Ernest Gellner and others describe as "the big gap" – the inequalities of technological power between the first and third worlds. For the frontier romancer, this "gap" seems to render the possibility of communication and consensus among the haves and have-nots inconceivable (in historical practice if not necessarily in theory). Thus, Cooper has Chingachgook suggest that the fate of the Indian has been sealed by the technological superiority of the white men and the inequality of the contest between the bullet and the arrow (30). Sanutee leads the Yemassee to attack the English in part out of a sense that this is their last chance "to arrest the progress of a race" which would eventually dominate the Indian by virtue of superior technology and military might (II, 13). For Helen Hunt Jackson, "industries and inventions" are the hallmarks of the white conquerors (*Ramona* 12). From different political and social perspectives, Jackson (in *Ramona*) and María Ruiz de Burton (in *The Squatter and the Don* [1885]) mourn the onslaught of Yankee technology as spoiling a more natural way of life in California. Ruiz de Burton describes the locomotive, that symbol of white American power, as a "round-eyed monster" shrieking and making a "distant rumble as if of a coming earthquake" (165). In *Seth Jones* (1860), a stripped-down, all-action version of *The Last of the Mohicans* for the dime-novel audience, Edward Ellis reframes this technological superiority in terms of an inherent intellectual difference: "When the Anglo-Saxon's body is pitted against that of the North American Indian, it sometimes yields; but when his mind takes the place of contestant, it *never* loses" (198). The superiority of the white mind is best indicated by its native curiosity: "[Seth] possessed the curious, investigating habits so generally ascribed to his race" (235). Reflecting a similar assumption, Sedgwick describes how Everell Fletcher "opened the book of knowledge" to Magawisca and "had given subjects to her contemplative mind, beyond the mere perception of her senses; had in some measure dissipated the clouds of ignorance that hung over the forest-child" (*Hope Leslie* 263). These (self-justifying) descriptions of the intellectual and cultural superiority of the Anglo-Saxon or white American assume a considerable racial divide and an imbalance of power precluding the possibility of interracial exchange or assimilation. The big gap in technology turns out to be a sign of racial difference, and that difference, whether originating in nature or nurture or both, is offered by these romances as the reason history has taken the course it has.[5]

Certain of these assessments of the Indians' demise are overtly racist. In response to the positive portrayals of Indians by Cooper and others and the suggestion that there is something tragic or perhaps even shameful in the decimation of the Indian people, Robert Montgomery Bird, Edward Ellis, and Edward Wheeler offered romances redolent of deep racial aversion.[6] In Bird's *Nick of the Woods*, Ellis's *Seth Jones*, and Wheeler's *Deadwood Dick*, Indians are unfeeling, bloodthirsty savages, without any respect for the value of human life. The arch-enemy of *Nick of the Woods*, Wenonga, the Chief of the Shawnees who has brutally murdered Nathan Slaughter's family, describes himself as a man without a heart (204). In the westerns that largely inherit the mantle of the frontier romance in the latter part of the nineteenth century, Indians are routinely termed "infarnal critters" "danged descendent[s] o' ther old Satan, hisself," who will stoop to such cruelties as the torture of women (*Deadwood Dick* 275, 279). There simply cannot be any rapprochement with such a "cowardly" and "devilish" race (*Seth Jones* 236, 214). To drive home the absoluteness of the racial difference, these tales repeatedly feature scenes of horrific cruelty. The charred corpse of a man who Seth Jones discovers has been burned to death while tied to a tree stands as a symbol of the Indians' inherent savagery (236). Of course, the student of American history knowing the similar horrors white Americans inflicted on Indians, black Americans, and others cannot help but see an unintended and grotesque irony in this condemnation of the Indian.

Despite their overtly different thematic aims, the frontier romances of both the more sympathetic and the openly hostile stripe often feature the brutal killing of a child as the evidence of a deep racial chasm. Cooper describes an Indian "dash[ing] the head of the infant against a rock, and cast[ing] its quivering remains to [the mother's] very feet" an instant before he drives his tomahawk into her brain (*Mohicans* 175). In *Nick of the Woods*, Bird has his frontiersman, Nathan Slaughter, describe such a scene to establish the evil nature of the Indian enemy and to set up an important qualification to the Quaker's pacifism. When Roland angrily denounces Nathan for standing by while a child is murdered, Nathan corrects him "when I stood in the corn and saw the great brutal Injun raise the hatchet to strike the little child, had there been a gun in my hand, I should – I can't tell thee, friend, what I might have done; but, truly, I should not have permitted the evil creature to do the bloody deed!" (149, 150). Such scenes stand as a kind of racial and moral litmus test. They divide the races, uniting whites of different classes and religions in opposition to the Indian, and they indicate the unavoidability of the racial conflict. While Sedgwick balances her Indian violence with a description of an English-led massacre of the Pequod people and is willing to credit the Indians' capacity for sympathy, she describes the savagery of an attack on Hope Leslie's home with graphic specificity, including the brutal crushing of a helpless infant (64–65). At a minimum, these violent images make the possibility of interracial connection seem practically impossible, but, I think, they also stand for an intuition variously held with differing levels of intensity by white authors and readers that the Indian people are different in kind – an intuition shared by Sedgwick as well as Bird.

The idea of a fundamental racial divide is repeatedly acknowledged by various characters in these romances. Sedgwick's Indian heroine Magawisca, for instance, affirms the impermeability of the racial divide: "the Indian and the white man can no more mingle, and become one, than day and night" (330). And when, after his daughter's death and funeral, Colonel Munro asks Hawkeye to tell the kind Delaware maidens who have honored his daughter "that the Being we all worship, under different names, will be mindful of their charity; and that the time shall not be distant, when we may assemble around his throne, without distinction of sex, or rank, or colour!" Hawkeye demurs that this would violate the Indians' sense of the natural order – it would be "to tell them that the snows come not in winter" (347). Despite its reformist intentions, Helen Hunt Jackson's *Ramona* does little to challenge the notion of an important and essential racial difference setting the Indian off from the white. Elated to learn that Ramona has "Indian blood in her veins," Alessandro repeats the fact to himself over and over, and, when she is first living in the wild, Ramona declares,

"I cannot believe that it is but two days I have lived in the air, Alessandro. This seems to me the first home I have ever had. Is it because I am Indian, Alessandro, that it gives me such joy?" (97, 209). In apparently accepting the determinative importance of a given or blood identity, Jackson comes very near her putative opponents, the Indian-haters, who urge the innateness of Indian savagery.

In two very different romances saturated with an aristocratic point of view, Simms's *The Yemassee* and María Ruiz de Burton's *The Squatter and the Don*, racial difference is cast in expressly hierarchical terms as a matter of the natural ascendance of the more powerful people. Simms's noble Indian Chief Sanutee fully understands

> that the superior must necessarily be the ruin of the race which is inferior – that the one must either sink its existence in with that of the other, or it must perish. He was wise enough to see, that in every case of a leading difference between classes of men, either in colour or organization, such difference must only and necessarily eventuate in the formation of castes, and the one conscious of any inferiority, whether of capacity or of attraction, so long as they remain in propinquity with the other, will tacitly become instruments and bondsmen. (I, 23–24)

Inequality inevitably results in domination and servitude for the inferior class. Inequality necessitates caste. Ruiz de Burton accepts what Sanutee fears – that Indians could be incorporated in "civilized" society as a subordinate class of servants in a position not unlike that held in the antebellum South by slaves:

> Our friendly Indians . . . tilled our soil, pastured our cattle, sheared our sheep, cut our timber, built our houses, paddled our boats, made tiles for our houses, ground our grain, killed our cattle, dressed their hides for market, and made our unburnt bricks; while the Indian women made excellent servants, took care of our children and made every one of our meals. (201)

Here Ruiz de Burton's sense of the properly subordinate role of the Indian in "civilized" society comes very close to the "great commanding truth" guiding the proslavery romances of the Old South. "[W]herever civilized man exists," as Caroline Lee Hentz puts it in her idealized novel of plantation life, *The Planter's Northern Bride* (1854), "there is the dividing line of the high and the low, the rich and the poor, the thinking and the labouring" (32). The overlap among frontier romances more or less sympathetic to the fate of the Indian suggests at least a suspicion and at most an ardent conviction that, whatever the reason, race is connected to power and power determines history just as it determines the outcome of the romances' battles.

## The plantation idyll: a romance of the Old South, slavery, and race

Whether it is embraced or reluctantly admitted, the formula equating superior power with national identity and both power and national identity with the white race corresponds with Chief Justice Roger Taney's infamous definition of citizenship in *Dred Scott*. According to Taney's constitutional etymology, the words "people of the United States," "citizens," and "sovereign people" are "synonymous terms" historically denoting those "who hold the power and conduct the Government through their representatives." In other words, citizenship is an attribute of political power, and political power flows along racial lines. Neither Indians nor African Americans possess the requisite power to be considered "constituent members of this sovereignty." However, there are certain differences in their status (Taney indicates that an individual Indian by leaving his or her tribe can become a "naturalized" citizen, an option he does not admit for African Americans) traceable to the two historical narratives Taney has in mind when comparing the subordinate groups. While "uncivilized," the Indians were nonetheless a "free and independent" people. From "the first emigration to the English Colonies to the present day," Taney says, they were treated with some measure of respect as a sovereign nation in their own right: "Treaties have been negotiated with them, and their alliance sought for in war." As a consequence of coming out on the losing end of armed conflict with British Americans, these formerly free and independent tribes reside "within the limits of the United States under subjection to the white race." By contrast, African Americans, Taney contends, "had for more than a century before [the framing of Declaration of Independence and Constitution] been regarded as beings of an inferior order" who could be legitimately forced into slavery. No people held this opinion "more firmly" than the English, who "seized them on the coast of Africa, and sold them or held them in slavery for their own use" and "took them as ordinary articles of merchandise to every country where they could make a profit on them, and were far more extensively engaged in this commerce than any other nation in the world" (*Dred Scott* 404, 407–08).

Taney's comparison of the degraded status of Indians and black Americans evokes a pair of related but different historical romances. The plot of the frontier romance – two nations fight and one is vanquished – has a certain clarity in regard to the issue of national identity. By the terms of the storyline, the conquered Indians are not and never were constituent members of the national populace. The romance of race and slavery is messier, more metaphysical, and, despite Taney's denials, more hopefully open-ended. He cannot simply class the "negroes" brought to this country more than a hundred years before the Revolution as an "alien" or "foreign" nation. Their story is not one of battle, defeat, and expulsion or quarantined subordination on "reservations" as a separate but subjugated nation within a nation. While disenfranchised (though not to the extent that Taney avers), black Americans were undeniably an integral part of the nation's populace, and, unlike the Indian whose subordinate status can be attributed by Taney to defeat in a war between nations, the permanently subordinate status of the "negro" is dependent on a bit of magic – the transformation of human beings into "merchandise" so that kidnapping becomes something akin to harvest or manufacture – an illusion that Taney senses is losing its grip on the nation's imagination. "It is difficult at this day," Taney admits, "to realize the state of public opinion in relation to that unfortunate race, which prevailed ... at the time of the Declaration of Independence" (407). Because "public opinion" on this issue is changing, to maintain the propriety of slavery and racial caste, Taney has to urge that the only legally relevant opinion is the proslavery one of the men who framed the Constitution, "Any other rule of construction would abrogate the judicial character of this court, and make it the mere reflex of the popular opinion or passion of the day" (426). Not comfortable with simply dismissing the shifting currents of popular opinion on this issue, pro- and anti-slavery novelists offered competing romances of race, slavery, and the Old South.

The proslavery romance of the Old South responds to the winds of change in public opinion by creating a vision of a timeless agrarian paradise characterized by gracious and unhurried living in harmony with nature and benevolent relations between those who have power and those who don't. The caring and organic qualities of this world, its slow pace – the intimacy of its inhabitants with each other, its toleration of indolence on the part of the laborer as well as the landlord – stand in sharp contrast to the aggressiveness and artificiality of the Northern mercantile or capitalistic system. If overcome by market forces, technological innovation, and individual ambition, the pastoral society of the South will be replaced by something far uglier, crueler, and less natural, a society emblematized by the factory and the mill. In this capitalistic society, as de Tocqueville observed, all notions of sympathetic or quasi-familial emotional connections and duties between people have been stripped away, reducing the central human relation to the simple and often brutal exchange of labor for pay: "The manufacturer asks nothing of the workman but his labour; the workman expects nothing from him but his wages. The one contracts no obligation to protect, nor the other to defend; and they are not permanently connected by either habit or duty." The centrality of economic exchange and acquisition of wealth to this world works against the creation of "mutual traditions or mutual hopes" (qtd. Davis 87–88). We get a glimpse of this brave new world in Rebecca Harding Davis's *Life in the Iron-Mills* (1861):

> The mills for rolling iron are simply immense tent-like roofs, covering acres of ground, open on every side. Beneath these roofs Deborah looked in on a city of fires, that burned hot and fiercely in the night. Fire in every horrible form: pits of flame waving in the wind; liquid metal-flames writhing in tortuous streams through the sand; wide caldrons filled with boiling fire, over which bent ghastly wretches stirring the strange brewing; and through all, crowds of half-clad men, looking like revengeful ghosts in the red light, hurried, throwing masses of glittering fire. It was like a street in Hell.    (45)

In this capitalistic and industrial hell, all signs of humanity and human feeling are effaced. For instance, in his story "The Tartarus of Maids," Herman Melville describes how in a paper mill "The human voice was banished from the spot. Machinery – that vaunted slave of humanity – here stood menially served by human beings, who serve mutely and cringingly as the slave serves the Sultan. The girls did not so much seem accessory wheels to the general machinery as mere cogs to the wheels" (182). In conjuring the idyllic, pastoral, and passionate world of the plantation as the antithesis to a hellish life dominated by capitalism and industry, the romancer of the Old South blithely ignores the economic reality that Southern plantations sold their cotton to Northern textile mills. Melville's appalled narrator, a seed seller wanting to purchase paper for his business, embodies the ubiquitous complicity of all participants in the market system in the creation of this hellish world. Even the yeoman farmer buying those seeds supports the satanic mill.

Like the frontier romances which drew upon such documentary accounts as John Filson's description of Daniel Boone's adventure, the romance of the Old South, as Lewis Simpson has pointed out, had its own documentary models. John Pendleton Kennedy's *Swallow Barn* (1832), William Gilmore Simms's *Woodcraft* (1852), and Thomas Nelson Page's *In Ole Virginia* (1887) inherited from Robert Beverley's *The History and Present State of Virginia* (1705) a vision of the South as a "secure world redeemed from the ravages of history, a place of pastoral independence and pastoral permanence" (Simpson 16–17). Of course, like the wilderness of the frontier romance, the unchanging and idyllic plantation world appeals precisely because it is either lost to or imperiled by the forces of history and change. From Sir Walter Scott's *Rob Roy* to Margaret Mitchell's *Gone with the Wind*, one of the emotional payoffs of the historical romance is its bittersweet celebration of a world that once seemed to be timeless but which has been overcome by the tides of change. As John Pendleton Kennedy puts it in prefatory material he appended to *Swallow Barn*, the romance of the Old South seeks to exhibit a picture of country life in the South that is threatened by "progress." The pre-modern authentic and more essential existence located by the frontier romance in the wild is repositioned by the romance of the Old South to the "sunny luxuriance of her old-time society – its good fellowship, its hearty and constitutional companionableness, the thriftless gayety of the people, their dogged but amiable invincibility of opinion, and that overflowing hospitality which knew no ebb." With the advent of capitalism and its technological marvels, the steamship, telegraph, and railroad, the piquant and striking characteristics of this distinctively Southern world are being replaced by a bland universalism which, in turn, is robbing the national identity of its savor: "An observer cannot fail to note that the manners of our country have been tending towards a uniformity which is visibly effacing all local differences . . . What belonged to us as characteristically American, seems already to be dissolving into a mixture which affects us unpleasantly as a tame and cosmopolitan substitute for the old warmth and salient vivacity of our ancestors" (Kennedy 8–9). The better, more authentic world Kennedy would preserve in his romance is characterized by its love of stasis and its fear of progress.

In its ramshackle and unkempt appearance (a feature of Southern farms and towns often read by Northerners from Frederick Law Olmstead to Harriet Beecher Stowe as a sign of a lack of moral character), Swallow Barn, the plantation for which Kennedy's romance is named, embodies inactivity, indolence, and a resistance to the very notion of improvement. The cultivated land of the plantation is interpenetrated with swamps, streams, and forests, making it seem a very minimal intervention into the natural landscape. Human beings have left their marks, but these signs are not out of harmony with the environment. The human intrusion is here respectfully limited, willing to accept nature's resistance to cultivation and to tolerate a considerable degree of natural decay. The personality of the squire of the manor, Frank Meriwether (whose name suggests the change in climate and feeling as one moves from the North to the South), corresponds to and explains the condition of the plantation. Meriwether openly lacks any desire to impose his will on the land or his society. His preference is to let things be. He could "improve" his plantation, but he won't. He could run for Congress and change the country, but he won't (32). Meriwether is similarly uninterested in the possibility that certain improvements to his plantation might enhance his profits. He is content with his present mode of existence. Kennedy's descriptions of Meriwether and Swallow Barn enhance the organic feel of both. Their closeness to untrammeled nature is suggested by the degree of irregularity and chaos characterizing both the master and his plantation. They each have fallow as well as cultivated aspects in similar proportions. In its love of the uncultivated, the unmanicured, the romance of the Old South is deeply skeptical that human beings actually improve life through their interventions and schemes. Change, if it comes and if it is to be beneficial, must come gradually, less as a matter of human will and agency and more as a result of the tide of natural events.

The romance of the Old South is a paean to stasis. Stasis, however, requires a considerable degree of isolation from the rest of the world. As a result, Kennedy's idyllic plantation world is threatened by the new technologies of the steamship and the railroad facilitating interstate contact and commerce. Unlike Frederick Douglass who embraced the notion that the world was moving in a cosmopolitan direction in part due to the effects of the steamship, railroad, and telegraph in annihilating time and space, Kennedy's planter, Meriwether, is markedly anxious about the effect of these improvements: "This annihilation of space, sir, is not to be desired. Our protection against the evils of consolidation consists in the very obstacles to our intercourse . . . Dubbs of Dinwiddie made a good remark – That the home material of Virginia was never so good as when her roads were at their worst" (72–73).[7] Implicitly, part of what is at stake in such changes is the values of the Old South. Never having traveled much beyond the Old Dominion, Meriwether's values are true to his locale and upbringing. Untainted by heterodox opinions, he remains "kind and considerate" toward "his servants and dependents," and his slaves "hold him in most affectionate reverence, and, therefore, are not only contented, but happy under his dominion" (34). But just as the land can be threatened by economic development, so too the benevolence of these relations and the communal fellow feeling animating the Southern society can be threatened by exposure to other cultures, other values, and the cosmopolitan drift of modernity. Indeed, Frederick Douglass's life story, while an abomination from the proslavery perspective, nonetheless offers an illustration of the destructive impact of cosmopolitan influences on the relations of master and slave (Crane *Race* 104–30).

These plantation romances rewrite the formula of the frontier romance so that the Southern gentry are in the position of the noble savages or, shifting models, the position of Scott's Highland chieftains. This gentry and its way of life are under siege by the forces of change, but the contest itself is not depicted. Instead, the clearly desperate competition between a more static, local, organic, and caring way of life and an unfeeling industrial capitalism is assumed as the initial premise for a frankly sentimental journey back in time to a lost or nearly lost world. As is the case with other historical romances, the retrospective glance at this extinct or endangered world of the plantation is attended by a sense of loss. This melancholy intuition, however, does not indicate surrender. The threat to Southern traditions and institutions may be great, even insurmountable, but it does not lead to an acceptance that the values of this way of life are outmoded or obsolete. The Southerner is characterized, as Kennedy says, by his "dogged but amiable invincibility of opinion," and the romance of the Old South contains a considerable element of dogged critique and protest (8–9). It refuses to abandon the overarching or master principle that life closer to nature is better and that the closer to nature one gets the more inevitable and beneficial hierarchical social arrangements will seem.

There are at least two prominent problems in this romantic and idealized vision of the Old South as a pastoral society in harmony with nature and held together by the mutual affection and sympathy of all of its members. First, as Louis Rubin has pointed out, the more one mulls over the romancers' dream of an idyllic plantation life, the more its distinctly bourgeois and capitalist aspect emerges. The fantasy of a leisured existence on "the fresh green breast of the new world" is shared by Fitzgerald's Jay Gatsby as well as Faulkner's Thomas Sutpen (Rubin 47). Offered as a critique of the brutal and dehumanizing nature of the North's capitalist economic system and its selfish and materialistic values, the beau ideal of plantation life was in fact a sign "of the very acquisitiveness and social mobility that it is supposed to rebuke" – a connection that could be fleshed out historically by looking at the economic interdependence of Northern textile mills and Southern plantations (Rubin 49). Second, the benign and pastoral vision of the Old South is troubled even more fundamentally by the presence of slavery. To create and maintain a system of perpetual bondage requires the very human agency and artifice that the romances of the Old South so ardently deny. The dynamics of power suggested by the mere existence of slavery threaten to make the institutions and social arrangements of the Old South seem no more natural or organic than a society of factory workers, owners, and various merchants and middlemen bound only by economic interest or necessity.

The literary challenge faced by the proslavery romancer is to make the act of will involved in putting and keeping people in bondage disappear so that the peculiar institution will seem as natural and inevitable as the verdant greenery of the Southern landscape. For proslavery romancers and apologists, the solution was to make slavery as a family affair. In *Woodcraft* (1852), William Gilmore Simms responds to Harriet Beecher Stowe's portrait of slavery in *Uncle Tom's Cabin* (1852) as a despotic relation grounded in the power of one group to hold another in bondage. Simms's romance centers on the joint efforts of a master and servant, Porgy and Tom, to be reestablished on the family estate, Glen-Eberly, after the Revolutionary War. Porgy and Tom are held together not by force but by mutual affection which Simms, with a self-consciously humorous irony, figures as ownership, having Tom declare "Ef I doesn't b'long to *you, you* b'long to *me*! . . . *You* b'long to me Tom, jes' as much as me Tom b'long to *you*; and you nebber guine git *you* free paper from me as long as you lib" (581). The comedy here does not obscure the deeply held notion that the proper connection between master and slave is one of affection and loyalty not force. Years later, after the Civil War and Reconstruction, Thomas Nelson Page's story "Marse Chan" celebrates the happier days of the Old South, when time moved slowly and human relations on the plantations were characterized by trust and fellow feeling between masters and slaves. The familial nature of the connection between loyal servant and benevolent master meant that each took care of the other in hard times: "de same doctor come to see 'em whar 'ten' to de white folks when dey wuz po'ly" (10). The bond between the servant Sam and Marse Chan is an alloy of brotherly affection and the fealty of the dutiful subject to his rightful ruler. When Marse Chan is born, his father, "ole marster,"

> put de baby right in my arms (it's de truth I'm tellin' yo'!), an' yo' jes'
> ought to a-heard de folks sayin', "Lawd! marster, dat boy'll drap dat
> chile!" "Naw, he won't," sez marster; "I kin trust 'im." And den he sez:
> "Now, Sam, from dis time you belong to yo' young Marse Channin'; I
> wan' you to tek keer on 'im ez long ez he lives. You are to be his boy from
> dis time. An' now," he sez, "carry 'im in de house." An' he walks arfter
> me an' opens de do's fur me, an' I kyars 'im in my arms, an' lays 'im
> down on de bed. An' from dat time I was tooken in de house to be Marse
> Channin's body-servant.   (5–6)

Such affection and loyalty can be neither bought nor commanded.

As proslavery apologist George Fitzhugh understood, by comparing the master/slave relation to the parent/child or spousal relations, the subordination involved in slavery can be made to seem natural, inevitable, and benign. The fact of subordination, by itself, need not cause any alarm. After all, who would treat a young child as competent to make her own decisions and live independently without regulation by an adult? Who would pretend that the regulation of such a child by a caring adult is tyrannical? Of course, to accept the application of this principle to black adults depends on one's acceptance of a natural and inevitable inequality between the races. Comparing human society to ant colonies or bee hives, Fitzhugh argues that inequality is the great and ubiquitous rule of nature (*Sociology* 25–26, 177–79). Benevolently authoritarian institutions, such as slavery and marriage, represent the only moral way of addressing the pervasive and apparently natural inequalities characterizing humankind as well as nature's other life forms. The family's innately hierarchical structure, with the husband and father at the head, for Fitzhugh, offered a model for all natural and just forms of government. The naturalness of the family's hierarchical arrangement disproved the social compact theory of Locke and his American disciples: "Fathers do not derive their authority, as heads of families, from the consent of wife and children" (*Cannibals* 353). Social contracts, equality, natural rights, and the consent of the governed, as well as the right of revolution to sweep away corrupt human institutions, were the destructive fantasies of abstract or visionary thinkers, such as Jefferson, who knew only how to tear down not how to construct a society. Real prophets, like Moses, built a just social order based upon the natural fact of inequality and the understanding that justice only comes in the paternalistic form of the strong protecting the weak.

Thomas Dixon's romances of the Reconstruction era, *The Clansman* (1905) and *The Leopard's Spots* (1902), and D. W. Griffith's filmic adaptation of *The Clansman*, *The Birth of a Nation* (1915), depict in floridly racist terms the social chaos and violence wrought by overturning the benevolent hierarchical social arrangement of the Old South. The kindly and noble plantation owner is deposed by carpetbaggers and opportunistic, clownish freedmen. In the absence of the caring regulation of slavery, a malign strain of black man flourishes who preys upon the isolated and vulnerable white women in the rural South. The Ku Klux Klan (a name which refers to the romantic legends of Scottish Highlanders) arises to put things back into some semblance of order, but gone forever are the happier days of a familial relation between the races. From a different vantage point, María Ruiz de Burton's romance of the destruction of Old California, *The Squatter and the Don* (1885), offers a strikingly similar account of the social and economic consequences of replacing the paternalist and aristocratic order with unregulated capitalism. Don Mariano Alamar's thoughtful stewardship is replaced by the Treaty of Guadalupe-Hidalgo with the nightmare of Yankee greed and the rule of the mob. The squatter canaille who seize Don Mariano's land are not different in kind from their upper-class analogues the Railroad monopolists, Stanford, Huntington, Hopkins, and Crocker, who use their tremendous wealth simply to acquire more wealth and power without regard to the welfare of the people. Don Mariano's wisdom about the types of agriculture best suited to the climate and the land as well as his intelligent capacity to see the possibility of compromise and adjustment of competing interests and needs is drowned out by the selfishness impelling both the squatters in San Diego County and the robber barons in San Francisco (88–96). The productive and orderly pre-treaty world in which each has an appropriate and productive place and role is replaced by a world turned upside down.

## The romance of race and republicanism

Turning the world upside down was precisely what certain novelists had in mind, and they produced counter-romances recasting national identity not as a matter of blood but as a fulfillment of the egalitarian and democratic aspirations of the American Revolution. Like Frederick Douglass's 1852 address "What to the Slave is the Fourth of July," these counter-romances, such as William Wells Brown's *Clotel* (1853) and Lydia Maria Child's *A Romance of the Republic* (1867), represented the nation as suffering from a deeply split personality, caught between radically opposed conceptions of society and law. The nation's history was full of evidence suggesting that the white majority read the abstract values announced in the Declaration of Independence not as universal principles but as their particular birthright, yet, for Douglass, Brown, Child, and many others, the words themselves seemed open-ended, capable of being grafted onto an alternative narrative of national identity. They suggested a different kind of hero, a different set of perils and triumphs, and a different kind of nation.

The Fugitive Slave Act of 1850 did much to inspire the sense that the time had come to recast the national narrative in more fundamentally just terms. Intensifying the penalties for harboring or aiding fugitive slaves and greatly enhancing the ability of Southerners to reclaim their human property, this enactment seemed, for many Northerners, to take what was the disgrace of a discrete and backward region and make it national. In response, Senator Charles Sumner from Massachusetts expressly invoked the power of literature to rewrite American history: "The literature of the age is all on [the slave's] side. Songs, more potent than laws, are for him . . . They who make the permanent opinion of the country, who mould our youth, whose words, dropped into the soul, are the germs of character, supplicate for the Slave" ("Freedom National" 184). Sumner conceived of the fugitive slave's story as particularly affecting and heroic – the perfect subject for romance:

> Rude and ignorant they [the fugitive slaves] may be; but in their very efforts for Freedom they claim kindred with all that is noble in the Past. Romance has no stories of more thrilling interest. Classical antiquity has preserved no examples of adventure and trial more worthy of renown. They are among the heroes of our age. Among them are those whose names will be treasured in the annals of their race. By eloquent voice they have done much to make their wrongs known, and to secure the respect of the world. History will soon lend her avenging pen. Proscribed by you during life, they will proscribe you through all time.

Sir, already judgment is beginning. A righteous public sentiment palsies your enactment. ("Freedom National" 184)

The justice of the fugitives' claims to freedom is linked in this passage (as it is in romances by Douglass, Brown, and Child) to the affective power of their exciting, adventurous, compelling narratives of personal heroism. The force of the reader's recognition of the fugitive slaves' humanity and moral strength is proportional to the affective success of their narratives. Behind Sumner's appreciation of the power of literature to open the public's mind by stirring its heart is an implicit appreciation of literary innovation. Literature can offer persuasive new conceptions of old truths ("all that is noble in the Past"). Creating a new heroic icon, the black patriot struggling for freedom, the fugitive slave narrative breaks the egalitarian and democratic ethos of the American Revolution out of its racial chrysalis.

Interestingly, Sumner's comments do not distinguish between autobiographical and fictional accounts of the fugitive slave's life – presumably both the documentary and novelistic versions strike him as heroic romances worthy of the age. This ambiguity usefully reminds us of the hybrid nature of these genres. As Cindy Weinstein points out in "The Slave Narrative and Sentimental Literature," proslavery advocates often contended that slave narratives were not authentic to the extent that they seemed like novels. Harriet Jacobs's seven-year imprisonment, for instance, struck some as resembling the implausible and amazing events of the romance, as did Ellen Crafts's imitation of a white man in making her escape from slavery. Ironically, the factual events and details drawn from documentary accounts give considerable romantic power to the novels of William Wells Brown and Lydia Maria Child. Whether documentary, fictional, or a blend of the two, Sumner fully appreciated the political power of the narratives we depend on to illustrate our abstract political values.

In contrast to the slow-moving and static life depicted in the romance of the Old South, anti-slavery writers tended to use movement as a figure for the social and political transformation the writers wanted to engender. For instance, in his address "The Slumbering Volcano" (1848), Frederick Douglass gives a telling sketch of Madison Washington (the romantic hero of Douglass's novel, *The Heroic Slave*) aboard *The Creole*:

> About twilight on the ninth day, Madison, it seems, reached his head above the hatchway, looked out on the swelling billows of the Atlantic, and feeling the breeze that coursed over its surface, was inspired with the spirit of freedom. He leapt from beneath the hatchway, gave a cry like an eagle to his comrades beneath, saying, we must go through. (Great

> applause.) Suiting his action to the word, in an instant his guilty master
> was prostrate on the deck, and in a very few minutes Madison
> Washington, a black man, with woolly head, high cheek bones,
> protruding lip, distended nostril, and retreating forehead, had the
> mastery of that ship, and under his direction, that brig was brought
> safely into the port of Nassau, New Providence.   (155)

This passage rather neatly breaks into two parts, the prelude to action, which is described in universal terms as the inspiration of a nature not at rest but in motion, and the sequel, which describes the resultant transformation: a reversal of both personal and political fortunes. Douglass figuratively connects natural movement (the mobility of ocean and wind) to Madison Washington's surging physical movement and vocalization of revolt in a "cry like an eagle." The result is a personal and political transfiguration: the black Washington becomes the republican hero. The movement of the wind and water represents the "natural" intuition that slavery is wrong, that freedom is man's normal state. And Washington's metamorphosis, like that of Douglass himself, dramatically embodies the natural and innate process of development characterizing human existence. The historical incident Douglass has chosen as his subject has the additional symbolic benefit that it involved the seizure of a mode of transportation, emblematic that on the most fundamental level the slave's quest is for freedom of movement.

The winding and elaborate storylines of Brown's *Clotel* (1853) and Child's *A Romance of the Republic* (1867) are marked by a striking amount of domestic and foreign travel, and this physical movement is accompanied by another kind of movement, the crossing and blurring of race lines through miscegenation. Miscegenation generates many of these romances' fantastic and melodramatic elements. It produces the anomaly of visually white people defined by law and custom as black, and this, in turn, allows for moments of great pathos and drama when the hidden racial identity of a character is revealed. Representations of racial mixing also pointedly remind the reader that one effect of the white majority's racist conceptions of identity is to create the threat of "black blood" passing as and intermingling further with "white blood." Interracial romantic relations give the lie to assertions that race proscription – the walling off of the black race either by permanent bondage or by segregation and racial caste – is the natural and inevitable product of the inherent inferiority and subhuman character of the black race. Such romantic attraction suggests that the racial divide is more a product of the imagination than a natural or innate reality. George Washington Cable's *The Grandissimes* (1880), Frances Harper's *Iola Leroy* (1892), Mark Twain's *Pudd'nhead Wilson* (1894), Pauline Hopkins's *Contending Forces* (1900), Charles Chesnutt's *The Marrow of Tradition* (1901), and James Weldon Johnson's *The Autobiography of an Ex-Coloured Man* (1912) variously invoke the symbolic power of the child of miscegenation to reveal the hateful artifice involved in racial oppression. In many respects, Brown and Child are the progenitors of this line of American fiction.

Brown's *Clotel*, the first novel written by an African American, draws on a wide array of documentary material (as well as other fiction – he borrows the basic plot line from a story by Child entitled "The Quadroons"), such as slave narratives, newspaper articles, advertisements, letters, legal tracts, and religious publications. Brown's own fugitive slave narrative is attached to the romance as a kind of introduction. This collage-like mix of documentary material and fiction is clearly intended to lend plausibility to the extraordinary events of Brown's narrative. Inspired by the, then unconfirmed, rumors that Thomas Jefferson had fathered children by one of his slaves, Sally Hemmings, *Clotel* begins with the auction of Jefferson's slave mistress, renamed by Brown as Currer, and their daughters, Clotel and Althesa. Horatio Green, a Virginia gentleman, buys Clotel, falls in love with her, and establishes her in Richmond as his wife in substance if not in law. Clotel insists on the form of marriage though she knows that it lacks legal substance. Currer is sold to a parson transplanted from the North to Natchez, Mississippi, and Althesa eventually is sold to Dr. Henry Morton. Morton, another transplanted Northerner, falls in love with Althesa and marries her, not realizing that Southern law does not sanction his marriage. Later when he and his wife die of yellow fever, their beautiful daughters are shocked to discover that they are legally "black" and subject to seizure and sale (185). One commits suicide rather than submit to the sexual advances of her master, and the other dies of a broken heart when her lover is shot while trying to rescue her. Horatio and Clotel have a daughter, Mary, and for a time, Clotel's life is relatively happy. However, Green subsequently marries a white woman to advance his career, and Clotel is sold while Mary is kept behind to wait on the vengeful Mrs. Green. Clotel and a male accomplice, an intelligent dark-skinned slave named William, escape to the free state of Ohio. In an incident patterned on the famous escape of Ellen and William Craft, Clotel poses as a white gentleman attended by William, playing the role of servant. William continues north to Canada, but Clotel returns to Virginia, determined to rescue her daughter. She is captured in Richmond and taken to Washington, DC. She escapes again, but, cornered on a bridge over the Potomac, she leaps to her death. Mary has a happier fate than her mother. She is rescued from slavery by a smitten Frenchman, who spirits her away to Europe and marries her, then conveniently dies, leaving the well-fixed widow free to wed George Green, her long-lost love, when they meet again by chance in Dunkirk ten years later.

Brown clearly invokes the affair of Jefferson and Sally Hemmings not only for its provocative aspect but also because it highlights the stark inconsistency between aspiration and practice at the heart of the American republic. When Clotel is sold and later when she dies, he reminds us that this is the daughter of the "writer of the Declaration of American Independence," the man who declared that "all men are created equal" and "endowed by their creator with certain inalienable rights; that among these are life, liberty & the pursuit of happiness" (53). In her bravery and resourcefulness, Clotel proves herself fully worthy of the sentiments expressed in the nation's foundational document. She is a veritable republican hero fighting for liberty, willing to give her life that others may be free. And, in telling Horatio Green that she would not try to keep him if he wished to leave her ("If the mutual love we have for each other, and the dictates of your own conscience do not cause you to remain my husband, and your affections fall from me, I would not, if I could, hold you by a single fetter"), Clotel echoes the Declaration's insistence on the fundamental importance of consent ("the consent of the governed"), insisting on the voluntary basis of legitimate forms of connection between competent adults, in direct contradiction of proslavery (and anti-republican) conceptions of a society held together and structured hierarchically by innate inequalities of power (69). Instead of essentialist notions of race as a borne-in-the-blood determinant of human behavior and ability, Brown portrays race as a kind of dramatic role one can inhabit, imitate, and perform. Clotel's versatile imitation of a white man challenges the inescapable fixity ascribed to gender and racial roles. Just as a "black" person can grow up "white" and be for all intents and purposes white, so too can a "white" person grow up "black" and take on all the characteristics and features assigned as innate to the race. As Brown states in *The Black Man* (1863), "Development makes the man" (35–36).

The startling reversal of racial fortunes through which white is made black and black is made white preoccupies Child's *Romance of the Republic* (and after Child's romance, Twain's caustic satire of Reconstruction, *Pudd'nhead Wilson*, and Johnson's *The Autobiography of an Ex-Coloured Man*). By featuring very light-skinned mulatto characters, the author working with such reversals risks the racist response that such characters are more white than black and their white "blood" accounts for their beauty, intelligence, and dignity. Despite this risk, Child and others could not resist the power of this figure as an illustration of the artifice involved in racial categorization and the importance of environment to a person's development and sense of "innate" identity. A legally white character raised as black feels himself to be black, and the waving of a legal wand reversing that identification has no immediate impact on the intuitive sense of self other than shock. Such moments powerfully suggest that, whatever its biological aspects, the category of race as used in distinguishing between classes of American society is a social construction – anyone can be made black or white.

The heroines of *A Romance of the Republic* are two sisters, Rosa and Flora Royal, Southern belles who have been raised by their father, Alfred, in a state of luxurious semi-isolation. When Alfred dies, however, they learn that in fact their mother was black, that they are black, and that they are the property of their father's estate. Consequently, Alfred's many creditors can pursue the young women as payment of their father's debts. Gerald Fitzgerald, a cad who schemes to possess both Rosa and Flora, pretends to rescue them from this desperate fate. Having courted Rosa for some time before Alfred's death, Gerald is well positioned to trick Rosa with a sham marriage and take her and Flora to his island plantation, Magnolia Lawn, where they can live in relative isolation off the coast of Georgia (75). Here Rosa becomes pregnant. When Gerald attempts to seduce Flora, she escapes with a kindly Northern widow, Mrs. Delano. Later when Gerald brings his legal bride, Lily Bell, to the island, Rosa discovers his imposture and, in a delirious rage, exchanges her "black" baby with Gerald's legitimate heir. With help, Rosa escapes the island, and makes her way to Europe where for a short time she has a phenomenal success as an operatic soprano. She is eventually united with the good-hearted Alfred King and reunited with Flora, who marries the gentle Franz Blumenthal. By the end of the novel, Rosa's exchange of babies has been disclosed and at least partially rectified.

Child's tale is romantically charged and highly melodramatic. Astonishingly cosmopolitan for people raised in isolation from the rest of the world, Rosa and Flora are fairy-tale creatures, exquisitely beautiful and accomplished princesses who are threatened by cads, like Fitzgerald, and troll-like thugs, like the aptly named Mr. Bruteman, who would possess and crush them. Child occasionally reminds us of the romantic aspect of her novel by alluding to Shakespearean romances, such as *A Midsummer Night's Dream* and *The Tempest*. Their father's home with its "Temple of Flora" where the young ladies receive visitors and the island plantation of Fitzgerald are magical places where anything can happen, birds can talk, and metamorphosis feels imminent. And transformations and mysterious presences do occur. Another bride appears on the island. Rosa's son becomes Lily's son. Throughout the novel, miraculous coincidences determine the characters' fates. While in Rome and starring in Vincenzo Bellini's passionate opera, *Norma*, Rosa suddenly spots Gerald Fitzgerald and his wife in the audience. This happenstance permits her to use the lyrics of Bellini's opera to condemn Fitzgerald, who "quails before" her fierce performance (231). Later, when he has the temerity to approach Rosa in her rooms, she is rescued by the sudden appearance of her true love Alfred King. These coincidences permit justice to be meted out with a theatrical symmetry. Gerald's father-in-law, a wealthy Boston merchant, refuses to aid a man being taken by force back into slavery, only to discover later that the victim he has condemned to bondage is his own grandson.

Like *Hobomok*, *A Romance of the Republic* stands out for its frank depiction of interracial attraction and its insistence that neither nature nor morality stands in the way of a happy interracial marriage. The ultimate "romance" of Child's novel lies in its depiction at the end of a contented interracial community gathered around the two sisters and bound together by a shared vision of moral worth, beauty, and justice. The reversals of fortune turning various characters white and others black work to break down or drain terms of racial classification of their social and legal significance as markers of difference and caste. The reversals and changes ostensibly teach us to judge ourselves and others by reference to character not complexion. However, by making her characters' moral natures unambiguous and relatively stable, Child reassures the reader that such social fluidity does not foreshadow social degeneration and chaos. Flora's and Rosa's inner natures are left intact despite the turbulence of their lives and circumstances. Some bad characters, such as Fitzgerald, get worse, and some good characters, like Alfred King, only become nobler, but the trajectory is established at the outset.

The only character to undergo any substantial change would seem to be Mrs. Delano, Flora's rescuer and surrogate mother. The dignified wealthy Boston matron becomes more vibrant, as a result of Flora's influence:

> It was beautiful to see how girlish the sensible and serious lady became in her efforts to be companionable to her young *protégée*. Day after day, her intimate friends found her playing battledoor or the Graces, or practicing pretty French romanzas, flowery rondeaux, or lively dances. She was surprised at herself; for she had not supposed it possible for her ever to take an interest in such things after her daughter died. But, like all going out of self, these efforts brought their recompense.   (146)

Inspired by the novel appeal of people of different backgrounds, values, and attitudes, Mrs. Delano is able to "go out of self," and the resultant transformation comes with a substantial enlargement of her sympathies to include people increasingly remote from her own background and experience. Mrs. Delano's contact with Flora converts her into an ardent abolitionist and opens her to emotional bonds with others even less like herself. By combining the essential moral consistency of the novel's main characters with the growth and development of Mrs. Delano (the character who may well have most resembled Child's intended audience), Child's novel adopts the balance of continuity and change usually characterizing the vision of the reformer. Child does not want to over-throw the principles of the republic, its essential moral character; she wants to see them fulfilled, and that fulfillment requires a Mrs. Delano-like process of enlargement and growth, so that the democratic and egalitarian ethos of the nation becomes universally applicable to all Americans.

## The philosophical romance: Poe, Hawthorne, and Melville

The subcategory of romance I have denominated as the "philosophical romance" and associated with novels by Poe, Hawthorne, and Melville shares traits with both the sensational romance and the historical romance.[8] Like the sensational romance (which is often marked by Gothic horrors), the philosoph-ical romance manifests a taste for the hallucinatory quality of certain shock-ing experiences, such as carnival-like freaks and oddities of nature, bizarre or inexplicable events, and acts of horrific violence. These experiences can have a striking afterlife in the imagination, lingering to challenge or dissipate the force of everyday reason. Like the historical romancer, the philosophical romancer is intrigued by the continuing appeal of legend and myth in the era of modern science. Projects associated with the age of progress (the by-word of the nine-teenth century), such as historical investigations, the documentary accounts of explorers and mariners, and well-known scientific experiments, can take on elements of the supernatural, the otherworldly, and the inexplicable, becoming somehow larger and more resonant. The amazing tale of some natural phe-nomenon, such as an albino whale with unusual features and a striking ability to evade capture, can, in the romancer's hands, become a spectral or cosmic force of uncertain origin and significance. If successful, such tales can reintro-duce something like magic to minds habituated to rationalism and stiffened by everyday mental operations.

If, as Hawthorne claimed, the characteristic that chiefly distinguishes the romance from other forms of fiction is its inclusion of some measure of the marvelous or extraordinary, then the lesser distinction between historical and philosophical romances is largely a matter of the nature and quantity of such marvels. The historical romance attempts to forge larger-than-life, archetypal figures who act out a narrative drama of epic proportions, like the *Iliad* or the *Aeneid*, working toward an idealized script of the identity, history, and ulti-mate destiny of a people. In the historical romance, the marvelous or legendary appears in the exceptional abilities of certain key characters, uncanny or provi-dential coincidences and connections between characters and events, fantastic escapes and climactic battles which seem to settle the fates of competing peoples. In the philosophical romance, such marvels are not only more frequent, but they tend to have either a supernatural, psychological, or metaphysical dimension, such as the appearance of the Flying Dutchman (a spectral ship manned by a dead crew) or a boy driven mad by falling overboard and being temporarily isolated in the immensity of the sea. The philosophical narrative tends to redirect our attention away from the specifics of history toward the human psyche or the meaning of existence. This is not to say that history does not figure in Poe, Hawthorne, and Melville. Poe's romance *The Narrative of Arthur Gordon Pym* draws on the history of nautical exploration. Hawthorne frequently turns to the history of his puritan forbears in his novels, such as *The Scarlet Letter*, and his short stories, such as "Young Goodman Brown." Melville uses historical incidents, such as the Battle of Bunker Hill, the slave revolt aboard the *Tryal*, and the *Somers* mutiny, as starting points for *Israel Potter*, "Benito Cereno," and *Billy Budd*, respectively. Yet, in each of these cases, history seems less a destination than a vehicle for an inquiry that is largely introspective and metaphysical.

The form of the philosophical romance reveals a striking taste for shadows and obscurity. Plot devices, such as Melville's keeping Ahab below decks and out of sight until the *Pequod* has sailed, not only create a sense of foreboding and suspense but also engender speculation about both the man and the accounts given of him by others (including that of an apparently mad prophet figure, Elijah, who warns Queequeg and Ishmael not to sign on with the doomed crew of the *Pequod*). Truth, in this case the truth of Ahab's nature, is below decks, out of sight, and in the shadows. At least partially hidden, it is not easily comprehended but deeply encoded and hard to decipher. Truth is to be found "in the back view of a residence, whether in town or country, [not] in its front," as Hawthorne's somewhat unreliable narrator, Miles Coverdale, puts it in *The Blithesdale Romance*: "[t]he latter is always artificial; it is meant for the world's eye, and is therefore a veil and a concealment. Realities keep in the rear, and put forward an advance-guard of show and humbug" (149). Transparent truths, such as obvious character types and clear-cut or unambiguous moral distinctions, are, for the philosophical romancer, cheaply and easily constructed and often false. Following Edward Eigner, we can place the philosophical romance at one end of a continuum ranging from mimetic novels describing the effect of experience to metaphysical novels exploring the nature of experience itself (2–3). Eigner presents a useful account of the changing alloy of philosophical concerns and a motley mixture of fictional genres in nineteenth-century fiction. Of course, when looking at the more metaphysical novels, it may seem odd, even perverse, to suggest that the pursuit of truth inevitably leads one to take on the habit of mind of the distrustful detective or spy, but this notion seems less objectionable if one recalls examples of intractable or difficult problems, where the relevant facts are shrouded in obscurity or seem endlessly complex and the issues at stake are diametrically opposed. An acknowledgment of even one important but impossible to decide moral or intellectual question may well cast a shadow of doubt over all transparent meanings and clear-cut distinctions.

Unlike the historical romance which depends for its epic effect on the reader's ready translation of its characters into archetypes and its events into larger themes, the philosophical romance loves to confront its readers and main characters with overt but obscure symbols, such as an oddly shaped birthmark. Allegorical emblems which can be easily translated into unambiguous and fixed meanings are not, as Poe put it, "judiciously subdued." The better kind of symbol, Poe says, is "seen only as shadow or by suggestive glimpses, and mak[es] its nearest approach to truth in a not obtrusive and therefore not unpleasant appositeness" ("Twice-Told Tales" 583). This kind of symbol generates a degree of what we might call interpretive friction, a struggle to comprehend, enhancing rather than diminishing the interpreter's sense of the symbol's importance. The scarlet letter worn by Hester Prynne in Hawthorne's novel is not just a scrap of aged fabric and stitching. It is plainly symbolic, something to be read and interpreted ("Certainly, there was some deep meaning in it, most worthy of interpretation"), yet its significance is elusive, "stream[ing] forth from the mystic symbol, subtly communicating itself to my sensibilities, but evading the analysis of my mind" (108). Such signs and portents draw us into interpretive shadows which may well resist conclusive understanding. The opening of Melville's "Benito Cereno" (1855), for instance, draws the reader into a consideration of overtly but obscurely symbolic details of the scene:

> The morning was one peculiar to that coast. Everything was mute and calm; everything grey. The sea, though undulated into long roods of swells, seemed fixed, and was sleeked at the surface like waved lead that has cooled and set in the smelter's mould. The sky seemed a grey mantle. Flights of troubled grey fowl, kith and kin with flights of troubled grey vapours among which they were mixed, skimmed low and fitfully over the waters, as swallows over meadows before storms. Shadows present, foreshadowing deeper shadows to come. (37)

The description's insistent repetition of the scene's greyness is a veritable emblem of indistinctness and interpretive difficulty. How are we to take our bearings when the sky and sea seem to merge in a general obscurity? Yet the obscurity is itself an invitation to interpretation, a mystery wanting solution.

The passage's payoff line telling us that these shadows or interpretive difficulties foreshadow deeper and more important interpretive difficulties to come could well be taken as a motto for the philosophical romance itself.

Later in the same tale, the Yankee protagonist, Captain Delano, is confronted by an old Spanish sailor on board the slave ship, the *San Dominick*. Throwing an elaborate knot he has made to Delano, the Spaniard urges him to "cut it quick." The knot and the sailor's statement indicate the mystery which Delano (and the reader) must unravel, but the difficulty of the solution facing the good Captain (and the reader) is suggested by Melville's description of the knot's complexity and of Delano standing there "knot in hand, knot in head" (66). The implicit homonymic pun of "knot" and "not" represents the blankness of the Captain's mind faced with this cryptic sign, and the extreme variety of knots, "double-bowline-knot, treble-crown-knot, back-handed-well-knot, knot-in-and-out knot, and jamming knot," indicate an intricate web of meaning, as though each knot has its own significance and forms part of a more complex whole. Standing as a symbol for the intractable interpretive problem, the old sailor's "Gordian knots" embody the philosophical romancer's conception of truth as an intensely felt but incomprehensible presence (66).

These romances don't necessarily or flatly contradict the idealist's vision of a two-story universe in which signs or symbols drawn from daily experience stand in some meaningful relation to larger truths; instead, the obscurity and multiple implications of their key symbols expresses their authors' doubt that the particular relation between the sign and the larger truth can ever be known with any finality or certainty. In their taste for ambiguity, the philosophical romances recall Montaigne, who urged his readers to live with uncertainty as a concomitant of a plurality of interpretations and beliefs: "Never did two men judge alike about the same thing, and it is impossible to find two opinions exactly alike, not only in different men, but in the same man at different times" (817). Like Emerson, the philosophical romancers understood that, while "[g]ladly we would anchor" in a final interpretation, "the anchorage is quicksand" ("Experience" 1196). The harder we "clutch" at interpretive or epistemological certainty, the more it slips through our fingers, because we are not given direct access to absolute or essential truths ("Experience" 1194).[9] Plainly balking the reader's desire for interpretive ease and the comfort of obvious significations, the philosophical romance anticipates certain examples of realist and modernist writing which similarly clog the reader's rush to paraphrase experience into unambiguous and transcendent truths, and manifests a vein of skepticism running through nineteenth-century American culture, continuing Montaigne's distrust of either rationalist or idealist certainty. As Montaigne puts it in "Of Experience,"

> Philosophy is very childish ... when she gets up on her hind legs and
> preaches to us that it is a barbarous alliance to marry the divine with the
> earthly, the reasonable with the unreasonable, the severe with the
> indulgent, the honorable with the dishonorable; that sensual pleasure is
> a brutish thing unworthy of being enjoyed by the wise man.   (855)

Montaigne subverts the "up-on-her-hind-legs" perspective by reminding us
that "on the loftiest throne in the world we are still sitting only on our own
rump" (857).

In his essay on Montaigne, Emerson, the chief mediator of this line of thinking in nineteenth-century America, characterizes the skeptic as accepting neither the absolutism of the materialist who would pretend that all is determined
by matter nor the absolutism of the idealist who would pretend that mind can
be walled off from the mess and mire of physical and social existence. As he
points out in "Experience," human existence involves both a "flux of moods"
and an intellectual capacity to rank "all sensations and states of mind" (1202).
Sensation disrupts the tendency to build philosophical castles in the air, and
thought disrupts the illusion that we can live merely in an animal state ("Montaigne" 243). The skeptic perceives and objects to the "evils of society" but casts
a doubtful eye on the rational projects "offered to relieve them" ("Montaigne"
242, 243).

The skepticism of the philosophical romance can be felt in its depiction of
events or occurrences defying or overwhelming rationality. Often, the primary
effect of these events is one of shock and horror (e.g., the cannibalism Pym
resorts to in *The Narrative of Arthur Gordon Pym* or the image of Captain Ahab
lashed to the head of Moby-Dick as he plunges into the depths of the ocean).
At other moments, the irrational may take the form of an unreasoning and
irresistible desire, such as Pym's impulse to leap into an abyss. It is precisely
"because our reason most strenuously deters us from the brink," the narrator
of Poe's "Imp of the Perverse" (1845) claims, that "we the more unhesitat-
ingly approach it" (1591). Such moments are calculated to focus the reader
less on what he or she knows or thinks and more on what he or she feels. The
moment of horror, for instance, by filling us with dread, redirects our attention away from the cool process of getting and using knowledge and moves
us toward an awareness of our beating hearts, throbbing heads, and clammy
skins. In philosophical terms, we might say that these moments of sensational
excess undermine the rationalist's attempt to separate the mind from the body,
the observer from the observed. In the moment of terror or repulsion, what
is "out there" in the phenomenal world and what is "in here" in the mind
seem inextricably bound together, mind and body are welded together in a
shared reaction, and the connectedness that is so striking in those moments

may well make us wonder whether mind and body, the observer and what is observed, can ever be detached from each other as the rationalist would pretend.

In reconnecting the mind and body, the philosophical romancer challenges not only the rationalist's notion of detached objectivity but also the idealist's notion of absolute and undefiled purity. Borrowing Emerson's description of the poet, we could say that Melville's Ishmael comes to appreciate in the "barbaric" markings and religious practices of his friend Queequeg "another carnival of the same gods whose picture he so much admires in Homer" (*Moby-Dick* 65–68, "The Poet" 196). Rejecting attempts to separate the "high" (sentiment and thought) from the "low" (physical needs and desires), Walt Whitman proclaims, "I am the poet of the Body and I am the poet of the Soul . . . I keep as delicate around the bowels as around the head and heart, / Copulation is no more rank to me than death is" (48, 53). Following William James, we might conceive of this line of thinking as arguing for a shift from the vertical viewpoint of "absolute and eternal mind" toward the horizontal perspective of one lying "flat on [one's] belly in the middle of experience, in the very thick of its sand and gravel" (*Pluralistic Universe* 756). For James, such a shift refocuses our attention on "the world of concrete personal experiences," a world which is "multitudinous beyond imagination, tangled, muddy, painful and perplexed" and which contrasts sharply with the "simple, clean and noble" world of rationalist and idealist philosophy. "The contradictions of real life are absent," James says, from the world your philosophy professor introduces you to: "Its architecture is classic. Principles of reason trace its outlines, logical necessities cement its parts. Purity and dignity are what it most expresses. It is a kind of marble temple shining on a hill" (*Present Dilemma* 495). Within a mental architecture of refinement, purity, and abstraction, the rationalist takes refuge from a world that is "intolerably confused and gothic" (*Present Dilemma* 496). But it is this haunted, confused, and uncertain world that Poe, Hawthorne, and Melville as well as Charles Brockden Brown and the sensational novelist George Lippard plunge us into. Its architecture symbol could be the haunted house or the carnival's funhouse, places of intense and highly volatile feelings and strange or troubling sense impressions.

In these novels, knowing and cognition often take the form of a physical sensation or feeling, such as baby Pearl's recognition of her father's voice in *The Scarlet Letter*. Pearl's recognition is beyond the normal bounds of comprehension and interpretation. Pearl does not and cannot *know* that Arthur Dimmesdale is her father, but she somehow *senses* his identity. The image of her stealing "softly toward him, and taking his hand in the grasp of both her own, la[ying] her cheek against it," appeals to a desire for a form of understanding that transcends or supersedes reason (169). Such intuition would indicate the possibility of meaning beyond that derived simply from either sense experience or rational process. Pearl's recognition of her father would seem to be based on spiritual or psychic intuition, attesting to the reality of forces beyond the calculus of reason.

Unlike the other romances, whether historical or sensational, the philosophical romance shows a striking willingness to stretch out or defer the action. In *Pym*, Poe induces claustrophobia in his readers by elongating each scene of Pym's suffering to an almost unbearable length. Similarly, Melville's "Benito Cereno" achieves a protracted suspense by deferring the revelation of the slaves' mutiny until the end of the main narrative. Anticipating a kindred effect in Henry James's fiction, Hawthorne's novel *The House of the Seven Gables* spends chapter after chapter in the emotionally and psychologically saturated description of the Pyncheon house, its inhabitants, and its grounds. This deferral of action suggests that these narratives are less interested in how the main characters act than in how they feel or what they perceive and think. The slower pace of these novels is often complemented by an inconclusive or open-ended conclusion. What Pym sees at the end of his narrative is never fully explained. What Dimmesdale exposes in the climax of *The Scarlet Letter* almost immediately becomes a subject of dispute among the witnesses. Miles Coverdale's confession of love for Priscilla in the very last line of *The Blithesdale Romance* does not so much end the tale as suggest a tale that could never begin because of the protagonist's radical inability to act. Stories such as "Benito Cereno" and "Bartleby, the Scrivener" reach endings fraught with significance of uncertain scope and direction. What do we finally learn from Cereno's depression and Babo's mute death ("Benito Cereno" 103)? Does the Wall Street lawyer's final ejaculation of "Ah, Bartleby! Ah, humanity!" resolve any of the ambiguities surrounding the strange life and death of his clerk ("Bartleby" 34)? Even in *The Confidence-Man*, which drives to as final an ending as any nineteenth-century novel, Melville cannot resist cryptically reopening the drama in the last line: "Something further may follow of this Masquerade" (260). This statement does not indicate a forthcoming sequel (Melville would not write another novel for decades); instead, it suggests the impracticability of freezing this shifting and carnival-like society in any ending.

## Edgar Allan Poe, The Narrative of Arthur Gordon Pym *(1838)*

Edgar Allan Poe (1809–49) was born in Boston. His parents, both actors, died when Poe was quite young, and he was raised by John and Frances Allan of Richmond, Virginia. In 1826, he entered the University of Virginia but was forced to leave after a dispute with Allan terminated his financial support. Afterward, Poe had an abortive enlistment in the US Army and was briefly enrolled at West Point. He held positions at a number of publications, such as the *Southern Literary Messenger* and *Burton's Gentleman's Magazine*. In a short adult life plagued by financial insecurity, depression, and alcoholism, Poe managed to produce numerous poems, essays, and short stories, as well as the novel *The Narrative of Arthur Gordon Pym* (1838) and a philosophical meditation, *Eureka* (1848). In 1837, Poe married his 13-year-old cousin Virginia Clemm. Virginia died in 1847. In October 1849, Poe was found unconscious on a Baltimore street. He died four days later.

The *Narrative of Arthur Gordon Pym* is strikingly complex and multilayered. On one level, playing to the reading public's taste for sensationalism and horror, *Pym* is a Gothic sea tale in which the eponymous hero undergoes a series of deeply terrifying and harrowing experiences. The market for such entertainments was evident in the success of the sensationalist penny papers, such as James Gordon Bennett's New York *Herald* and Benjamin H. Day's New York *Sun*, known for such shocking stories as the murder of a prostitute by a young man of means and the "discovery" of human beings and animals living on the moon. As its title page luridly advertises, Poe's novel features "mutiny," "butchery," "famine," "massacre," and "incredible adventures and discoveries STILL FARTHER SOUTH." Pym encounters such inexplicable and strange apparitions as a ship manned by corpses and a white being of gigantic proportions and mysterious character. By turns horrifying and fantastic, *Pym* is also densely and obscurely symbolic. It can be read, like Coleridge's "Rime of the Ancient Mariner," as an inquiry into the spiritual significance of earthly existence. Or it can be read as an allegory of slavery, dramatizing the disastrous effects of interracial contact and conjuring the specter of slave rebellion. On a more personal level, the novel contains many autobiographical signs and references, such as the similarity of Pym's and Poe's names and the parallels between Pym's close friendship with Augustus and Poe's close relation with his brother Henry.

A sailing mishap and rescue at the outset set the template for the narrative as a whole. Pym and Augustus go for a sail on Pym's boat after an evening of drinking. They are run over and subsequently rescued by *The Penguin*. Instead of frightening Pym, this near disaster whets Pym's appetite for adventure, and he stows away on the *Grampus*, a vessel commanded by Augustus's father and on which Augustus serves as an officer. Hidden below decks, Pym almost starves when a bloody mutiny prevents Augustus from bringing him food and drink. With the help of Dirk Peters, a "half-breed Indian," Augustus and Pym overcome the mutineers. But a storm subsequently reduces the *Grampus* to a mastless hulk, and they float aimlessly without food and water. On the brink of starvation, Augustus, Pym, Peters, and Parker (a surviving mutineer) draw straws to see who will be sacrificed to become food and drink. Parker loses and is consumed by the others. Then Augustus dies. After describing the rescue of Pym and Peters by the *Jane Guy*, the narrative takes a break from these more horrific and fantastic events and scenes, shifting to more matter-of-fact descriptions of navigation and exploration. Pym successfully urges the commander of the *Jane Guy* to push southward toward the Antarctic. In their journey, they encounter a barren island with a ledge resembling "corded bales of cotton," an omen of the allegorical slave rebellion to come. They discover the island of Tsalal and the Tsalalians, who are jet black, muscular, and primitive. Captain Guy and the Tsalalian Chief Too-Wit enter an agreement to harvest and dry a kind of mollusk, but the moment of concord proves illusory as the natives go on a murderous rampage, killing captain and crew. Pym and Peters escape and miraculously make their way home by way of a mysterious cataract and an immense being of absolute whiteness.

This feverish blend of Gothic romance and exploration narrative is ostensibly offered as factual. An excerpt of his tale, Pym tells us in the Preface, was initially published as fiction under the name of "Mr. Poe." On finding that the public was "not disposed to receive [his story] as fable," Pym decided to bring out a complete and accurate account of his real life adventures. It's hard not to smile at the convolution involved in Pym's reasoning (and Poe's parody of the documentary narrative), but the Preface's juxtaposition of fact and fiction, authenticity and fraud, also works in a serious direction to connect the invention of what isn't with the discovery of what is. Scholars have shown how *Pym*'s nautical chapters (10 through 15) draw heavily on such factual accounts as Jeremiah N. Reynolds's *Address, on the Subject of a Surveying and Exploring Expedition to the Pacific Ocean and South Seas* (1836) and Reynolds's *Voyage of the Potomac* (1835) (Tynan 35–37). By interweaving his tale's fantastic inventions with apparently straightforward descriptions of navigation and natural phenomena, Poe suggests a kinship between his own imaginative compulsion and the scientific curiosity of the explorer. But what is the nature of this connection or kinship? Confronting this question, it helps to recall other novels similarly disguised as nonfiction, such as Hawthorne's *The Scarlet Letter*, James Weldon Johnson's *Autobiography of an Ex-Coloured Man*, and Vladimir Nabokov's *Pale Fire*. Like *Pym*, each of these later novels pretends to reveal an authentic real-life story, and each tells of a concealed reality, such as a true or second identity not known to others – something hidden, as Poe puts it in *Pym*, "*under the garb of fiction*" (4). While working in inverse directions, both imaginative fabrication and scientific penetration require the presence of hidden significance. In Poe's view, the artist constructs worlds of obscure or complex symbolism teasing us with suggestive glimpses of truths that remain largely and satisfyingly concealed in shadow (hence, Poe's dislike of straightforward allegory in which the symbol too transparently represents some truth or idea – in Poe's terms, an "unpleasant appositeness"). The scientist or explorer works in the opposite direction, seeking to penetrate such shadows yet also relishing the obscurity that makes such penetration challenging and the consequent discovery unprecedented.

By referring to real exploration narratives, Poe reminds his reader of voyages of discovery, proving that the Earth is round or revealing the existence of lands, peoples, and natural wonders previously unknown to the explorers. Poe's description of Pym's encounter with a primitive race on an island with valuable natural resources may also put the reader in mind of how exploratory voyages exposed certain parts of the world to imperial conquest and how those imperial ambitions shaped the course of history. Simultaneously, however, Pym's voyage to the edge of the world is a journey inward to the depths of his psyche. The voyage out is a voyage in – an exploration of the labyrinthine distortions and mutations of the human mind under extreme pressure, a recurring theme in Poe's fiction and poetry and one he shares with Charles Brockden Brown and Robert Montgomery Bird. In *Pym* (as in "The Fall of the House of Usher"), the inner mind's distortions and fragmentation resonate symbolically with external images of disintegration or destruction, such as the polar cataract Pym and Peters are sucked into and the Tsalalians' utter and senseless destruction of the *Jane Guy*.

Disconcertingly, the fluidities of Pym's mental states seem to be mirrored by an external world that is also continually changing, casting doubt on the distinctions between subjective and objective realities. In addition, the flux of both mental states and external circumstances raises questions about the existence of permanent or absolute truths. In an apparently shifting and metamorphic world, what can be said to represent an immovable truth? What aspects of self can I point to and say "that is the stable essence defining my true identity"? In *Pym*, Poe repeatedly tests whether our empirical categories and metaphysical distinctions can withstand his fantastic thought experiments in which opposites are brought together, and people and things seem to morph into their opposite. For example, intoxication and sobriety are brought into terrifying proximity at the beginning of the narrative, when Augustus, who should be unconscious with intoxication, is suddenly sober and ready for a nighttime sail. Once in the boat, however, his inebriation abruptly returns, endangering himself and Pym. The startling transformations between drunkenness and sobriety and Pym's suggestion that "a highly-concentrated" form of intoxication "frequently enables the victim to imitate the outward demeanour of one in perfect possession of his senses" threaten to destabilize if not erase the distinction (10). What starts out as a cozy hideaway for Pym on the *Grampus* becomes a prison. Instead of going on a lark, Pym has been buried alive. In the extremity of his suffering, Pym's dreams take a fantastic and metamorphic turn. His faithful dog, Tiger, becomes a rapacious monster, and, despite the fact that the dream vision is dispelled upon waking, it proves prophetic when Tiger does become something akin to his namesake and the monster of Pym's dream (28–29).

Even life and death seem to merge or overlap disconcertingly. Life imitates death when Pym impersonates a dead man to play upon the "superstitious terrors" of the murderous mutineers, and death imitates life when a Dutch ship manned by corpses is hailed by Pym and his starving comrades (77, 100). At first, the ship appears to be uninhabited; then, one man seems to be looking at them with "great curiosity . . . He seemed by his manner to be encouraging us to have patience, nodding to us in a cheerful although rather odd way, and smiling constantly so as to display a set of the most brilliantly white teeth" (100). On closer inspection, the ship proves to be peopled by twenty-five or thirty rotting corpses: "We plainly saw that not a soul lived in that fated vessel! Yet we could not help shouting to the dead for help! Yes, long and loudly did we beg, in the agony of the moment, that those silent and disgusting images would stay with us, would not abandon us to become like them, would receive us among their goodly company!" (101). This scene, with the near-dead calling out to the dead for aid, suggests the startling closeness of death and life.

In each of these examples, Poe applies a great deal of imaginative pressure to the notion of essential divisions separating one state of being from another. The intellectual and emotional stakes involved in challenging or threatening these boundaries are quite high. Our analytic and rational processes fundamentally depend on the ability to identify and classify people, things, and concepts by virtue of certain elemental distinctions. How can we proceed in any analytic inquiry without being able to separate one thing from another? Being able to spot such basic and definitional differences may also inspire a kindred confidence that we can reach some categorical certainty about immutable truths and values. The ultimate thrust of Descartes's famous thought experiment of doubting everything was to arrive at a point of no doubt, a place of classificatory certainty, where he could identify himself as the being doing the doubting. If the boundaries apparently separating different, even opposed, aspects of reality prove to be fluid and permeable, then knowledge and being are destabilized – what I know and what I am become uncertain.

Ultimately, Poe does not go so far as to erase these fundamental boundaries, such as the difference between life and death. The closeness and apparent ease with which one state imitates another does not negate the distinction between the opposed concepts. The stranger on board the Dutch ship who seems to be smiling and nodding is doing neither of these things. His "smile" is really a set of teeth which are exposed because his lips have been eaten away (103). The definitional distinctions remain intact, yet Poe has pressed the opposed ideas together with such intensity that our confidence may be shaken. Like a person in a horror movie reminding herself that what she sees is not real, we can be haunted by the specter of indeterminacy even as our rational minds see that the fundamental distinctions are still intact. It's hard, after Pym's dream and Tiger's subsequent transformation, to shake the sense that Tiger had always had some latent monstrous potential lurking within, and barely separate from, his identity as a faithful pet. After reading that Augustus was so far along in the process of decay that his body literally falls apart when he dies, it's hard not to feel as though living is just another name for dying (127).

This intense pressing together of distinct concepts is brilliantly emblematized in the water of Tsalal. Accompanying Chief Too-Wit on shore, the men of the *Jane Guy* are astonished by the appearance of this strange water:

> Upon collecting a basinful, and allowing it to settle thoroughly, we perceived that the whole mass of liquid was made up of a number of distinct veins, each of a distinct hue; that these veins did not commingle; and that their cohesion was perfect in regard to their own particles among themselves, and imperfect in regard to neighbouring veins. Upon passing the blade of a knife athwart the veins, the water closed over it immediately, as with us, and also, in withdrawing it, all traces of the passage of the knife were instantly obliterated. If, however, the blade was passed down accurately between the two veins, a perfect separation was effected, which the power of cohesion did not immediately rectify. The phenomena of this water formed the first definite link in that vast chain of apparent miracles with which I was destined to be at length encircled.   (168–69)

The ensuing bloody violence between the all black Tsalalians and the men of the *Jane Guy* ensures that, at least on one level, we will read this passage as an emblem of race.[10] The watery substance, like the human species, is all one, yet the divergent or different strands within that substance remain discrete and unmixable regardless of their proximity. The passage symbolically suggests that the different races must and will remain discrete, yet racial difference is only one of the many oppositions or dichotomies that the narrative takes up, such as sobriety and drunkenness, life and death. The figurative juxtaposition of black and white runs throughout the narrative, from the *Penguin*, the ship that runs down and rescues Augustus and Pym, to the contrast of the blackness of

Tsalal (which means "to be shaded" or "dark" in Hebrew and "to be shade" in its ancient Ethiopian root), to the ashy whiteness of the tale's final climax. The color contrast of black and white stands for all of these dichotomies, indeed, for the very concept of antitheses itself. And the cosmic or metaphysical mystery central to Poe's tale is his speculation that one can arrive at one state by penetrating its opposite. Pym's notion that extreme drunkenness can produce (at least temporarily) sobriety or the way that Pym and Peters pass through a land of darkness to arrive at a place of complete whiteness mirror on a grander scale the theory held by Poe's documentary inspiration Jeremiah Reynolds that the Earth was hollow and could be entered through vortices at its poles. While the separate identity of opposed conceptions is never erased, throughout Poe's romance a mysterious or unseen connection, dimly felt but never fully comprehended, haunts the literal and figural polar opposites we rely on to take our bearings and navigate experience.

### Nathaniel Hawthorne, The Scarlet Letter (1850)

Hawthorne (1804–64) was born on the fourth of July in Salem, Massachusetts. One of his ancestors had been a judge in the Salem witchcraft trials, memorialized by Hawthorne as the cursed founder of the Pyncheon family in *The House of the Seven Gables* (1851). Hawthorne graduated from Bowdoin College where his classmates included Franklin Pierce and Henry Wadsworth Longfellow. After college, Hawthorne turned to writing and studying colonial history. In March 1837, Hawthorne published *Twice-Told Tales*. The book received critical notice in England as well as the United States. In 1838, Hawthorne met his future wife, Sophia Peabody. He worked in the Boston Custom House in 1839 and 1840, and later became surveyor of revenue for the Port of Salem, a job he celebrates losing in "The Custom House" chapter of *The Scarlet Letter* (1850). From 1853 to 1857, he served as consul at Liverpool. In addition to *The Scarlet Letter*, Hawthorne's novels include *The Blithesdale Romance* (1852), *The House of the Seven Gables*, and *The Marble Faun* (1860) (published in London under the title *Transformation*).

The Scarlet Letter begins in the middle of the novel's main action. Though her husband is absent and presumed dead, Hester Prynne has had a child, and she refuses to identify the father to the civil and religious authorities. As punishment, Hester is forced to wear a scarlet "A" and she must endure a public shaming in the town square. Her husband turns up in Salem calling himself Roger Chillingworth, and he obtains from Hester a promise not to reveal his identity. Chillingworth rightly, it turns out, suspects the Reverend Arthur Dimmesdale to be Hester's lover and the father of little Pearl. Chillingworth obsessively and covertly pursues Dimmesdale, who seems to wither away steadily as the secret of his transgression is maintained and as Chillingworth tends to him in the role of a physician. Late in the narrative, Hester proposes to Dimmesdale that they flee with Pearl to Europe, but this is not to be. At the climactic moment, Dimmesdale acknowledges to the community that he is Pearl's father. His confession seems to break the spell binding the three adults and the child in an increasingly torturous psychological standoff. Having found redemption in his confession, Dimmesdale dies in peace. Chillingworth is effectively finished off by Dimmesdale's death, and he too dies, leaving his estate to Hester and Pearl. Hester and Pearl remove to England where Pearl is raised and educated. Hester eventually returns to Salem where her charity and good works will radically transform the meanings associated with the "A" she wears by choice on return.

Like *The Narrative of Arthur Gordon Pym*, Hawthorne's romance examines the coexistence of ostensibly opposed concepts, such as submission to authority and rebellion, tradition and innovation, religious orthodoxy and antinomianism. Clearly reflecting Hawthorne's abiding interest in history, these pairings can be grouped within a larger categorical opposition of continuity and change. Where Pym's adventures take him into a fantastic realm seemingly distant from any specific history, Hester Prynne's drama is intimately bound up with the puritan history of Hawthorne's forebears and it bears signs of the revolutionary ferment sweeping Europe and climaxing in 1848.[11] As Hester emerges from the prison and mounts the scaffold where she will be subjected to public censure, she passes a wild rose bush growing just outside the prison. This bush is said to grow on the spot where Anne Hutchinson (1591–1643) entered the prison, and its proximity suggests a kind of mystic connection between Anne and Hester. Tried and exiled for her nonconformist preaching, Hutchinson and her followers were labeled "antinomians" (against law) and, for many, represented the notion that individuals could derive and follow their own understanding of divine will rather than the orthodoxies of scripture and the religious authorities. Passing the rose bush and standing on the scaffold, Hester is pained by her public exposure but not submissive. Her "haughty smile" and "glance that would not be abashed" as well as the "gorgeous luxuriance" of the "A" she has embroidered signify continued defiance (123). By associating Hester with Anne Hutchinson, Hawthorne raises the stakes involved in his heroine's disobedience and defiance. Hester's act is considerably more serious than a mere sin or crime committed by one who subscribes to the social and legal norms of her community. Rather, both her "sin" and her unrepentant attitude are akin to a rejection of those norms. Hester's defiance raises one of the novel's central questions: can continuity in the form of social orthodoxies and conventions coexist with dissent and resistance? Or must one side of the antithe-sis overwhelm the other? Both principles have positive and negative aspects. Continuity in the form of adhering to traditional conventions and norms produces order and affirms membership in the larger group, but it can also be stifling and tyrannical. Change may come with welcome innovations and progress, but it may also produce chaos and work to unravel the social fabric.

On the one hand, Hawthorne explicitly rejects stasis as an option. The rep-etitious and stagnant lives of the Custom-House officials are a perfect emblem of a society utterly patterned and controlled by long-standing customs (89). Some degree of change is necessary: "Human nature will not flourish, any more than a potato, if it be planted and replanted, for too long a series of gen-erations, in the same worn-out soil. My children have had other birthplaces, and, so far as their fortunes may be within my control, shall strike their roots into unaccustomed earth" (93). On the other hand, *The Scarlet Letter* does not endorse revolution. Hester's proposal to Dimmesdale that they flee to Europe, a complete rejection of the orthodox position condemning their affair, does not succeed. Instead, Dimmesdale confesses and dies, and Hester returns to wear the "A" to the end of her days thereby completing their penance. For human nature to flourish, it would seem that change and continuity must coexist. One cannot, in Hawthorne's view, simply erase the force of time-honored customs and start over, but one also should not abandon the attempt to revise tradition and alter the course of the present. Thus, Hester's wearing of the "A" signifies a degree of obedience and submission to tradition, but she also transforms its significance, turning it into a different kind of symbol, "in the lapse of the toil-some, thoughtful, and self-devoted years that made up Hester's life, the scarlet letter ceased to be a stigma which attracted the world's scorn and bitterness, and became a type of something to be sorrowed over, and looked upon with awe, yet with reverence too" (271).

For Hawthorne, symbols, such as Hester's "A," offer a perfect site for explor-ing the coincidence of continuity and change. Continuity of usage and meaning is required for the comprehension of symbols. For instance, we must have some consistent notion that a particular set of marks represents an alphabet to begin to read the "A" as something more than a decorative pattern, and our under-standing of this particular use of the letter "A" requires some passing familiarity with past penal practices of marking or branding culprits with the letter of their crime. By itself, however, such continuity cannot compel either a static or a single interpretation of the symbol. The wild roses growing outside the prison, for instance, can be interpreted as a "token that the deep heart of Nature could pity and be kind to" those in custody, but these roses can also be seen as a sign of Anne Hutchison or of Hester's "wild" or outlaw passion for Dimmesdale, a multiplicity of plausible associations militating against the reduction of the rose to any particular or final meaning (119). The very idea of an unchanging reading of a particular symbol becomes hard to imagine when one is faced with manifold plausible readings.

The inevitability of multiple readings of potent symbols is vividly illustrated by the crowd's diverse reactions to Dimmesdale's "confession" scene. At the critical moment, it seems as though Dimmesdale has torn open his shirt to reveal an "A" miraculously burned in his flesh, a double of the fabric "A" on Hester's breast. Curiously speaking of himself in the third person, as though the person speaking and the person sinning were not the same, Dimmesdale "bids" the crowd "look again at Hester's scarlet letter! He tells you, that, with all its mysterious horror, it is but the shadow of what he bears on his own breast, and that even this, his own red stigma, is no more than the type of what has seared his inmost heart!" (265). While this passage ostensibly insists on a platonic correspondence between the symbols, Hester's "A" and Dimmesdale's "A," as well as on an absolute correspondence between these symbols and the moral state they signify, the skeptical spectator (or reader) might well wonder whether, for all his talk of typological or allegorical equivalence, Dimmesdale has in fact adequately and concretely confessed his sin. Instead of making a full and detailed confession of his transgression, he has gestured to a symbol on his breast, but gestures and philosophical abstractions tend to be imprecise and ambiguous. And this instance is no exception.

While "most of the spectators" say they have seen a scarlet letter on the minister's breast, some deny there was any mark there (267–68). In addition, there is a wide variety of speculation about the meaning or cause of any such mark – some arguing that Chillingsworth has made it appear by means of "magic and poisonous drugs," some saying it has been caused by the "tooth of remorse" (268). Both of these lurid explanations involve supernatural forces, beyond the reckoning of Church leaders or nineteenth-century science. Members of the church hierarchy do not acknowledge Dimmesdale's "A." They shape their accounts of the event so as to protect the young minister's reputation and that of the Church as well. In their view, Dimmesdale has not confessed to any personal sin but has only made a generalized acknowledgment of the worthlessness of "man's own righteousness" in the eyes of God (268). Hawthorne may not be willing to let Dimmesdale and Hester "get away" with their adulterous affair, but there is a covert antinomian sympathy in his description of how the clergy's self-interest leads them to incorporate error in what will become the orthodox account of these events. Our knowledge that God's law is interpreted by humans opens it up to doubt, not necessarily doubt about the existence of God, but doubt about the reliability of human access to the divine intent behind the law.

In addition, the Church's official denial of the "A" burned in Dimmesdale's flesh suggests that the vivid image represents the specter of otherworldly or emotional forces inimical to the orthodoxy's rationalism.

Cruelty enters interpretation in the attempt to confine a human being to a particular symbolic significance, such as the equivalence drawn between the baby Pearl and the scarlet letter, reducing Pearl to being merely a sign of human weakness and depravity. Hawthorne gives many instances of the allegorizing mind's readiness to compress the complexity of a human being into a single overriding symbolic significance: the willingness of preachers and parents, for instance, to make Hester into "the type of shame" and "woman's frailty" (142). Hawthorne's novel also, however, illustrates the impracticability of confining any person or even any symbol forever to a single, limited meaning. Pearl is too wild and too changeable to signify anything consistently, and Hester's exemplary and selfless conduct is such "that many people refused to interpret the scarlet A by its original signification. They said it meant Able; so strong was Hester Prynne" (202). Just as religious "lore" and practice shift over time, so does interpretation of symbols (187). The imaginative power of the scarlet letter to generate meaning and feelings proves to be distinct or severable from its origin as a brand of shame for the sin of adultery. Neither Pearl nor the "A" can be successfully reduced to a single meaning, and neither Pearl nor the "A" are static in their significance. Instead, Hawthorne's symbols seem to suggest that the interpretive project of finding or making meaning involves a considerable degree of volatility and variation.

Transformation of characters, as well as of interpretations or symbolic associations, is one of Hawthorne's major concerns in the novel. Borrowing from Coleridge's comments on Wordsworth, we might say that Hawthorne's romance "was intended for such readers only as had been accustomed to watch the flux and reflux of their inmost nature, to venture at times into the twilight realms of consciousness, and to feel a deep interest in modes of inmost being" (406–07). In *The Scarlet Letter*, Hawthorne describes such internal dynamics as a kind of torment – a writhing and convulsive process. When Chillingworth recognizes his wife on the scaffold, he briefly, almost unnoticeably, undergoes an Ovidian metamorphosis, not unlike those changes endured by Pym or Charles Brockden Brown's Edgar Huntly,

> A writhing horror twisted itself across his features, like a snake gliding swiftly over them, and making one little pause, with all its wreathed intervolutions in open sight. His face darkened with some powerful emotion, which, nevertheless, he so instantaneously controlled by an effort of his will, that, save at a single moment, its expression might have passed for calmness. (129)

The descriptive terms, "writhing," "twisted," and "intervolutions," signify a very active process through which Roger Chillingworth's outer features for a moment correspond to his inner torment.[12] In this moment of recognition, a terrible process of transformation has begun. After a time, Hester can read the physical signs of this mutation: "Hester . . . was startled to perceive what a change had come over his features, – how much uglier they were, – how his dark complexion seemed to have grown duskier, and his figure more misshapen, – since the days when she had familiarly known him" (166). His newly discovered and malign project of vengeance has distorted his features (in much the same fashion as Dimmesdale's conscience sears an "A" on to his breast). By describing how Chillingworth's scientific curiosity (his pursuit of medical science into the realms of "antique physic" and Indian cures) becomes a means of destruction (much as Aylmer's scientific obsession does in "The Birthmark"), Hawthorne aims to challenge a too sanguine faith in the separation of opposed terms such as matter and spirit or reason and madness (171–72). These oppositions prove to be thresholds over which beings pass as they are transformed.

Like Poe and Melville, Hawthorne is interested to explore what we might call ontological confusion, the exploration of whether antithetical ideas or states of being, such as love and hate, are really separated by firm and certain boundaries. Looking at the interdependent, intensely intimate, and passionate relation between Dimmesdale and his persecutor Chillingworth, Hawthorne speculates whether love and hate might not prove to be

> the same thing at bottom. Each, in its utmost development, supposes a high degree of intimacy and heart-knowledge; each renders one individual dependent for the food of his affections and spiritual life upon another; each leaves the passionate lover, or the no less passionate hater, forlorn and desolate by the withdrawal of his object. Philosophically considered, therefore, the two passions seem essentially the same, except that one happens to be seen in a celestial radiance, and the other in a dusky and lurid glow. In the spiritual world, the old physician and the minister – mutual victims as they have been – may, unawares, have found their earthly stock of hatred and antipathy transmuted into golden love. (269)

Denying any essential or "philosophical" difference between love and hate, Hawthorne seems to imagine the distinction as crucially depending on the perspective of the viewer, the position from which love is "*seen*" "in a celestial radiance" and hate is "*seen*" "in a dusky and lurid glow." Given their similitude, he considers it possible that one can morph into the other.

Metamorphosis or transformation, Hawthorne recognizes, such as the alchemy that Chillingworth has studied, represents a fundamental challenge to the categories and rules we use to organize existence. It cuts across supposed barriers dividing opposites and unravels notions of order. Pearl would seem to be the ultimate example in the novel of the conjunction of the metamorphic and the lawless. She is described as having a mercurial personality, constantly in flux, and she seems to be able in an almost witch-like fashion to invest material reality with her own metamorphic spirit:

> The spell of life went forth from her ever creative spirit, and communicated itself to a thousand objects, as a torch kindles a flame wherever it may be applied. The unlikeliest materials, a stick, a bunch of rags, a flower, were the puppets of Pearl's witchcraft, and, without undergoing any outward change, became spiritually adapted to whatever drama occupied the stage of her inner world . . . The pine-trees, aged, black, and solemn, and flinging groans and other melancholy utterances on the breeze, needed little transformation to figure as Puritan elders; the ugliest weeds of the garden were their children, whom Pearl smote down and uprooted, most unmercifully. (152–53)

As Chillingworth aptly observes, Pearl has no "reverence for authority, no regard for human ordinances or opinions, right or wrong" (182). But Pearl's mutability and her lawlessness cannot be seen as healthy. Under a kind of spell, she seems hardly "human," at times, even to her mother (151). Pearl's quicksilver personality and wildness is directly related to the secret of her paternity, and once Dimmesdale acknowledges her as his own, the spell is broken. This does not mean an end to Pearl's transformation. Indeed, she is transformed into a human child by Dimmesdale's gesture, and afterward she is able to be educated and socialized. But transformation after this disclosure takes on a different tone, it becomes more moderate, predictable, and ostensibly healthy, unlike her earlier uncanny and freakish mutations.

The unhealthy or problematic form of transformation would seem to involve the denial of the social context which in large part defines and labels the characters and attributes certain identities and meanings to them. When Hester and Dimmesdale agree in the forest to flee Salem, in effect rejecting their community's categories, labels, and rules, they become unrecognizable in certain critical ways. Pearl will not recognize Hester without the "A" and won't approach Dimmesdale without an acknowledgment of his relation to her mother. To resist the definitions imposed on one by one's community would seem in Hawthorne's novel to put the very fact of one's identity at risk (234–37). When Dimmesdale reenters Salem after this forest meeting, his shock at the apparent "mutability" of familiar individuals and places he sees seems to be a clear projection of his own mutability (239–40). He has come back from the forest a changed man. But this change is pathological and disorienting. He has trouble distinguishing dream from reality. The positive form of transformation, embodied in Hester's return to Salem, requires that one accept society's judgment before one can transcend it.

*The Scarlet Letter* does not, like *The Narrative of Arthur Gordon Pym*, leave us with a mysterious connection between opposed concepts; rather, Hawthorne's narrative implicitly argues for a salutary if difficult balance between forces pulling in opposite directions. Tradition, history, established religion, and membership in a cohesive community pull in the direction of conformity, continuity, and orthodoxy. Individual inspiration and the free play of the imagination pull in the direction of rebellion, change, and heterodoxy. Refusing to endorse one or the other side of this opposition to the exclusion of the other, Hawthorne's novel suggests that we do and must live in the paradox that both sides of this dichotomy are necessary to our well-being and that we are constantly in a process of transformation as a result. Like Emerson, Hawthorne understands that our desire for "permanence" is accompanied by a different need for "circulation" and "change" (Emerson "Experience" 1196). Hawthorne does not adjudicate between these competing pressures but rather conceives of our endurance of the conflict as revelatory of the hybrid nature of truth and value – it must and always contains something of continuity and something of innovation or change.

### Herman Melville, Moby-Dick; Or, The Whale *(1851)*

Herman Melville was born in 1819 in New York City, a descendant of English and Dutch families. His father, a man of grand tastes and less than grand economic resources, eventually was ruined and died in the midst of his family's financial crisis in 1832. This reversal of fortunes effectively ended young Herman's relatively comfortable middle-class existence as well as his formal education. These early crises of financial instability and his father's death clearly impressed Melville with a sense of the transitory and insecure nature of existence. When he muses in *Pierre* (1852) that "In our cities, families rise and burst like bubbles in a vat," Melville probably had his own family in mind (13). Like his friend Hawthorne, Melville was keenly aware of the turbulent and fraught nature of life in nineteenth-century America. "In this republican country," as Hawthorne puts it in *The House of the Seven Gables* (1851), "amid the fluctuating waves of our social life, somebody is always at the drowning point" (35). After a succession of different jobs, he served as a cabin boy on a voyage to

Liverpool, a trip he memorialized in *Redburn* (1849). A few years later, he sailed on the whaler *Acushnet*, an experience he would draw from in writing *Moby-Dick*. His experience as a seaman included jumping ship in the Marquesas and Polynesian Islands, adventures he fictionalized in *Typee* (1846), *Mardi* (1849), and *Omoo* (1847). *White-Jacket* (1850) was inspired in part by his naval experience on the frigate *United States*. Melville's literary career has its own dramatic ebb and flow. Initially popular, his appeal began to ebb after *Moby-Dick* (1851). His deeply introspective and autobiographical novel *Pierre* (1852) did not help to rekindle popular enthusiasm for his fiction. After his satiric portrait of a carnivalesque American society, *The Confidence-Man* (1857), he abandoned fiction for years. His last piece of sustained prose fiction, *Billy Budd, Sailor*, an almost existential drama about the impossibility of justice, was written much later and published posthumously in 1924.

Despite its range of reference, complex symbolism, and its sheer length (its "blubber" as Melville termed it), the storyline of *Moby-Dick* can be briefly and simply recounted. Ishmael, a young seaman with no whaling experience, ships on the whaler, the *Pequod*, under the command of Captain Ahab. Ahab, it turns out, is not particularly concerned with acquiring whale oil, the voyage's economic aim; instead, he is obsessed with the destruction of Moby-Dick, a sperm whale which, in a previous encounter, sheared off the lower half of one of Ahab's legs. Eventually the men of the *Pequod* and the great white whale clash. The ship and her boats are destroyed, and Ishmael alone survives. Bound by a whaling line to the leviathan, Ahab is dragged below to a watery death.

This relatively straightforward narrative line is layered with multiple allusions, diverted into sundry digressions and meditations, and crowded with densely symbolic descriptions. In terms of its allusions, Melville's whale story can seem a veritable compendium of Western culture, calling to mind Perseus, Prometheus, Odysseus, Job, Jonah, Hamlet, Lear, Goethe's Faust, Byron's Childe Harold, Montaigne's cannibals, Coleridge's ancient mariner, and Turner's seascapes. Melville's tale also draws on scientific and documentary sources such as J. N. Reynolds's magazine article on Mocha-Dick:

> an old bull whale, of prodigious size and strength. From the effect of age, or more probably from a freak of nature, as exhibited in the case of the Ethiopian Albino, a singular consequence had resulted – *he was white as wool!* . . . Numerous boats are known to have been shattered by his immense flukes, or ground to pieces in the crush of his powerful jaws; and, on one occasion, it is said that he came off victorious from a conflict with the crews of three English whalers, striking fiercely at the last of the retreating boats, at the moment it was rising from the water,

> in its hoist up to the ship's davits. It must not be supposed, howbeit, that through all this desperate warfare, our leviathan passed scathless. A back serried with irons, and from fifty to a hundred yards of line trailing in his wake, sufficiently attested, that though unconquered, he had not proved invulnerable.   (379)

Reynolds's description, based on first-hand accounts, conjures the image of a powerful beast that is intelligent, angry, and vengeful. Mocha-Dick is relatively simple, a manifestation of the destructive power of nature, bearing little if any metaphysical significance. In *Moby-Dick*, the white whale is beautiful as well as fierce, mysterious as well as recognizable, and the whaling enterprise is by turns poetic and commercial, playful and deadly serious, eventually coalescing into an obsessive quest to destroy a manifestation of nature that seems to threaten human conceptions of meaning and value.

*Moby-Dick* is also an education tale. With the novice whaler, Ishmael, as our guide, we follow and learn from his initiation into the world of whaling with its strange and striking customs and polyglot citizens. We are introduced to this world of elemental forces, powerful creatures, and intrepid mariners through a range of perspectives, including the scientific approach of the cetological chapters, which aim at an analysis and classification of the leviathan; the commercial viewpoint of Peleg and Bildad, the *Pequod*'s owners; Ishmael's romantic desire to experience a transcendent truth in the wild; and Ahab's apocalyptic vision of the whale as a sign of the malign or empty nature of existence. A vast and varied amalgam of materials, Melville's novel shifts in voice from Ishmael's first-person narration to that of a third-person omniscient narrator (after the first hundred pages or so, the narrator starts telling us things Ishmael could not have witnessed, such as the behavior and dialogue of the officers at meals); it shifts in tone from the quiet, disinterested tone of a natural historian to the blood and thunder rants of Ahab (in anger, Ahab doesn't just threaten to kill a man, he threatens to "clear the world of [him]," suggesting a kind of cosmic erasure) (133). The novel's main action is repeatedly interrupted by meditations and digressions. In its fragmentary and collage-like collection of disparate materials – literary, mythic, religious, scientific, and historical – *Moby-Dick* has a distinctly proto-modernist aspect, resembling James Joyce's *Ulysses* and Ralph Ellison's *Invisible Man* far more than it does a contemporary text such as Susan Warner's *The Wide, Wide World* (1850).

*Moby-Dick* is also unconventional in its theme, pushing in an agnostic direction more forcefully than any other American novel of its era. Melville's novel pursues the meaning of existence with an epic intensity, traversing its wide variety of perspectives in search of signs of order and divine sanction only to arrive at uncertainty and doubt. Floating on a coffin, Ishmael, like Job, survives to tell the tale of the *Pequod*'s destruction, but what has he learned? What have we learned? What is the meaning of the tale? The various human ventures – romantic, biblical, scientific, commercial – represented by the *Pequod* and her crew have disappeared utterly. Every atom of the ship, every crew member, with the exception of Ishmael and Queequeg's coffin, has disappeared under "the great shroud of the sea" which rolls "on as it rolled five thousand years ago" (535). In the face of such utter extinction, one wonders what meaning there can be save the raw fact of the transitory nature of existence itself – for a time these people and this ship had being, they existed. For a sense of how strikingly ambiguous Melville's ending is for its time, one has only to turn to the end of Harriet Beecher Stowe's *Uncle Tom's Cabin* (1852). Stowe's enormously popular novel leaves no doubt about the moral and religious import of its ending. Slavery is wrong, condemned by God's if not man's law. A Christ-like martyr, Uncle Tom is bound for heavenly glory, and the wicked slave holder, Simon Legree, is doomed to eternal perdition. What does not reach a satisfying resolution in earthly life will in the next, and justice – the protection of the weak, punishment of the cruel and selfish, and reward for the faithful and generous – prevails in heaven if not on Earth. By contrast, Ishmael's survival and the "universe" that permits it would seem "a vast practical joke" (226). Why is he spared? Why don't the sharks and sea-hawks attack? Why would providence spare him to tell this tale?

The answer to these questions may be found in the fact that we feel compelled to ask them. While *Moby-Dick* does not arrive at a conclusive reading of reality or ascribe a particular meaning to human existence, Melville's novel leaves little doubt that human beings are, by their nature, meaning seekers and meaning creators, compelled to "throw out questions and answers," to borrow a phrase from Whitman (164). In Chapter 99, "The Doubloon," Melville dramatizes the human impulse to interpret reality in the crew's multiple readings of the gold coin Ahab has nailed to the mainmast as a reward for the man who sights Moby-Dick. Ahab sees himself and his fate in it. Starbuck reads it as symbolizing the Trinity and a providential vision of life and death. Stubb, the happy pagan, finds astrological signs indicating a "jolly" ending. And Flask sees a "round thing made of gold" worth so many cigars (412). Largely determined by each interpreter's personality and particular viewpoint, the multiplicity of these strikingly different interpretations seems to cut against the possibility of a definitive reading; otherwise, the readings would agree in some particulars. Melville's acknowledgment of the inevitable multiplicity of interpretation echoes Montaigne's skeptical view of people "who think they can diminish and stop our disputes by recalling us to the express words of the Bible. For our mind finds the field no less spacious in registering the meaning of others than

in presenting its own" ("Of Experience" 813). If we view the varied interpretations of the doubloon as symbolizing different faiths, then the influence of
personal predisposition and interest on such beliefs would seem to make the
project of faith doubtful; yet, Melville insists, such things must be interpreted:
"some certain significance lurks in all things, else all things are little worth, and
the round world itself but an empty cipher" (409). To avoid the unbearable
option of treating the world as an empty cipher, we read it. Pip's observation of
the many interpreters of the doubloon – "I look, you look, he looks; we look, ye
look, they look" – suggests how irresistible this process of interpretation is even
as it refuses to single out one of the interpretations as better than the others
(an equality driven home by Pip's comparison of the lookers to bats) (413). By
suggesting that this urge to interpret reality is irresistible if not accurate in any
final or absolute sense, Melville focuses our attention on an intersection and
potential conflict between what we know and our built-in impulse to assign
meaning or value to what we know.

In the chapter entitled "The Whiteness of the Whale," Melville models this
tension, by showing how a particular bit of knowledge, a fact, inspires a veritable flood of associated meanings and values. On the simplest level, whiteness is merely one of Moby-Dick's known traits, a genetic accident that can
be used to identify him, but, as Melville's chapter suggests, it is a fact that
inevitably inspires interpretation. The whale's unusual whiteness must also be
seen as an emblem of the whale's nature and a sign of some ultimate theme
symbolized by the whale. In the span of a few pages, like one of Whitman's
catalogues, whiteness is associated with, among other things, beauty, purity,
justice, ancient civilizations, a variety of religious symbols as well as the alba-
tross of Coleridge's "Rime of the Ancient Mariner," lamb's wool, murder, the
crest of breakers, and snow. It is both all-color *and* the utter absence of color,
the mystic sign of God's love *and* the "all-color of atheism" (196). Like Emerson, Melville would seem to conceive of this ample and metamorphic stream
of associations as evidence that the defining "quality of the imagination is
to flow, and not to freeze" (Emerson "The Poet" 1188). It also paradoxically
evidences both the idealist's quest to push through the surfaces of things to
some ultimate knowledge of their essential nature *and* the impossibility of
fixing any of these associations to particular essential and unchanging truths.
The fact that we can compellingly associate whiteness both with the presence
and the absence of God tends to empty it of any essential connection to a
deeper, more permanent truth – the truth of whiteness. Rather than being
something we can penetrate so as to get at its absolute or ideal meaning, whiteness becomes the catalyst for a stream of responsive associations, which, in
its fluid and "multiform" energy, parallels the metamorphic energy of nature.

Even the more scientific cetological digressions do not lead to a final and clear understanding of the whale but leave us with unanswered questions: does the whale spout vapor or liquid? Where does the whale's skin begin and end? How exactly are we to classify the different kinds of whale? In plunging the reader into the sheer abundance and variety of the leviathan's mysterious characteristics, the cetological materials come to resemble a stream of poetic associations and metaphors – a process that increases rather than dispels the creature's mystery.

The inherent human drive to create meaning out of knowledge should, it would seem, make us question the finality of any particular assertion of meaning – not because knowledge cannot occur (Moby-Dick is, after all, verifiably white), but rather because our impulse to find meaning never arrives at a final destination. It is part of our nature to spring off from mere fact gathering and analysis into imaginative flights manipulating and vastly exceeding the bounds of empirical reasoning. We are unable to examine facts or bits of factual evidence neutrally. Instead, we must be delighted or appalled, finding in them signs of "the Christian Deity" or "the charnel-house within" (196). Whatever the association and regardless of whether the meanings we "find" correspond in some absolutely verifiable way to the facts we are interpreting, we insist that these facts must signify some larger meaning. The power of this impulse to assign such meaning to experience would seem to make ontology (the study of being) not epistemology (the study of knowledge), in Melville's view, the more pertinent and rewarding line of philosophical inquiry for the student of humanity.[13]

If we set aside, as I think Melville wants us to do, epistemological questions, such as how we know what we know or how we verify the meanings that we assign to events or facts, then something very remarkable happens to the quest for ideal meanings or metaphysical truths of existence: they become unstable, metamorphic, and multiple. They become aspects of our responsiveness to experience, rather than any fixed essence "out there" in reality. Instead of looking for static and conclusive correspondences between symbols and particular meanings, we can view meaning as an attribute of human nature, a built-in need to imagine the events of life and the parts of the universe as connected in some meaningful fashion. Melville anticipates William James's rejection of "the absolutely empty notion of a static relation of 'correspondence' . . . between our minds and reality" and his recognition that "[i]n our cognitive as well as in our active life we are creative. We *add*, both to the subject and to the predicate part of reality. The world stands really malleable, waiting to receive its final touches at our hands. Like the kingdom of heaven, it suffers human violence willingly. Man *engenders* truths upon it" (*Pragmatism* 35, 112).

*Moby-Dick* dramatizes several reasons to conceive of meaning as something we cannot resist making rather than as some verifiable substrate of the physical universe that we can ascertainably and positively know. The sheer variety and contradictory nature of the meanings we derive from experience would seem to argue against the possibility of arriving at a clear and certain vision of the inner essence of reality. In addition, the multiple and metamorphic nature of reality itself would seem to complicate any claim to knowing such ultimate meanings. The whale is both a creature of great beauty and a terrible destructive force. Queequeg is "a creature in the transition state – neither caterpillar nor butterfly" (46). Father Mapple is both a mariner and a preacher, and his chapel is a fortress and a ship as well as a place of worship (55). Ahab is sick and not sick, a good man and not a good man (92–93). Searching for the essence of a person or thing, such as the "blackness of darkness," does not lead to verifiable conclusions (*Moby-Dick* 28). Instead, as Ralph Ellison suggests in his brilliant riff on *Moby-Dick*, the search for essential truths, such as the "Blackness of Blackness," leads only to a shifting series of contradictions: "black is" and "black ain't," "black will" and "black won't," "black will make you . . . or black will un-make you" (*Invisible Man* 9–10). "Nothing," Ishmael tells us, "exists in itself" (68). We find significance by comparing things, events, experiences. Warmth is not an absolute principle; it is a relation between more and less warm things or beings.

Ahab's desire to "strike through the mask" of phenomenal experience in order to reach some inner reality or animating principle is dangerous exactly in proportion to his certainty that there must be some final and fixed ultimate meaning attached to things (167). In *Moby-Dick*, multiple interpretations are not the problem, the quest for the final interpretation is. The alternative to Ahab's fear that there will be "naught beyond" the pasteboard mask of reality (here, the whale) is abandoning the correspondence theory of truth and accepting the ongoing and fluid process of meaning-making (167). While we differ in our interpretations, we are at least joined in the project of giving meaning to existence. This metaphysical project might be labeled "ontological heroics," borrowing the phrase Melville used to describe his lengthy conversations with Hawthorne during the composition of *Moby-Dick* (qtd. Delbanco 135). It is "heroic" in part because it is hard to give up the Ahabian quest for a certain and fixed answer to the cosmic riddle of existence. Choosing the heroics of being over the heroics of knowing requires an acceptance of uncertainty and change, and the attendant discomfort of never arriving at an ultimate and final conclusion. But there is joy in this project as well – tremendous energy and playfulness, and an appreciation of the metamorphic energy of the imagination's ability to find points of comparison and connection between beings.

There is something very affirming in setting aside the rationalist's insistence on separating the observer from the observed and giving oneself over to an ontological confusion of the "me" and the "not me." Meaningful connection may not prove to be verifiably knowable in some Ahabian and absolute sense, but it can be felt. Melville offers a luminous description of such "felt" connections in the "Squeeze of the Hands" chapter. Here squeezing the lumps of the whale's sperm, Ishmael feels himself merging with the sperm and the shipmates' hands he is indiscriminately squeezing. Ishmael's delirious confusion of the lumps of spermaceti and human hands releases an ecstatic (and sexualized) sense of connection:

> Such an abounding, affectionate, friendly, loving feeling did this avocation beget; that at last I was continually squeezing their hands, and looking up into their eyes sentimentally; as much as to say, – Oh! my dear fellow beings, why should we longer cherish any social acerbities, or know the slightest ill-humor or envy! Come; let us squeeze hands all round; nay, let us all squeeze ourselves into each other.   (398)

Here meaning comes as a half- or un-conscious feeling, something produced by "reverie" in which one's separate identity is "diffused" and replaced by a sense of connection between oneself and "every strange, half-seen, gliding, beautiful thing," "every dimly-discovered, uprising fin of some undiscernible form." All become manifestations of one soul. By their nature and the necessities of existence, such "reveries" are transitory, and Ishmael's "dream" of connection vanishes with the reassertion of the rational point of view, separating the dreamer and the sea into which he can fall and drown (162–63). Yet, despite their impermanence, these fleeting sensations of connectedness have the residual consequence of softening our prejudices and opening us up to different kinds of experience.

Melville is keen to illustrate that substantial transformations of our most fundamental belief systems do not require rational demonstration or proof positive. They can occur at the level of feelings, sensations, and intuitions. For instance, at his first sight of Queequeg, Ishmael is terrified and has no rational means to comprehend "the head-peddling purple rascal," yet, despite his terror, Ishmael does not require a thorough introduction or detailed account of Queequeg before spending the night with him (40). Instead, Ishmael's fear is allayed by a "kind and charitable" gesture on the cannibal's part and a sense that despite his barbarous markings he is "clean" and "comely looking" (43). Ishmael's comfort amounts to an intuition that Queequeg will prove to be a decent chap. After their night together and waking to find himself in Queequeg's embrace, Ishmael has "no serious misgivings" (45). This rapprochement has been achieved without conversation or any form of reasoning. The two men continue to be strangers to each other, yet they have become somehow intimately connected. They are "naturally and unbiddenly" drawn together *before* knowing each other, "married," as Queequeg puts it, *before* they have conversed at any length (67). Whether we approach this scene in expressly sexual terms or not, the link between Queequeg and Ishmael exceeds reason, bypassing words and defying social conventions. Their "premature" and "sudden flame of friendship" represents human connection as a matter of feeling and sensation. The power of such felt connections is suggested by the fact that his sudden friendship with Queequeg effectively breaks down Ishmael's prejudices, transforms his beliefs, and converts him into an "idolater" (69, 67–68).

Watching Queequeg get dressed, Ishmael observes that he "was a creature in the transition state – neither caterpillar nor butterfly" (46). Watching Ishmael with Queequeg, we may well conclude that he too is a creature in a transition state, as, indeed, we all are, in Melville's view – all being caught up in a continuing process of metamorphosis and driven as much by sensation as by reason.

## The sensational romance – a taste for excess

One of the striking developments in nineteenth-century fiction is the birth of the "dime novel" in the antebellum period. These exciting tales of urban and frontier adventure were written (and consumed) at lightning speed and sold for small amounts of money in great quantities throughout the remainder of the century. The dime novel's introduction was facilitated by widespread literacy and improvements in paper making and publishing technologies permitting low-cost production on a massive scale.

Scholars, such as Michael Denning and Shelby Streeby, have emphasized the importance of the dime novel's working-class audience to our understanding of the genre. Denning challenges the view that the dime novel began with tales of the frontier and the western but then degenerated into the detective story, the outlaw tale, and urban adventures (13–16). As Denning points out, dime novels featured urban tales from the outset, and he argues against negative assessments of the dime novel's depiction of urban settings and working-class dramas as a degeneration of the form. In favoring the epic of creating a new race in a new world, such critics, in Denning's view, betray a hostility to and denial of the centrality of class to nineteenth-century America. Denning describes the dime novel's master plot as a conflict between honest and decent workers and a corrupt elite – the laborer hero actually produces something for the material benefit of society while the accumulator villain pursues his own gain at society's cost and peril (73). In marked contrast to the genteel fiction of the period, "dime novels offered depictions of working class life, and a gallery of working class heroes" (79). Reinserting race issues, Streeby discusses the complex and varied ways in which popular novels expressed the era's predominant concerns of national identity and empire-building: "The sensational literature of this period responds, in other words, to a double vision of Northeastern cities divided by battles over class, race, national origin, and religion, on the one hand, and on the other to scenes of U.S. nation- and empire-building in Mexico, Cuba, and throughout the Americas" (5). According to Streeby, one of the cultural roles undertaken by this literature was to envision the creation of a white national identity through the process of excluding, subjugating, or conquering nonwhite peoples who were inevitably and properly not part of that identity (28). Class tensions could be muted by fictions reminding working-class readers that they were white Americans.

I term these popular fictions "sensational romances" for two reasons. First, they are "sensational" because their aesthetic focuses on shock, terror, and intense excitement – the abrupt reprieve from mortal peril, the sudden presence of the grotesque, startling metamorphosis, the freakish and the sublime. For instance, one of George Lippard's early novels, *The Ladye Annabel* (1844), (which was praised by Poe), includes scenes of necrophilia, torture, live burial, and alchemy (D. Reynolds *Lippard* 256–57). Moving quickly and featuring action rather than character development, such novels are designed to plunge the reader into a series of gripping sensations, not unlike those one experiences on an amusement-park ride. Second, they are "romances" because their storylines are marked by an insouciant disregard for plausibility, featuring highly improbable coincidences, characters with supernatural abilities or strengths, as well as unearthly or magical events. This category of romance includes westerns, adventure tales, and urban fictions greatly indebted to the Gothic novel.

The penchant for exaggerated sensations can be found in Edgar Allan Poe's *The Narrative of Arthur Gordon Pym* and Herman Melville's *Moby-Dick* as well as George Lippard's *The Quaker City* and Edward Wheeler's *Deadwood Dick*. Indeed, this appetite for the onrush of sensation making both mind and body vibrate with feelings and associations heedless of propriety and willing to plunge into the muck and mire of life runs right through the century from Charles Brockden Brown to Henry James. Pulled by the polyglot "allure" of the New York street scene and the city's "dauntless power," James attempts in *The American Scene* (1907) to sustain both the "fine notes" and the "loud ones, the whole play of wealth and energy and untutored liberty, of the movement of a breathless civilization . . . the contrasts of prodigious flight and portentous stumble" (65, 59, 87). This taste for excess leads writers such as James and Whitman to push against notions of refinement and artificial separations of the high and low matters of life. Thrusting his readers into the varied and multitudinous reality of life in nineteenth-century America, Whitman bluntly juxtaposes the sweaty peddler, dazed opium eater, and harassed prostitute with the president and his cabinet (719, 43). He directs the averted gaze of genteel America to the suicide, the slave auction, and the amputation, as well as the politician's speech or minister's sermon (36, 42). Sensational romancers, such as George Lippard and Emerson Bennett, sought to capitalize on the powerful grip that such unflinching images of their mongrel society could exert on the reader's imagination. In *The Prairie Flower* (1849), Bennett offers the spectacle of Fort Laramie's exotic and volatile society:

> Here may be found representatives of all nations and colors, meeting on an equal footing, often drinking and gambling together, many of whom may be put down as implacable enemies, and who, at another time and place, would think nothing of cutting each others' throats. Here occasionally may be seen the Ponka, the Pawnee, the Crow, the Blackfoot, the Sioux and the Shoshone – intermingled with the Spaniard, the Frenchman, the Mexican, the Anglo-Saxon, the Dutchman and Negro . . . The trapper comes in at certain seasons loaded with furs, and receives in exchange for them powder, lead, tobacco, whisky. &c., at the most exorbitant prices. Then generally follow a few days of dissipation – in feasting, gambling, drunkenness, and sometimes riot – when he finds all his hard earnings gone, and he is obliged to betake himself again to the mountains, to procure a new supply, to be squandered in the same reckless manner.   (53)

The presence of the "allure" of the street in Emerson Bennett as well as Whitman and James suggests a pervasive liking for experiences violating the usual notions of order, conventional propriety, and stable meaning – something akin to the attraction of the circus and freak show. George Thompson's "romance of city life," *Venus in Boston* (1849), is a telling example of the genre (3). Recounting the perils of a vulnerable and attractive young woman, Thompson's novel mines the scandals reported in the penny news, the licentious images of pornographic fiction, as well as the macabre and freakish displays of P. T. Barnum for material that will shock, appall, and titillate in equal measure.

But what is the significance of this predilection for the flood of sensation evoked by the different, strange, or outrageous? Of course, it signifies different things in different texts and contexts, but it would seem at a minimum to indicate a certain shared skepticism about the rationalist's attempt to categorize the world. The shared taste for an excess of sensation, whether it's conjured by Pym's horrific confinement in the hold of the *Grampus* or Byrnewood Arlington's nightmarish imprisonment in Lippard's Monk's Hall, expresses a measure of doubt about the power of rationality to fathom and parse all aspects of human experience. Such experiences exceed or defy logic and rational process. They swamp the ideal of a cool, empyrean, and objective perspective with the kind of raw pulsing emotion evoked by a well-made thriller or horror movie. And the popularity of such entertainments would seem to indicate that considerable pleasure is derived by the audience from such violations of the rational. The sensational romance may set out to expose certain social evils in lurid (and sometimes prurient) detail, but the overwhelming nature of the sensations of shock, horror, and desire aroused by these images casts doubt on the project of rationally planning a way out of these conflicts or horrors.

For instance, influenced by Eugène Sue's very popular novel *The Mysteries of Paris* (1842–43), Lippard's *The Quaker City* depicts wrenching scenes of urban poverty and scathing depictions of the corrupt ruling class in the city of brotherly love, but it is far from the muckraking, naturalistic exposé one would encounter at the end of the nineteenth century, such as Upton Sinclair's *The Jungle* (1906). More closely resembling the Gothic fiction of Charles Brockden Brown, Isaac Mitchell, and Edgar Allan Poe, Lippard's novel is a heady mélange of rape, murder, intoxication, supernaturalism, and hypnotism. His Hieronymus Bosch-like vision of Philadelphia as an unredeemable hell on Earth is so complete as to make apocalypse rather than reform seem the only solution. Gothic fantasy, metaphysical truth, and even reportorial accuracy come together in the sensational romance's portrait of the depths of human depravity.

While apparently sharing with the philosophical romances of Poe, Hawthorne, and Melville a skeptical awareness of the limits of rationalism, the sensational romance, at first glance, seems to be far less doubtful when it comes to asserting the meaning or moral lesson of its conflicts and adventures. The genre's storylines leave little room for moral ambiguity. A young man avenges the rape of his sister (Lippard's *The Quaker City*). Reduced to poverty and outlawry by the theft of their inheritances, characters return from the margins of society to strike back at their privileged or elite enemies (E. D. E. N. Southworth's *The Hidden Hand*, Edward Wheeler's *Deadwood Dick*, and John Rollin Ridge's *The Life and Adventures of Joaquín Murieta* [1854]).[14] Brave and decent frontiersmen overcome murderous Indians and malign "foreigners" (Edward Ellis's *Seth Jones*, Emerson Bennett's *The Prairie Flower*, and Charles Webber's *Old Hicks* [1848]). By the end of these tales, justice has been served by the villains' often horrific demise (Lippard's arch villain, Devil-Bug, for instance, is gruesomely squashed to death, and Wheeler's villains, Alexander and Clarence Filmore, are "strung up" for their crimes).

While rightly emphasizing how the sensational novel challenged certain aspects of "the sentimental-domestic genre," David S. Reynolds overlooks the moral transparency characterizing and connecting the two genres (*Quaker City* xxi–xxii). George Thompson's *Venus in Boston* begins with an image that could have been drawn straight from sentimental fiction, the poor orphan girl, Fanny, being befriended by a charitable old man whose sympathies are aroused by her desperate plight (4). Fanny's home "was a poor and lowly place, the abode of humble but decent poverty; yet the angel of peace had spread her wings there, and contentment had sat with them at their frugal board. True, it was but a garret; yet that little family, with hearts united by holy love, felt that to them it was a *home*" (5). This humble image of domestic moral harmony is vulnerable to the corruption of the city, potentially overwhelmed and destroyed by a measureless malignity in the more villainous members of her society, but the domestic image or ideal is not critiqued. As portrayed by Thompson, the sentimental ideal of the caring home needs protection not criticism.

Given the sensational romance's apparent lack of confidence in rationalism as well as its taste for excess, one may well wonder what the basis is for its confident idealistic visions of plainly good and bad characters, just deserts, and decent homes. The answer seems to be a form of romantic intuition which is frequently alloyed with racialist (and racist) assumptions about the essential nature of different kinds of people. We can "just tell" the good from the bad characters by the way they appear, their motions, physical attributes, and habits. For instance, the nobility of Capitola, the heroine of E. D. E. N. Southworth's swashbuckling adventure story *The Hidden Hand*, shines straight out of her eyes, "those clear windows of the soul," which show "only truth, honesty, and courage" (304). The tear of pity in a female character's eye in George Thompson's *Venus in Boston* is as sure a voucher of Alice Goldworthy's good character as it would be in the sentimental novels of Harriet Beecher Stowe and Susan Warner (9). In a similar fashion, bad characters are "hideously ugly," such as Thompson's aptly named Sow Nance (10). The monstrous villain of Lippard's *The Quaker City*, Devil-Bug, is compared to a huge insect created by Satan to test his powers of invention:

> It was a strange thickset specimen of flesh and blood, with a short body, marked by immensely broad shoulders, long arms and thin destorted [sic] legs. The head of the creature was ludicrously large in proportion to the body. Long masses of siff [sic] black hair fell tangled and matted over a forehead, protuberant to deformity. A flat nose with wide nostrils shooting out into each cheek like the smaller wings of an insect, an immense mouth whose heavy lips disclosed two long rows of bristling teeth, a pointed chin, blackened by a heavy beard, and massive eyebrows

meeting over the nose, all furnished the details of a countenance, not
exactly calculated to inspire the most pleasant feelings in the world. One
eye, small black and shapen like a bead, stared steadily in Byrnewood's
face, while the other socket was empty, shriveled and orbless.   (51)

Of course, there is something all too obvious, too definite, and troublingly
unexamined in drawing such equivalences between physical traits and moral
character, which often take the form of racial or ethnic stereotypes. "Indians,"
in Ellis's *Seth Jones*, are uniformly "dark and threatening" (237). In Lippard's
novel, the scheming Gabriel Von Gelt (whose name transparently signifies
his mercenary character) is indelibly marked by features indicating his Jewish
identity as well as his inner corruption (175). While satisfying a desire for clarity
and predictability, the correlation between outward mark and inward character
suggests a disturbingly deterministic model of existence in which complexion,
features, and physiognomy become destiny in a comic-book version of Platonic
correspondences.

However, the predictability of the sensational romance's storyline (villains
vanquished, heroes rewarded) and the unmistakable clarity of its signs of moral
character are not unalloyed and pure. Despite the fact that we may never have
been in doubt about either the end of the story or its moral significance,
the sensational romance's penchant for a disorienting stream of shocking or
strange images threatens to break in upon the overt allegorical clarity of the
storyline and its characterizations. In their desire to pull us into the funhouse of
their imaginations, these novelists indulge in a kind of piling up of sensational
detail, determined to push our affective response as far as it will go. We can see
a small instance of this tendency in a bit of description from Edward Wheeler's
western, *Deadwood Dick*. Consider Wheeler's portrait of a minor character,
Geoffrey Walsingham Nix, the father of one of the lead female characters:

> a little, deformed old man; humpbacked, bow-legged, and white-haired,
> with cross eyes, a large mouth, a big head, set upon a slim, crane-like
> neck; blue eyes, and an immense brown beard, that flowed downward
> half-way to the belt above his waist, which contained a small arsenal of
> knives and revolvers. He hobbled about with a heavy crutch constantly
> under his left arm, and was certainly a pitiable sight to behold.   (274)

As is the case with Lippard's description of Devil-Bug, the accumulation and
exaggeration of these details – crossed eyes, humpbacked, lame, yet armed to
the teeth – appeal to a "more is more" aesthetic, a desire to push the description
into the dream-like realm of the fantastic. In its proliferation of exaggerated
descriptive details, the passage creates a kind of kinetic movement. Nix is not
inert. He is under pressure, bent, deformed, pushed in different directions,

downward by humpback and lame leg, but also oddly vertical with long neck and flowing beard.

Sometimes the movement figured in such violent descriptions is literal. Lippard, for instance, has a predilection for images of convulsion – physically and viscerally graphic depictions of extreme change in the physiognomies of his main characters. When the novel's avenging hero, Byrnewood Arlington, is gassed by Devil-Bug, his face turns "ghastly pale, one moment; the next it flushed with the hues of a crimson flame. His large black eyes dilated in their glance and stood out from the lids as though they were about to fall from their sockets. His mouth distended with a convulsive grimace, while his teeth were firmly clenched together" (118). Similarly, in describing the rage of Capitola's benevolent, if fiery, guardian (aptly nicknamed Old Hurricane), Southworth emphasizes paroxysmal movement:

> Reader! did you ever see a raging lion tearing to and fro the narrow limits of his cage, and occasionally shaking the amphitheatre with his tremendous roar? or a furious bull tossing his head and tail, and ploughing up the earth with his hoofs as he careered back and forth between the boundaries of his pen? If you have seen and noted these mad brutes, you may form some faint idea of the frenzy of Old Hurricane, as he stormed up and down the floor of the front piazza.   (120)

Such comparisons suggest a keen appetite for the kind of radical transformation and metamorphosis we associate with Ovid. Overcome and transfigured by great passion, the person becomes something other than him/herself. Though he would seem to be fundamentally or inherently bad, Count Albert, the villain of Webber's *Old Hicks*, has been made into a strange and monstrous alloy of savagery and civilization by his "lust of gold and slaughter" and close contact with the Indians (255). Lest the reader assume that such metamorphosis is limited to the wicked characters, Webber has his heroic narrator describe his own transformation in battle: "The raging lust of destructiveness was fairly aroused, and nothing but blood! blood! blood! could the thirsty eye-balls see ahead . . . This horrible passion once aroused, and all the tender seeming of our life grows hateful, and is gulfed – lost, in the fiery vortex we are rushing through, and in which earth and heaven are at once confounded" (263). The kinetic qualities of these descriptions introduce an element of mutability into these romances' confident and transparent correlation of character and moral value. They suggest the possibility that just as the reader may be overwhelmed by sensation, transported to a fantastic realm unlike that of daily life, so can a person's sense of self and ethical direction be overcome by passions and forces beyond his control.

The moral idealism of the sensational romance, its assumption of a clear and fixed correlation between character and moral significance, is subtly qualified by the form's frequent invocations of metamorphosis and disguise. Things and people who seem to transform before our eyes suggest that what seems obvious and stable may not be. While his fundamentally flawed moral nature is never in doubt, there is still something additionally and disconcertingly fluid about Lippard's wealthy and handsome cad, Fitz-Cowels, who turns out to be neither wealthy nor handsome. Indeed, his self-presentation is all an act, a fabrication of padding, make-up, costume, and bold imposture. Seeing him out of his disguise reminds one of Swift's harsh satiric vision of the whore Corrina at her toilet in "A Beautiful Young Nymph Going to Bed" (155–56). Seth Jones, the eponymous hero of Ellis's forest adventure, is revealed to be not a rough and uncouth scout, but a gentleman in disguise (262). Capitola is not the ragged newsboy she appears to be at the beginning of *The Hidden Hand*, but an adventurous young lady. The villain of George Thompson's *Venus in Boston*, the Chevalier, is impossible to read as to origin, background, even his age: "he was one of those singular persons whose external appearance defies you to form any opinion as to their age, with any hope of coming within twenty years of the truth" (57). The reader's sense of how to evaluate these characters is not directly subverted by these transformations and disguises, but our certainty that Capitola is good and that the Chevalier is bad is shadowed by the presence of change.

Often this change is mourned as when John Rollin Ridge's outlaw/hero, Joaquín Murieta, tells a friend, "as he brushed a tear away from his eyes, 'I am not the man I was; I am a deep-eyed scoundrel, but so help me God! I was driven to it by oppression and wrong'" (50). Oppression has transformed Murieta from a peaceful, educated young man born to respectable parents into a man of violence. But such personal mutations are also presented in more affirmative terms, even recommended. In imagining the sudden revelation of Seth Jones's real identity as the educated Eugene Morton, Ellis implicitly suggests the possibility of a real transformation along parallel lines. Perhaps the reader of the dime novel, like Horatio Alger's Dick Hunter, could undertake this upward metamorphosis. Even the monstrous Devil-Bug is allowed a fleeting instant of positive transformation as he remembers "the fair woman, who had loved him. Loved the outcast of mankind, the devil in human shape! . . . For a moment the soul of Devil-Bug was *beautiful*" (339).

While frightened of change, these novels are also drawn to it. Many of the transformations they imagine are monstrous, but some are ennobling. Murieta may regret his more innocent past, but, in his outlaw incarnation, he is an exciting avenger of the wrongs of the common people. Lippard's romance, which given its author's credentials as a reformer (he was an early supporter of women's rights and the founder of an early labor union), has surprisingly few positive images of transformation and change. Yet, some characters do undergo something akin to a conversion experience. After helping in Lorrimer's scheme to seduce Mary, Bess, one of Devil-Bug's many accomplices, repents and helps Mary escape Monk Hall.

The sensational romance's appreciation of change is expressed by the appetite for adventure and imposture shared by good as well as bad characters. Consider, for instance, the similarity and mutual attraction of Capitola and the villainous Black Donald. She "likes men whose very names strike terror into the hearts of commonplace people!" (156). Both embrace danger, and both are willing to defy social convention, though, to be sure, Black Donald's defiance is far more serious. Both clearly enjoy using disguise and metamorphosis to achieve their aims (Capitola as a boy and later as Clara Day; Black Donald as a peddler and later as a camp preacher [157, 218]). Edward Wheeler's hero Deadwood Dick, like so many in westerns and detective stories, is more not less appealing for his willingness to dispense with legal and social convention as well as his fearlessness and skill in battle. His version of heroism comes costumed in black, and that association with darkness conjured by his clothing adds to rather than subtracts from his allure. The adventurous woman who dresses as a man and fights duels as well as the heroic outlaw dressed in black preserve the notion of clear moral significances but connect it to a volatility of appearances suggestive of social change. The sensational romance plays to its audience's expectations of good heroes, bad villains, and unambiguous endings with obvious moral import, but its metamorphic energies, and the rush of sensations it seeks to evoke, suggest a cultural reexamination of the divisions between good and evil and the possibility that the culture's values, its sense of happy endings, are under revision.

# Chapter 2

# The sentimental novel

## What is the sentimental novel?

People discussing the sentimental novel often begin by observing the genre's remarkable commercial success. Sentimental novels, such as *Uncle Tom's Cabin* (1852) by Harriet Beecher Stowe, *The Wide, Wide World* (1850) by Susan Warner, and *The Lamplighter* (1854) by Maria Cummins were best-sellers when the mass market for novels was a relatively new phenomenon (Davidson 16–37, Gilmore 46–54). Nathaniel Hawthorne famously complained, "What is the mystery of these innumerable editions of the Lamplighter, and other books neither better nor worse? – worse they could not be, and better they need not be, when they sell by the 100,000" (Fern xxxiv). More recently, critics have sharply differed on the significance of the genre's popularity – some seeing it as a sign of the sentimental novel's expressive power and others as evidence of the culture's vapidity (e.g., Tompkins 124, Douglas 114).[1] These discussions often overlook a revealing point of connection between the sensational romance and the sentimental novel. Before the extraordinary sales of *Uncle Tom's Cabin* (estimated at 5 million before the Civil War), the biggest seller in American fiction had been George Lippard's *The Quaker City* (1845) (Gilmore 54). A marketing expert trying to understand the comparable popularity of such ostensibly different productions would be quick to note that they share an emphasis on powerful emotion. Both genres seek to produce in the reader an overwhelming emotional reaction, and both genres are willing to shock the reader in order to generate the desired intensity of feeling. A kitten is boiled in Maria Cummins's *The Lamplighter*. *Uncle Tom's Cabin* includes scenes of gruesome brutality and torture. And the eponymous heroine of Fanny Fern's *Ruth Hall* (1855) confronts sexual harassment and the prospect of prostitution. However, while the production of powerful emotion would seem to be an end in itself in a novel such as *The Quaker City*, in sentimental fiction it has an unmistakable moral and religious dimension.

Perhaps more than any other single factor, sentimental novels are defined by their depiction of the conversion moment, the moment when a flood of emotion transforms the individual, revealing moral truths and human connections previously ignored by or invisible to the convert. In the sentimental novel, characters (and readers) are swept away by a powerful current of feeling, a feeling intuitively known to be heaven sent. This emotional rush reveals the existence of a better, more caring self, and offers direct access to the values that give life meaning. Trueman Flint, the heroic lamplighter in Cummins's novel who adopts the benighted orphan Gerty, "never" hears her sad story "without crying" (239). His tears are an indisputable sign of his good character and an illustration of the sympathetic feeling that ought to direct individuals and societies. In *Uncle Tom's Cabin*, when Topsy, an orphan slave, expresses her sense that she is so bad as to be unlovable, little Eva spontaneously bursts out, "O, Topsy, poor child *I* love you!" and lays "her little thin, white hand on Topsy's shoulder" (245). The effect on Topsy (and, Stowe hopes, on her readers) is immediate:

> The round, keen eyes of the black child were overcast with tears; – large, bright drops rolled heavily down, one by one, and fell on the little white hand. Yes, in that moment, a ray of real belief, a ray of heavenly love, had penetrated the darkness of her heathen soul! She laid her head down between her knees, and wept and sobbed, – while the beautiful child, bending over her, looked like the picture of some bright angel stooping to reclaim a sinner.    (245)

This scene, like many others in sentimental fiction, recalls biblical associations of children and heaven (Matt. 18 and 19). In her redemptive capacity, the child is linked to less worldly ways of perceiving the world, a readier expression and reception of love, and a native understanding of the moral significance of sympathy. The apparently untutored and immediate reaction of the tender-hearted child seems like a sign of the inherent goodness of the human heart. Apparently intractable or impossibly complex problems become suddenly clear and simple when illuminated by the child's intuitive compassion.

In their portrayal of an innate capacity for fellow feeling, sentimental novelists were influenced by the moral sense psychology elaborated by the Earl of
Shaftesbury, Joseph Butler, Frances Hutcheson, David Hume, and Adam Smith.
For these eighteenth-century philosophers, John Locke's concept of right reason – an empirical calculus of sense impressions and inductive reasoning – was
incomplete. It left out the emotional and aesthetic aspects of human nature.
Human beings were inherently capable of deriving exquisite happiness and
pleasure from sympathy and self-sacrifice. For Shaftesbury, Locke's dismissal
of innate moral ideas was tantamount to a rejection of virtue. Shaftesbury
contended, instead, that the heart is the seat of an innate moral sense that
determines right from wrong as the visual sense determines beauty from ugli-
ness. Adam Smith and David Hume extended the moral sense concept by
characterizing sympathy as an activity of the imagination, which enables us to
go beyond our own person and understand another's suffering. For Thomas
Jefferson, the possession of a sympathetic moral sense defined humankind.
Following Hutcheson, Hume, and Smith, Jefferson found that "nature hath
implanted in our breasts a love of others, a sense of duty to them, a moral
instinct, in short, which prompts us irresistibly to feel and to succor their
distresses" (Crane *Race* 21–23).

Sentimental fiction similarly posits the existence of the moral sense but
conceives of it in overtly religious terms, often using the figure of the angelic,
otherworldly child to exemplify it and to illustrate its power to relieve human
suffering. In his temperance novel, *Ten Nights in a Bar-Room* (1854), T. S. Arthur
measures the depths of Joe Morgan's alcoholism by comparing his condition
with the innocence of his daughter, Mary (23–24). Particularly touching is
Arthur's description of Mary calling, "Father," into the darkened bar where Joe
has drunk himself into a stupor. Mary's innocence and her unconditional love
for Joe remind the reader of Christ and his heavenly Father whose love does
not abate despite our failings. The contrast between Mary's purity and Joe's
debased condition aims also at arousing the reader's indignant condemnation
of the tavern as a source of human degradation and sorrow (33). Like Stowe's
little Eva, Mary is doomed to a short life, but she is still able to redeem her
father through love and heavenly insight before she dies. The disfigurements
wrought upon her father's face by drink do not prevent Mary's better form
of perception from seeing "only the beloved countenance of her parent" (62).
Knowing full well that she has been fatally injured in the bar, Mary obtains her
father's promise not to return to the tavern until she is better. Joe's promise
becomes in effect a temperance pledge (62–64, 71).

While their affective punch is apparently direct and simple, these scenes do a
number of things simultaneously. First and foremost, they offer straightforward

representations of intuitive compassion.[2] When Topsy bluntly declares that no one does or can love her, Eva immediately responds with affection and kindness, throwing Topsy an emotional lifeline. Similarly, undeterred by the darkness of the tavern and the debased condition of her father, Mary's love effectively penetrates Joe's alcoholism. But these aren't just rescue scenes in which a helpless victim is protected, comforted, or healed. These are conversion scenes. In Arthur's and Stowe's novels, high emotion drives toward a once-and-for-all reversal of life patterns and behaviors, and the depictions of these radical transformations are designed to produce an echo-like change in the reader who is similarly moved by the scene. Eva's loving reaction sparks a seismic shift in Topsy's life, winning the little girl's soul for Christ. Having recognized Topsy's humanity by her love, Eva can enjoin Topsy to do better, to know right from wrong, and to act accordingly. In Stowe's calculus of sentiment and religious faith, love is the prerequisite for moral responsibility. Without love, Topsy's humanity is denied, and, without the recognition of Topsy's humanity, moral responsibility does not make sense. From this moment forward, Topsy is a changed child, not perfect, but always on an upward course, evolving into a better state of mind and behavior. Miss Ophelia, who has witnessed Eva's ministration to Topsy's parched soul, is vicariously moved to become a loving surrogate parent. Joe Morgan's life is similarly redeemed by his dying daughter's love, which sustains him as he suffers the pains of withdrawal and delirium tremens (76–79). Mary's love becomes the touchstone for his life in sobriety. Change is thus central to the sentimental narrative. The emotional power of such scenes is designed to represent and engender a complete personal transformation. As we shall see, these moments of sympathetic catharsis, or purifying emotional transport, can also be connected to or thought of as inspiring social and political renewal.

Conversion, of course, is a religious concept, and sentimental fiction is marked by its framing of powerful sympathetic feelings in expressly Christian terms. Eva, "The Little Evangelist" of Stowe's novel, touches Topsy and draws her near, just as Christ reached out to the children errantly held back by his disciples (Matt. 19:14–15). Compassionate feelings are repeatedly identified with Christian inspiration in this fiction. In Cummins's *The Lamplighter*, Trueman Flint describes compassion as the surest guide to religious duty (229). In Frank Webb's *The Garies and Their Friends* (1857), sympathy inspires a benign owner to free his slave, George Winston. George's repeated response "God bless you!" signals the role of religious inspiration on the issue of slavery – real Christianity which is intrinsically sympathetic pulls in an abolitionist direction (13). The emotional impulse to aid those in need, such as the orphaned Ellen Montgomery in Susan Warner's *The Wide, Wide World*, is something akin to a message from God – divine instruction as to how to act toward others. Part of Ellen's role in advancing the religious themes of Warner's novel is to make divine will seem palpable in the sympathy that various characters, such as Mr. Van Brunt, feel for Ellen (87, 91–94, 412–13). Indeed, sentiment is so clearly and ubiquitously tied to religion in this fiction that one might well describe these novels as Christian fiction which merely features sentiment as a means of religious insight. However, although apt in many respects, such a characterization would obscure this fiction's emphasis on emotion as a nonsectarian vehicle of moral change.

Written from a wide variety of Christian (Protestant) perspectives, sentimental fiction generally stresses positive feeling before religious form. These novels are replete with characters who do not practice any orthodox liturgy but who are nonetheless profoundly moral and devout. Good-hearted characters, such as Trueman Flint and Uncle Tom, do not need to go to church to know right from wrong or to love and bear witness to God. Sympathy and other positive emotions precede and are of far greater import than the mere observation of religious forms. Gerty Flint doesn't need catechism to pray: her inchoate and untutored longing "for God and virtue" is "a prayer" (Cummins 245). Such observations do not erase the substantive denominational differences between these writers but rather point to a commonality: a shared accentuation of the role of sympathy and kindly affective response in directing one to a higher truth and moral obligation. Even Warner's *The Wide, Wide World*, one of the more orthodox and overtly pious of these novels, puts the substance of sympathy and proper feeling before the doctrine of any particular creed. Warner's scenes of religious instruction take place in homes, on walks, and on the deck of a passenger boat, and her religious mentors are lay people. In its depictions of the spontaneous and powerful surge of redemptive emotion ending all questioning and argument, replacing doubt with blessed certainty, sentimental fiction carries on the evangelical tradition of the Great Awakening described by Alan Heimert.

Looking at religious thought in the period leading to the Revolution, Heimert maps a split between an emphasis on rationality (associated with the educated and upper classes, High Church liturgy, and deism) and a stress on emotional fervor (associated with the lower parts of the social order, Low Church liturgy, evangelicalism, and an ardent belief in scripture). He sees this division as exerting a continuing influence in the nineteenth century (Heimert 3, 5–6). Of course, such dichotomies often do not remain pure or stable. Over time, the supposed opposites may tend to draw nearer to each other and mix or merge. For instance, Fanny Fern's *Ruth Hall* and Maria Cummins's *The Lamplighter* encompass both a rational, pragmatic program of incremental self-improvement (think here of Benjamin Franklin's rationalist approach to "moral perfection") and a belief in the power of emotions to reveal moral truths (think here of Jonathan Edwards's belief that the "affections" hold the key to religious truth) (Franklin 63–72, Edwards 10–15). From the evangelical tradition, the sentimental novel inherits a compelling argument for following one's own intuitive and emotional registration of divine inspiration, a principle which, as Heimert observes, has revolutionary potential. The individual's faith in his or her access to divine will through emotion provides a sense of authority independent from time-honored traditions and leads, in certain cases, to a lack of respect for the established social order. While much of *The Wide, Wide World* focuses on Ellen Montgomery's need to learn submission to God's will, Warner shows how one's passions can readily and appropriately fire up into revolutionary zeal, as when Ellen tells her domineering Scottish uncle, "And if I had been in the American army I would have fought *you* with all my heart" (506). Inspiration of this emotionally charged type is not as cautious as the rationalist approach, which continues to seek evidence and maintains a degree of uncertainty, potentially maiming its ability to produce radical or innovative action.

Of course, as noted by Heimert and others, evangelical endorsements of high emotion and rebirth have provoked considerable opposition and skepticism. For contemporaries fearing radical change, the Calvinist ministry seemed "fond to a madness" of "popular forms of government" (Heimert 12). Novelists, from Henry Fielding to Mark Twain, mocked what they saw as the simplistic moral universe of the sentimental writer. In our own era, many have observed how the emphasis on feeling rather than thought can be used by skilled demagogues to advance a fascist political agenda. And the average person may well doubt whether the apparent feelings of certainty generated by strong emotion always lead to the best ethical conclusions. Working through difficult or complex ethical problems frequently entails a considerable degree of uncertainty and hesitancy, especially when the stakes are high, and often the best solution is not known beforehand but emerges from the contest between opposed points of view.

Another line of criticism contends that the emotional fervor touted by the sentimental writers is too facile, too easily put on and off like an article of clothing. For instance, Wendell Phillips, an ardent abolitionist, warned that the emotion aroused by *Uncle Tom's Cabin* may well prove insufficient to motivate real anti-slavery action: "There is many a man who weeps over Uncle Tom and swears by the [proslavery New York] Herald" (Gossett 168). What happens when the moment of passion subsides, when the tide of sympathetic feeling ebbs? Have one's behavior and attitudes been actually and meaningfully changed? When not caught in the grip of overwhelming emotion, does a different, less intense kind of feeling take over? Do these more moderate feelings guide us? Or are we sent in search of ways to rekindle the moment of evangelical fervor over and over again? How does sentiment help us deal with less dramatic challenges, such as everyday bad behavior or the banal confusions that come up in life? And how do we address cases where strong emotions seem to pull in opposing directions or in a direction of uncertain or questionable morality (such as the desire for vengeance)?

For our purposes, a useful way of categorizing such criticisms and questions is to see them as posing the challenge of a certain form of realism to the idealism underpinning sentimental fiction. As we shall see in the next chapter, this philosophical contrast helps to illuminate some of the defining features of realist fiction. Generally speaking, the philosophical realist works empirically to derive knowledge from the rational analysis of sense impressions, taking an exploratory or inductive rather than paradigmatic or deductive approach to experience and remaining open to uncertainty rather than claiming to arrive at any final or unchanging conclusions. In its literary form, realism tends to eschew allegory, which usually depends on some version of the Platonic or idealist two-story universe, in which the particulars of the lower story more or less clearly emblematize the universals of the upper story. Not believing in the two-story schema or lacking confidence in being able to ascertain the ideals of the second story, realists turn to the particulars of experience to find meaning in a process much too uncertain and muddled for allegory's purposes. Idealism, by contrast, conceives of experience as a readable revelation of absolute values and God's plan (in its religious versions). Influenced by Plato's conception that the particulars of the tangible world are imperfect copies of more perfect ideals (e.g., all the tables in the world are imperfect representations of the ultimate heavenly table), the idealist regards ideas of truth and right, goodness and beauty, not only as aspirations but as knowable ideals which are imperfectly shadowed forth in everyday experience.

Sentimental fiction applies emotion to this philosophical orientation, portraying the sympathetic heart as the best means of access to the moral and philosophical ideals dimly or partially represented in the particulars of experience. As Jane Tompkins reminds us, when viewed from the perspective of those sharing this faith, it is "realistic" to believe in one's emotional intuition (127). Once awakened, the feeling hearts of even such apparently depraved characters as Sambo and Quimbo, the slaves Simon Legree uses to torture Uncle Tom, can penetrate the ephemera of appearances and glimpse divine truth. For Stowe and other sentimental writers, fellow feeling engenders a superior and more accurate view of what matters in everyday life. When thinking about this genre's claim to reveal the most important truths of human experience, we should keep in mind the fact that sentimental fiction often moves back and forth between fictional invention and biographical or autobiographical reportage. Fanny Fern's *Ruth Hall*, for instance, draws extensively on its author's life story. And as Ann duCille, Cindy Weinstein, and others have pointed out, the sentimental novel is often best read as part of a dialogue with documentary slave narratives – each borrows from the other and both claim that the emotions can reveal important and indubitable moral truths, such as the injustice of slavery. Perhaps because of their authors' overriding faith in the heart as a medium of moral certainty and the clear importance of the social issues being addressed, sentimental novels and slave narratives often display an insouciant disregard for the boundaries between fiction and nonfiction.

The idealism of sentimental fiction, its belief in absolute and fixed values, is reflected in the unambiguous nature of its characters – their relative transparency and typicality. In *The Wide, Wide World*, Ellen Montgomery's emotional and moral survival and growth depend on her ability to see people clearly for what they are. When little Ellen goes to a department store, she recognizes the malign character of a sales clerk, Mr. Saunders, straight away; it is plain in his "tone and manner," "slovenly exterior," and "disagreeable" eyes (46). And when she is rescued from Saunders's rudeness by an older gentleman, Ellen can intuitively rely on his "kind tone of voice" and friendly manner as reliable proof of his good character (48). The appearances and manners of the two characters stand in a perfect and dependable relation to their moral characters (318). Similarly, in Frank Webb's novel *The Garies and Their Friends* (1857), Mr. Walter's good character is as manifest in his noble physiognomy as Mr. Stevens's corrupt nature is manifest in his "cunning-looking eyes," and his "cadaverous skin," and his twitching, "thin compressed lips" (124). Webb takes pains in his story of racial violence in antebellum Philadelphia to deny that racial difference can be read as a sign of moral character, but his novel is nonetheless replete with appearances transparently signifying moral character. Indeed, this transparency of moral character is essential to the project of conversion. As Alice Humphrey informs Ellen, "Christians are the only Bible some people ever read; and it is true; all they know of religion is what they get from the lives of its professors; and oh! were the world but full of the right kind of example, the kingdom of darkness could not stand" (239). In *The Lamplighter*, when Gerty Flint eventually blossoms into a beautiful young lady, her beauty is tied to her transparency, her "tell-tale" face which "speak[s] the truth and proclaim[s] the sentiment within" (318). In each case the transparency and fixity of the character signified by legible outward signs lends support to an idealist conception of absolute and fixed values – the idealist predicate for the sentimental novel.

The idea of fixed and absolute values is alien to the realist world of Theodore Dreiser's *Sister Carrie* (1900), where all value, including the merit or worth of the main characters, seems to fluctuate in the competitive marketplace of desire. In the sentimental novel, real value, unlike market value, is something fixed and knowable. When in *The Wide, Wide World* Mrs. Montgomery, Ellen's mother, sells a beloved keepsake, a ring, for $80, we are told that this amount represents "about three-quarters of its *real value*" (emphasis added, 28–29). On one level, this remark may simply be intended to indicate that Mrs. Montgomery could have received more for her ring, but, in a novel full of religious idealism and moral absolutes, the term "real value" would seem to suggest something different from and transcending the fluctuations of the second-hand jewelry market. Mrs. Montgomery uses the $80 she obtains for her precious keepsake to buy Ellen a few nice things for her life with the stern and austere Aunt Fortune. The "real value" of this bit of commerce lies in its illustration of the unwavering and unconditional love between mother and daughter. In sentimental fiction, the changeable nature of the market reveals the falsity of worldly values in contrast to the priceless fixity of real value. In her sentimental proslavery novel, *The Planter's Northern Bride* (1854), Caroline Hentz paints free market capitalism as the antithesis of compassion and permanent values. Threatened by competition, illness, and disability as well as driven by materialistic appetites and envy, workers are constantly in motion trying to better their situation, moving from one position to the next. As a result, society is destabilized, and the quality of life (for both worker and employer), which depends in Hentz's view on a high degree of stability, is substantially eroded. For instance, the traveler cannot find a good meal in Northern hotels because the kitchen staff is always new, and the kitchen staff is made discontent and unhappy by the incessant movement and competition (259–60, 265). Not only does the marketplace not value human life, but it also makes a wholesome social order impossible.

The religious and emotional ideals of the sentimental novel are static and unchanging, and the typical sentimental novel's protagonist seeks a kind of spiritual and emotional calm by faithfully adhering to these moral absolutes. This is the quest of both Ellen Montgomery and Uncle Tom. For Ellen, this quest begins when her mother holds out the idea of Christ as a refuge "where changes do not come and they that are gathered there are parted no more forever" (41). The earthly version of this heavenly stasis is a kind of emotional and psychological contentment which is invulnerable to outrage, insult, and changes of circumstance. If she succeeds in submitting to God's will, Ellen will be "content" and "beautifully placid" (189, 190). The ultimate example of this ideal in American sentimental fiction has to be Uncle Tom's unwavering spiritual equilibrium during his torture by Simon Legree. Tom's final torment comes when he won't reveal the hiding place of two female slaves. In a rage at Tom's refusal to speak, Legree vows to "count every drop of blood there is in you, and take 'em, one by one, till ye give up!" (358). Divinely inspired – his "brave, true heart was firm on the Eternal Rock" – Tom is calm, patient, and unmoved throughout this hellish abuse, even forgiving Legree in the midst of his rage and cruelty (357–59). And when young George Shelby comes to the rescue, too late, and is grief-stricken at the sight of Tom's mangled body, Tom responds, "Don't call me poor fellow!" "I have been poor fellow; but that's all past and gone, now. I'm right in the door, going into glory! O, Mas'r George! *Heaven has come!*" (362). For Stowe, Tom has found a peace that transcends rational understanding and cannot be threatened by changes of circumstance and condition, including death itself. He has attained the unmoved and unmoving spiritual center of a tumultuous and changeable world.

This brings us to one of the central paradoxes of the sentimental novel: it values permanence and stasis as signs of transcendent value, but it is full of movement and transformation. The ultimate goal may be union with unchanging and absolute ideals, but this aim is achieved by way of considerable motion, effort, ongoing development, learning, conversion, lapse, and renewed conversion. For some, conversion – the once-and-for-all spiritual awakening and choice – ironically has to be experienced several times before it seems to take and become permanent. While the sentimental novel's protagonists are inherently good, these characters frequently must go through some process of growth, steadily improving themselves and moving toward the full realization of their good natures. The plot of the sentimental novel is organized around the main character's reversal of spiritual fortunes (a reversal which often has material and social aspects as well).

In addition to the primacy of emotional transport stimulating conversion, sentimental fiction contains many signs of a Franklinian emphasis on prudence, thrift, hard work, and education. At the beginning of *Uncle Tom's Cabin*, we watch as Tom practices reading his Bible, a skill that will stand him in good stead in his hardships and suffering. Ellen Montgomery's moral improvement moves in tandem with her educational progress. Under Alice Humphrey's patient instruction, Ellen is not only learning to be less rebellious and willful, she is also learning French, arithmetic, English grammar, and history. Similarly, in *The Lamplighter*, Gerty Flint becomes a better person as she becomes more polite, better educated, and an improved housekeeper. In Gerty's religious, educational, social, and economic progress, Cummins's novel, like many others in this genre, suggests a model for obtaining a respectable and secure middle-class life. And by imbuing the self-improving character with sympathy and a native religious feeling, the sentimental novel seeks to give the project of self-improvement a moral anchor and significance.

## Theme and variations: a young woman's story

The narrative template or storyline most associated with the sentimental novel is that of a young woman struggling to make her way in life without the support of a traditional family. Nina Baym has described how novels such as Susan Warner's *The Wide, Wide World*, Maria Cummins's *The Lamplighter*, and Fanny Fern's *Ruth Hall*

> all tell, with variations, a single tale. In essence, it is the story of a young girl who is deprived of the supports she had rightly or wrongly depended on to sustain her throughout life and is faced with the necessity of winning her own way in the world. This young girl is fittingly called a heroine because her role is precisely analogous to the unrecognized or undervalued youths of fairy tales who perform dazzling exploits and win a place for themselves in the land of happy endings. She also fits the pattern of comic hero, whose displacement indicates social corruption and whose triumph ensures the reconstruction of a beneficent social order.   (11–12)

The key to these young women's triumphs lies in their achievement of self-mastery. Sometimes this enhanced self-control or self-discipline results in a considerable measure of independence (as in the cases of Gerty Flint or Ruth Hall); sometimes it results in a kind of idealized self-abnegation (as in the case of Ellen Montgomery). Targeted at young people, young women in particular, these novels are didactic, instructing readers in the development of good character and the reciprocal nature of emotional connections and moral obligations. The domestic ideal of finding and maintaining a caring and healthy home is central to the sentimental novel's drama.[3]

We can better identify and understand many of the key elements of sentimental fiction by looking closely at Warner's, Cummins's, and Fern's novels. The comparison of these writers' work also reveals a trend in the fiction (and the era) toward a greater emphasis on the independent judgment and moral and intellectual agency of women.

### Susan Warner, The Wide, Wide World (1850)

Susan Warner's father, a lawyer, lost most of his money in the Panic of 1837. After this financial blow, Susan and her sister, Anna, took up writing. They authored religious novels, stories, and songs, such as "Jesus Bids Us Shine" and "Jesus Loves Me" (Warner 587–92). Susan's very popular novel, *The Wide, Wide World*, tells the tale of a little girl, Ellen Montgomery, who is severed from her family at a very young age and grows up without a mother (or a father, for that matter, though his absence does not seem to be a loss of the same magnitude for Warner). At the beginning of the novel, Ellen's mother is very ill, and a doctor has prescribed travel abroad as a restorative (though he doubts she will recover). Because caring for Ellen would further tax her mother's weakened and frail condition, Ellen must remain behind, staying with her Aunt Fortune in the country. Not a particularly warm person, Aunt Fortune has little use for her niece's affectionate, spirited, and imaginative nature. During her time with Aunt Fortune, Ellen receives news that her mother and father have died. After Aunt Fortune marries the man who has been managing her farm, the kindly Mr. Van Brunt, Ellen goes to live with the Humphreys. Unfortunately, Alice Humphrey, the gentle young woman who has been caring for and teaching Ellen, dies, leaving Ellen to fill in as the woman of the house. Letters turn up unexpectedly indicating that Ellen's parents had wished that she would go to live with her aristocratic maternal relatives in Scotland (Ellen's grandmother and Uncle Lindsay). With much sadness, Ellen loses yet another home and leaves America to live with her newly discovered relations in Scotland. The Lindsays find Ellen altogether too "American" and too pious, and seek to reshape Ellen's character in a more fashionable direction. As far as her conscience permits, Ellen complies with good grace to the Lindsays' demands. As originally published, the novel concludes by indicating that Ellen's patient endurance in the Lindsay household will be rewarded by her return to America and a resumption of her life with the Humphreys. Warner (or her publisher) omitted a final chapter (perhaps because of the novel's great length) describing in some detail the luxurious and happy home that Ellen comes to as John Humphrey's bride (8).

The novel's storyline moves Ellen from the city to the country and from the United States to Scotland and back, and each of these moves poses a new challenge for Ellen. She is jarred by the contrasts between her mother's warmth and Aunt Fortune's practicality and between the Humphreys' piety and the Lindsays' worldly and aristocratic outlook. In each case, Ellen must not only adapt to new circumstances and customs, but she must also submit to new forms of discipline – the imperatives of each new set of surrogate parents. The psychological drama running through each of these moves is framed as a matter of discipline. Ellen has to learn to curb her impulses and desires and submit wholly to God's will (11). Particularly difficult for Ellen are those moments in which she must restrain her desire to object to insult, threat, or injustice. Warner gives little sanction to even the more justifiable forms of self-assertion. Ostensibly (though, as we shall see, not entirely), she wants to argue that only by self-sacrifice will Ellen achieve a good life. Ellen's task, her challenge, is to learn to keep her nature in check and to submit to sorrow and the dictates of a higher authority.

*The Wide, Wide World* opens with young Ellen musing as she looks out the window on a rainy city street, lost in rapt observation of passersby, horses, and carriages (9). The mind of the child, amorphous, open, and waiting to take shape and direction, is not unlike that of the reader who waits for the novel to give shape to his or her imaginings. Distinguished by her intellectual curiosity and desire to learn, Ellen is able to take aesthetic pleasure in a wide variety of experiences. When Ellen goes for a walk with Nancy Vawse, she expresses her curiosity about lichen, to Nancy's surprise ("Tain't worth looking at"), and, when Ellen stares with wonder at a flock of ducks passing overhead, Nancy is perplexed and contemptuous (120). Ellen's imaginative ability (e.g., her ready transformation of a little brook into Niagara Falls) connects her to both Warner and the reader (122). Magnifying and finding significance in small or common details, drawing comparisons, making allusions, and creating virtual worlds out of the experiences before her, Ellen's talents are kindred with those of both the writer and reader of novels.

Warner uses the pattern of repeated adoptions and rescues to advance both Ellen's self-mastery and her story. Beginning with Ellen's separation from her mother, the good parent or guardian is replaced by the unsympathetic surrogate, a substitution that intensifies Ellen's loss and threatens to plunge her into despair. From these low points, Ellen is repeatedly rescued by a more loving caretaker. Thus, Ellen's separation from her mother is made more painful by the insensitivity and thoughtlessness of the family with which she is forced to travel – Margaret Dunscombe and her mother. Fortunately, the gentle and kindly George Marshman appears, offering Ellen a respite from the uncaring Dunscombes. Later, Alice Humphrey similarly comforts Ellen and gives her a refuge from Aunt Fortune's harsh and unloving treatment. At the novel's conclusion, John Humphrey saves Ellen from the Lindsays by marrying her. This pattern of separation and adoption happens so frequently that Ellen wonders "how many times one may be adopted" (504). But, in each case, Ellen has something to learn. The appearance of the better, more loving guardian comes with a renewal of Ellen's spiritual progress. When George Marshman takes Ellen under his wing while they travel together up the Hudson River, he gives her important religious instruction as well as kindness. Similarly, Ellen not only finds emotional relief with Alice Humphrey but also a demanding spiritual and academic education. The overarching effect of these substitutions and their role in furthering Ellen's spiritual progress is to reinforce the reader's sense of a providential hand directing the details of Ellen's life, bringing her low only to raise her up.

Ellen does make progress, learning to set aside her own will. Submitting to earthly authority figures, whether they are sympathetic (Alice and John

Humphrey) or unsympathetic (Aunt Fortune and Uncle Lindsay), prepares Ellen to submit to divine authority. Increasingly as the narrative progresses, she finds peace in relinquishing her will. For instance, turning a decision over to John Humphrey leaves Ellen genuinely happy and content (471). Warner seems willing to give Ellen some latitude to differ from or disagree with other people, such as her Uncle Lindsay, but Ellen must differ in respectful silence and deferential modesty. Blunt or outspoken self-assertion is not permitted, and conquering her impulse to declare her own views and feelings proves to be the chief test of Ellen's spiritual progress. When she vehemently objects to her uncle's taking of a copy of *Pilgrim's Progress* given to her by John Humphrey, her conscience rebukes her, "you spoke improperly; he is justly displeased, and you must make an apology before there can be any peace" (553). Again and again, Ellen is brought into conflict with others as a result of her self-assertion. Each time the lesson is that she will have no peace until she yields, setting aside whatever imperatives her "passionate" nature has seized on, even if that means enduring patent injustices and unfair treatment.

In this terrestrial realm, such wrongs can only be directly addressed by men. Indeed, the good male characters have a considerably easier time of it in Warner's novel. They are entitled to assert their rights and openly rebuke wrongdoers, even with violence when necessary (e.g., the kind older gentleman in the department store appropriately reprimands the malign clerk, Saunders, for his mistreatment of Ellen, and, later, John Humphrey physically chastises the same "scoundrel"). The only direct action Ellen can properly undertake is entreaty and moral suasion. By attaining a feminine ideal of moral purity and selflessness, Ellen can acquire a kind of iconic power as a symbol of proper feeling, and, like the modest and deferential Alice Humphrey, Ellen will be able to inspire others to emulate her. As a follower of Christ, she has moral agency (e.g., the power and responsibility to help others in need), and, as a young woman and later as a wife, her household roles will include many domestic duties and responsibilities. But these forms of agency do not apparently come with a corollary set of civil rights and powers. The form of authority and agency Ellen possesses as a Christian woman would seem to lack any direct worldly application other than charity. No direct connection is drawn by Warner between the goodness of women, such as Ellen's mother and Alice Humphrey, and public opposition to social or political wrongs. Later in this chapter, we shall see how Harriet Beecher Stowe takes up this feminine ideal and modifies it so as to permit women some engagement with the world of law and politics.

Warner's portrait of Ellen's apparent success in accepting submission, however, is complicated by certain tensions and contradictions. Most importantly, Warner is not wholly immune to the appeal of Ellen's critical judgment, her passionate objection to unjust or spiteful behavior, even her rebellious tendencies. For instance, Warner seems disposed to laugh at Ellen's cheeky, albeit silent, reaction to Aunt Fortune's declaration that "she thanked Heaven she could always make herself contented at home; which Ellen could not help thinking was a happiness for the rest of the world" (333). And Warner is willing to grant some sort of exception to Ellen's program of self-effacement for her ardent defense of the American Revolution: "if I had been in the American army I would have fought *you* with all my heart, uncle Lindsay" (506). Ellen's "extraordinary taste for freedom" and her refusal to cede control of her affections and conscience to her uncle, her belief that there are "some things he cannot command," represent a form of self-assertion apparently meeting with Warner's approval (510, 515). So, while Ellen's main task in self-improvement lies in returning good for ill (e.g., being kind to Margaret Dunscombe despite her spiteful behavior toward Ellen) and stifling her outrage over the oppressions of her Aunt Fortune or her Uncle Lindsay, at times and under certain circumstances, there appears to be some allowance for Ellen to express her desire for freedom and her intuitive sense of equity and justice. With Warner's novel as a guide, women would seem to be faced with the rather substantial challenge of combining the ethos of the American Revolution (e.g., the Founding Fathers' insistence on the individual's moral authority and insight) and the Christian goal of self-sacrifice.

The complexity and difficulty of the balance Ellen must achieve between self-denial and self-assertion would seem to derive, at least in part, from the religious conception of free will. Ellen must *choose* to negate her will, to stifle her objections. When Aunt Fortune unjustly strikes her, Ellen must consciously undertake to humble herself and set aside her outrage (165). In order to make the choice of self-denial, Ellen must have the same kind of moral agency, insight, and free will assumed by the Founding Fathers as authorizing the American Revolution. She must be competent to know right from wrong and have the ability to act on that knowledge. Or, to put it another way, Ellen must have the agency requisite to enter a contract, a voluntary agreement adjusting and structuring the relations of the parties to the bargain. That Ellen has this agency can be seen in Alice's seeking of Ellen's "consent" when asking her to spend the holidays with the Humphrey family. Alice does not simply command Ellen to come (226). However, though such agency is the prerequisite for Ellen's salvation and her spiritual improvement – she must choose Christ – her course of improvement entails a progressive abandonment of agency, a ceding of will. The tension here between the exercise of free will and the ultimate goal of ceding agency is manifest in Warner's conception of contractual exchange as a means of achieving an anti-contractual or gratuitous end. By definition, a purely gratuitous act, an unearned or unmerited kindness, for instance, eludes the logic and scope of contract. The answer to Ellen's conflicts with other people appears to be that she must act in a non-contractual or gratuitous fashion, giving love and kindness without receiving anything of value in return. Yet, this lesson in charity is framed as though it were a matter of exchange. In her dealings with her difficult aunt and imperious uncle, Ellen has to learn that she must not insist on a kind of fair trade of like treatment for like treatment. She must learn to return humility for pride, love for callous disregard. The relation remains reciprocal, structured as a kind of religiously informed bargain. Alice instructs Ellen that it is worth "paying a price in suffering to find how much kindness there is in some peoples' hearts" (204). The quid pro quo recommended by this better form of exchange is a big spiritual reward for "a little self-denial" (e.g., Ellen reads to her grandmother and is rewarded by the satisfaction of her grandmother's tearful appreciation [245]).

Thus, Warner mixes a large measure self-effacement with a few elements of self-assertion, and her representation of a purely charitable relation to others takes the form of a contractual exchange in which one's kindness earns a spiritual quid pro quo. These incongruities suggest that the values Warner recommends cannot be attained, at least in this world, in an absolutely pure or unalloyed form. Indeed, it is hard to imagine how Warner could portray Ellen's spiritual progress without some of these contradictions and inconsistencies. Idealist notions of religious absolutes are hard to graft onto the rapidly changing world Ellen inhabits. Some contamination seems inevitable. Similarly, a straightforward and unqualified deference to higher authority is difficult to maintain without occasional qualification in the face of the petty and major tyrannies Ellen encounters. Finally, Ellen's project of self-abnegation is unavoidably made more complex by a model of human development which is predicated on the notion that one betters one's self through a series of acts, choices, and agreements.

### *Maria Cummins,* The Lamplighter *(1854)*

Unlike Gerty Flint, the heroine of her most famous novel, Maria Cummins grew up in a financially secure and well-connected family. Her father was a judge, and the Cummins family lived in Dorchester, a prosperous suburb of Boston. Cummins never married. First published in 1854, *The Lamplighter* was very popular, selling 40,000 copies in the first month and 100,000 by the end of the year (Gilmore 54). Famously, *The Lamplighter*'s success spurred Nathaniel Hawthorne to complain to his publisher that "America is now wholly given over to a d—d mob of scribbling women" (Fern xxxiv). Like Warner's *The Wide,*

*Wide World*, Cummins's novel tells the tale of an orphaned girl who is cared for and effectively adopted, first by Trueman Flint, who rescues Gerty from the brutal Nan Grant, and second by the blind and angelic Emily Graham. Trueman provides Gerty with an extremely humble but wholesome home, and, with the help of Willie Sullivan and his mother, Trueman is able to help start Gerty on the road to a happy life. When Trueman dies, Gerty is taken under the wing of the gentle Emily Graham. Eventually, after many trials, including her rejection of the marriage proposal of an eligible but feckless young man, Gerty becomes an independent and true-hearted young woman capable of tremendous bravery and self-sacrifice. By the novel's conclusion, Gerty has been discovered by her long-lost and prosperous father and is married to her childhood friend Willie.

While the storyline of *The Lamplighter* bears an obvious general resemblance to that of Warner's novel, there are several significant differences. In comparison with *The Wide, Wide World*, Cummins's narrative seems positively worldly. Instead of focusing on her protagonists' submission to the will of Providence, Cummins takes pains to describe Gerty's and Willie's efforts to improve their practical lot in life as well as their spiritual well-being. Cummins's endorsement of thrift, hard work, and perseverance as means of advancement has a secular, Franklinian ring to it largely absent from *The Wide, Wide World* (249). Ellen Montgomery's story seems to take place at some distance from the larger social context, but Gerty's narrative directly engages the changing social texture of the times. Such change can be felt in Cummins's description of the advent of the steamship and railroad. In contrast to the days of stagecoach travel, when "the driver was a civil fellow, each passenger a person of consequence," "[n]ow, on the contrary, people moved in masses; a single individual was a man of no influence, a mere unit in the great whole" (422–23). Later in the novel, Gerty has to enter and contend with a middle- and upper-class society that increasingly resembles a resort where "all are in motion" and "in pursuit of amusement" (444). In this mobile society, there are "counterfeits," disguises, and a rising degree of anonymity. Indeed, middle- and upper-class people have removed from the city to the suburbs to become more anonymous (310). The greater worldliness of *The Lamplighter* can also be felt in the romantic plots that become dominant in the last half of the book. Where romance is almost entirely absent from Warner's depiction of Ellen's and John's feelings for each other, Cummins entangles her heroine in romantic intrigue. Gerty is pursued by a shallow young man, whom she rejects, and she has to struggle with a misapprehension that her beloved Willie has forgotten her and fallen for another – a traditional device of the love story.

The domestic scene has a different and more prominent aspect in Cummins's novel as well. It is less static, less a given, and more a matter of creation and partnership. In *The Wide, Wide World*, Ellen Montgomery is thrust into different homes and domestic arrangements over which she has little, if any, influence and control, and which are largely static and unchanging. Even the prosperous and happy home Warner originally imagined as Ellen's reward at the end of the novel is already fully furnished and arranged when she crosses its threshold. As Ellen walks through it staring in wide wonder like a child in a fabulous shop, she simply and completely accepts the arrangements, decorations, and furnishings as a given, not presuming or desiring that anything might be changed. By contrast, in Cummins's novel, a home would seem to be something one must dedicate oneself to creating. Though aged and poor, Trueman Flint chooses to provide a home to Gerty, to be her father, and Gerty works hard to become "quite a nice little housekeeper." These choices and labors result in the creation of a new family and a new home. Trueman is "astonished" by Gerty's transformation of their home, and Gerty is overwhelmed by Trueman's "adoption": "bursting into a paroxysm of joyful tears, [she] gasped out the words, 'Shall I stay with you always?' 'Yes, just as long as I live,' said True, 'you shall be my child'" (230–34). Cummins emphasizes the idea of making in homemaking and represents that endeavor as a reciprocal partnership between voluntary agents who are mutually blessed by the joy they give to each other in their joint endeavor to make a home and to be a family. As Cindy Weinstein has pointed out, Cummins's imagining of the domestic brings mutual consent and joint effort to the fore as means of making a family (45–65). In *Family, Kinship, and Sympathy in Nineteenth-Century American Literature*, Weinstein compellingly describes how the consensual dimension of sentimental fiction displaces the biological family with families formed by the voluntary affective connection of love.

Cummins's novel represents a substantial revision and extension of the sentimental story of a young woman's development, moving markedly in the direction of independence and self-assertion and showing a greater appreciation for the protagonist's moral authority. Like Ellen Montgomery, Gerty's main developmental challenge is self-control, in particular control of her anger (239). Her temper is associated with her previous brutal and degrading condition while in the care of Nan Grant (240). Emily Graham helps to "cure" Gerty of this "dark infirmity," by instilling in her "the power of Christian humility . . . the humility of *principle*, of *conscience*, – the only power to which native pride ever will pay homage" (263, 271). Like Ellen, Gerty must "learn to bear even injustice, without losing your self-control" (292). She must resist the temptation to return spite for spite (293). The reward for such "self-sacrifice" is the greater joy of helping others (284). However, self-assertion is not quelled here in the same way and to the same degree as it is in *The Wide, Wide World*. Self-sacrifice in *The*

*Lamplighter* can entail or require rebellion and self-assertion, as when Gerty decides to help the ailing Mrs. Sullivan rather than going on a trip with Emily Graham and her father (326). When Mr. Graham, a benefactor and authority figure, objects, Gerty refuses to prove "traitor to [her] own heart, and [her] own sense of right" (329). Cummins presents Gerty's polite but firm defiance of the wishes of such authority figures as Mr. Graham as noble and meritorious. Gerty's rebellious impulse works toward plainly good ends, and the rightness of her dissent argues implicitly for the independent moral agency of all young women.

### Fanny Fern, Ruth Hall *(1855)*

A highly autobiographical work, the storyline of *Ruth Hall* (1855) follows the broad contours of the early life of its author, Sara Willis, who published under the pen name of Fanny Fern. Sara Willis was the daughter of Nathaniel and Hannah Parker Willis. Her father was a successful publisher, and her older brother was a poet and editor. When her young husband died of typhoid fever in 1846, Sara and her two daughters found themselves nearly destitute. She received little support from her relations and attempted unsuccessfully to provide for her family as a teacher and seamstress. In this difficult period, Sara remarried. This alliance proved to be disastrous, and, after two years, Sara left her husband. Sara struggled then succeeded in her effort to support herself and her children by her writing. Sara's brother rejected her writing and refused to help her, just as Ruth Hall's brother does in the novel. With the notable absence of the remarriage and divorce, the events in *Ruth Hall* follow the broad outline of Sara Willis's life. *Ruth Hall* is about the challenges faced by a young widow trying to support her family. As family and friends either abandon Ruth or fail to rise to the challenge of aiding her, her story is perforce one of self-sufficiency. She must overcome the long odds against financial success as a writer, surmount the callous disregard of brother, father, in-laws, and many others, and contend with greedy and unscrupulous editors. The mere fact that the eponymous heroine of Fern's novel is not a married woman is a clear signal that the genre of the sentimental novel is being pushed even further in the direction of endorsing female independence and moral agency. Elizabeth Cady Stanton, one of the great advocates of women's rights, wrote that "The great lesson taught in *Ruth Hall* is that God has given to woman sufficient brain and muscle to work out her own destiny unaided and alone" (Fern xliii).

While not quite as popular as Stowe's *Uncle Tom's Cabin*, Warner's *The Wide, Wide World*, or Maria Cummins's *The Lamplighter*, Fern's novel was a best-seller, selling 70,000 copies in the first year of publication, and it won the praise of one skeptical reader of sentimental fiction, Nathaniel Hawthorne, who commented:

> In my last, I recollect, I bestowed some vituperation on female authors. I have been reading *Ruth Hall* and I must say I enjoyed it a good deal. The woman writes as if the devil was in her; and that is the only condition under which a woman ever writes anything worth reading.   (Fern xxxiv–xxxv)

*Ruth Hall* is, as Hawthorne's appreciation suggests, markedly different from other sentimental novels. First, on a formal level, the structure of the novel is distinguished by its fragmentary quality. It reads like a set of relatively discrete scenes or moments of dialogue often with little or no narrative explanation of how we have moved from one moment to the next. Instead, the reader is left to fill in the necessary connective matter. Second, unlike most American sentimental fiction, Fern's novel combines scenes of heart-wrenching pathos with satire, and acerbic portraits of the hypocrites, fools, and scoundrels in Ruth's life. Third, unlike *The Wide, Wide World, The Lamplighter,* and *Uncle Tom's Cabin,* Fern does not emphasize the transformation of the individual through religious inspiration and discipline. Ruth is as mature, caring, and good at the beginning of the narrative as she is at the end. And her adversaries, such as her vain and selfish brother and her churlish mother-in-law, are grossly flawed throughout. Fourth, the novel neither begins in childhood, nor ends in marriage. Instead, it ends with Ruth's success in obtaining independence and a valuable identity supplementary to her former roles as wife and mother. In this last move, Fern seeks to merge Ruth's passion for family, her absolute dedication to her domestic duties, with her independent and unconventional vocation as a writer.

Many aspects of this novel are quite conventional to the sentimental genre. Like Gerty and Ellen, Ruth has an intuitively religious nature. She cannot see the beauty of "sea, sky, leaf, bud, and blossom," "listen to the little birds," or "inhale the perfumed breath of morning, without a filling eye and brimming heart." She instinctively and reflexively gives thanks "to the bounteous Giver" (25). As in other sentimental novels, children are here associated with the heavenly perspective: "Blessed childhood! the pupil and yet the teacher; half infant, half sage, and whole angel! what a desert were earth without thee!" (54). Urging her daughter, Daisy, to put down a caterpillar, Ruth observes, "what an ugly playfellow," but Daisy responds as Eva or Christ might, "Why – God made him" (37). In scenes such as Ruth's tearful recollection of Daisy's death as she holds "a little half worn shoe, with the impress of a tiny foot," Fern's novel dramatically portrays the emotional values that constitute the core of the sentimental project – the undeniably positive feelings, such as the love of mother and child, which the sentimental novelist believes connect all members of the human family (53–54). The hand of divine providence is present and manifest throughout Ruth's travails and suffering. Even in the moments of Ruth's keenest sorrow and greatest loss, she is cared for by "He who seeth the end from the beginning" (50). When she cannot bear the burden of the death of Daisy, her first child, she lays "[t]he weight her slender shoulders could not bear . . . at the foot of the cross" (25). Like other sentimental novels, *Ruth Hall* is filled with morally transparent characters. Ruth's goodness is unmistakably legible in her tender heart and ready tears, and, by contrast, the marked absence of such tears and feelings are equally indicative of the malign nature of her adversaries, such as her mother-in-law and her brother.

However, *Ruth Hall* also dares to disrupt or break out of the conventions of sentimental fiction. For instance, Fern delicately but unmistakably registers the sexual desire felt by the newly wed Ruth for her husband, Harry:

> [Ruth] moved about her apartments in a sort of blissful dream. How odd it seemed, this new freedom, this being one's own mistress. How odd to see that shaving-brush and those razors lying on her toilet table! Then that saucy looking smoking-cap, those slippers and that dressing-gown, those fancy neckties, too, and vests and coats, in unrebuked proximity to her muslins, laces, silks and de laines! Ruth liked it. (11)

That last short sentence speaks volumes, acknowledging many things unspoken in other sentimental fiction. Even more striking for a present-day reader, perhaps, is Fern's suggestion of a sexualized jealousy on the part of Harry's mother, who, after surreptitiously going through Ruth's bureau drawers, objects, "What is the use of all those ruffles on her underclothes" (10). As the heroine of a sentimental novel, Ruth is also sharply distinguished by her native aversion to "common female employments . . . bead-netting, crochet-stitching, long discussions with milliners, dress-makers, and modistes, long forenoons spent in shopping, or leaving bits of paste-board [i.e., personal cards], party-giving, party-going, prinking and coquetting, all these were her aversion" (56). Ruth's impatience with such occupations anticipates by decades Kate Chopin's portrait of Edna Pontellier.

But Fern's most provocative innovation has to be the way she transforms the moment of conversion, the central pivot of the sentimental novel, from a religious event into a professional and vocational epiphany. Brought low by poverty and threatened with the permanent loss of her children, Ruth is suddenly inspired to try writing as a means of support: "I can do it, I feel it, I will do it." She tells Katy, one of her children, "when you are a woman you shall remember this day" (145, 147). It is no accident that this inspiration comes to Ruth in the month of July (one thinks of the fact that Henry David Thoreau takes up his abode in the woods near Walden Pond on 4 July). Ruth's determination to succeed by writing becomes, in effect, a declaration of independence. The revolutionary import of her decision to pursue a career as a writer and thereby to gain economic independence is hinted at when a character observes that Ruth has "the spirit of '76' flashing from her eyes" (244). Fern's innovation of the sentimental genre and Ruth's rebellion are both qualified by the fact that the sentimental heroine, who would prefer simply to be a happily married wife and mother, was driven to her radical course of action by necessity. Ruth tells one of her daughters, "no happy woman ever writes" (225). Viewed one way, this statement records a simple fact – dire economic circumstances drove Ruth to write (it is her excuse). Viewed another way, it represents a gesture toward the more conventional notions of femininity usually found in the sentimental novel. In any case, it does not mute Ruth's pride in her accomplishment.

Ruth's ultimate triumph is cast in both sentimental and worldly terms. Ruth is deeply gratified by the emotional comfort and spiritual guidance her writing has brought to others. One of her readers tells her that he is "a better son, a better brother, and a better husband, and a better father" for having read her articles, praying that she be "rewarded by Him to whom the secrets of all hearts are known" (235). But Ruth is also rewarded in more temporal or earthly terms. Every character who rebuffed Ruth's requests for aid or attempted to obstruct her quest for independence receives his or her comeuppance. Ruth's brother, Hyacinth, is publicly humiliated by his refusal to help his impoverished and talented sister. Her hostile mother-in-law, Mrs. Hall, is embarrassed to find that the book she so enjoys was written by the daughter-in-law she has so thoroughly scorned (260–61). A cousin who cruelly commanded that Ruth's child not address him in public regrets the insult as he cannot now avail himself of her aid (258). Ruth's success as a writer brings considerable financial security, proudly represented by her ownership of shares in a bank (269). Becoming a savvy businesswoman as well as an accomplished author, Ruth's self-transformation has significant practical dimensions. In her dealings with editors (by and large not a particularly sympathetic group), Ruth proves herself to be fully capable of managing her own negotiations in a clear-eyed and business-like fashion. Rejecting Ruth's appeal to his sense of friendship and sympathy, a greedy editor brushes such considerations aside as irrelevant to business. He condescendingly explains to Ruth the harsh rule of supply and demand, only to find himself hoisted on his own petard and incapable of urging friendship and loyalty on Ruth when she tells him she has already accepted a better offer (188, 189–90).

Comparing *The Wide, Wide World*, *The Lamplighter*, and *Ruth Hall* highlights several aspects of sentimental fiction. Education is clearly an important theme. In addition to studying the basic academic subjects, Ellen and Gerty have to learn certain basic social and religious lessons as well. While such scenes of formative schooling have already transpired before Fern's novel begins (the novel opens with Ruth on the eve of her wedding), literacy and education play a critical role in Ruth's triumph as a writer. All three novels emphasize family, but the family one is born into (think here of the dearth of aid Ruth receives from her father and brother) appears to be less important than the family one creates – the mutually nurturing and consensual relations that one establishes with others. All of the novels valorize religiously inspired fortitude, such as that sustaining Ruth when Daisy dies, and this ability to endure sorrow is nurtured by moments of emotional transport in which the protagonist is swept away by sympathetic emotion to a richer and better sense of life. Comparing these novels, one also observes that they become progressively secular. The focus on religious piety diminishes, and worldly matters become more prominent. The ideal of womanhood would also seem to be in flux, becoming markedly less passive. The insistence on submission is increasingly replaced by an endorsement of the heroine's assertion of her moral and intellectual agency. Finally, looked at as a continuum, these novels become less enamored of permanence and more tolerant of change. The active and shifting world of publishing that Ruth Hall successfully plunges into and conquers is at a fair remove from the happy prearranged home Warner envisions as Ellen Montgomery's reward.

## Sentiment and reform: *Uncle Tom's Cabin*

Apparently preoccupied with the individual's emotions and his or her spiritual state, the sentimental novel might well seem to direct our attention toward inward private matters and away from broader social concerns.[4] Certainly, sentimental fiction has often focused on the development of the individual and the domestic scene. However, certain nineteenth-century writers recognized that the moment of sympathetic catharsis and conversion central to the sentimental novel might be reconceived more broadly as the emotional awakening of an entire society, a pervasive rush of fellow feeling leading to the transformation of the nation's legal and social norms. Among other things, sentimental fiction has been used to argue for temperance, against prostitution, for the relief of the poor, and against the removal of American Indians. The most famous and influential of the efforts to turn sentiment outward in the direction of political, legal, and social reform is Harriet Beecher Stowe's *Uncle Tom's Cabin* (1852). In *Uncle Tom's Cabin*, Stowe applies the techniques of the sentimental novel to the most provocative issues of her day – race and slavery. Critical characterizations of Stowe's anti-slavery fiction as separating the values of home from those of the legislature or marketplace tend to miss the interconnection between sentiment and public policy that Stowe wants to advance.[5] Her emotionally charged narrative episodes, such as little Eva's expression of love to Topsy or Uncle Tom's martyrdom, are designed to enlist our sympathies in a general recognition of the moral invalidity of slavery and the legal claims of black Americans to freedom.

*Uncle Tom's Cabin* is organized around two plot lines. One is the northward escape of George and Eliza Harris and their son from slavery to freedom, which has many of the elements of the romantic adventure novel. Eliza Harris's harrowing escape across the icy Ohio River and the heroic resolve of George Harris and Phineas Fletcher to fight the slave catcher Tom Loker on a rocky promontory recall similar scenes of romantic heroics in James Fenimore Cooper's *The Last of the Mohicans* (1826). The other is the dark, southward journey of Uncle Tom from less to more extreme forms of slavery and ultimately to martyrdom and transcendence. Both plot lines take the reader through a variety of different Northern and Southern homes. Some of these, such as Uncle Tom and Aunt Chloe's humble cabin, the Birds' cozy home, and the Quaker home of Rachel and Simeon Halliday, are orderly, warm, and welcoming, manifesting the good values of the kind-hearted families who live in them. The plantation homes of the Shelbys, the St. Clares, and finally Simon Legree, by contrast, are corrupted to varying degrees by slavery. The deeper into the peculiar institution we go, the more a lack of order and good feeling characterizes the home, until we arrive at the domestic nadir of the novel, Legree's plantation, which seems in its hellishness to be virtually an anti-home, barren of all domestic comforts and harmony.[6]

As Stowe anticipated, the broad appeal of her novel derives in large part from the iconic power of her characters, their appearances, actions, and words, whose clear and firm outlines and vivid details are readily translatable into definite moral significances. The moral pattern of compassion and Christian forbearance embodied in Uncle Tom is set against the type of tyrannical power represented by Simon Legree. The dramatic interactions Stowe stages between these antithetical types are designed to trigger in the reader an emotional conviction of slavery's moral and legal invalidity. This conclusion, Stowe hopes, will seem conclusive and unimpeachable to the reader not because it is based on superior argument and evidence, but because it springs unbidden from

the well of sympathy innate to human nature. For Stowe, as for other sentimental novelists, sympathetic feelings are akin to a message from God telling
us the difference between right and wrong. To be morally legitimate, individual behavior, social norms, and legal rules must not contradict these feelings.
Stowe famously posits the authority of this form of moral intuition in her
novel's "Concluding Remarks":

> [W]hat can any individual do? . . . They can see to it that they feel right.
> An atmosphere of sympathetic influence encircles every human being;
> and the man or woman who feels strongly, healthily, and justly on the
> great interest of humanity, is a constant benefactor to the human race.
> See then to your sympathies in this matter!   (385)

Sympathy, at least as it is conceived in the sentimental novel, works by identification. One person sees the parallel between his or her experience and that of
another, and is then capable of feeling sympathetically for the other's suffering
and plight. Gerty Flint indicates the importance of identification to sympathy
when she tells Mr. Phillips, an appealing but sorrowful man she has met on
a trip to New York, "I should not know how to feel for others; if I had not
often wept for myself, I should not weep for you now" (Cummins 435). In
effect, sympathy is the product of an always implied question, "how did I or
how would I feel when in a position similar to this unfortunate character?"
In sympathizing with the challenge Willie Sullivan faces as the sole breadwin-
ner in his family, Willie's employer recalls his own experience as a friendless
young man trying to support a poor mother (Cummins 280). In *Ruth Hall,* the
heart of the good editor John Walter "readily vibrates to the chord of sorrow"
struck by Ruth's writing because he has experienced "desolation of his own"
(Fern 185). Of course, the apparent requirement of identification for sympathy
raises questions. Are we incapable of sympathy when there is no ready basis
for comparing our own experiences to those of the other person? How closely
related must the experiences be for sympathy to be possible? How much like
us must the other person be before we can identify with and feel sympathy for
that person?

By taking up the issues of slavery and racial difference, Stowe plunges head-
long into these questions about sympathy. She attacks the potential obstacle of
racial difference to interracial sympathy by diminishing differences and height-
ening similarities. The "imploring *human* eye" and the frail, trembling *human*
hand" as well as the fundamental resemblance between black and white families should, Stowe hopes, draw her white readers into an identification with the
fugitive slave (emphasis added, 77). When her flight from slavery takes Eliza
Harris and her child in desperation to the Birds' Ohio home, Eliza's ladylike

manners and speech and the common ground of parental feeling prevent racial difference from blocking the Birds' (and the reader's) sympathy. The Birds, like Eliza, have lost a child. Mr. Bird "had never thought that a fugitive might be a hapless mother, a defenceless child, – like that one which was now wearing his lost boy's little well-known cap" (77). The image of the threatened child and the parent fighting to protect him, Stowe hopes, will be readily recognizable and familiar enough to overcome whatever barrier racial difference poses to the readers' sympathies and to conjure their most emotionally intense registration of the inequity of slavery.[7]

The utility of the image of the child in danger as a trigger of identification and sympathy across racial lines was not lost on African American novelists, such as Frank Webb and Charles Chesnutt. In *The Garies and Their Friends*, Frank Webb's version of the Mrs. Bird character is able to sympathize with a young black boy named Charlie because she has lost a son named Charlie (147). In the melodramatic climax of Chesnutt's *The Marrow of Tradition* (1901), the parallel between the loss of a black child and the threatened life of a white child forces a white woman to recognize her family connection with a black half-sister she has spent a lifetime rejecting. Of course, accepting the necessity of resemblance for sympathy leaves open the possibility of a certain limit to sympathy – at some point, the other person may seem too alien, too different for resemblance, and consequently, for sympathy to occur.

When the sentimental home is expanded into a sentimental community, the political limits of sympathy with its attendant requirement of resemblance become more conspicuous. In *Uncle Tom's Cabin*, Stowe presents the Quaker community of Rachel and Simeon Halliday as a model community united and animated by its members' shared sympathetic awareness of right and wrong. Rachel Halliday leads this benevolent and peaceful polis not by virtue of some power that she possesses, but by reason of the moral authority manifest in her "loving words, gentle moralities, and motherly loving kindness," which solve "spiritual and temporal" problems (117). Punishment, threatened or actual, is not needed to obtain obedience and order from the children in this community. All Rachel has to do is touch the children's intuitive sense of right and wrong with gentle directions, such as "Hadn't thee better?" "The danger of friction or collision" within Rachel's busy but harmonious community is erased by the fact that there is an almost perfect identity in the members' moral responses to questions, problems, and necessary tasks (121). Revealingly, two outsiders, George Harris, a fugitive slave, and Phineas Fletcher, a convert to Quakerism, interrupt the community's consensus of pacifism, sympathy, and self-sacrifice with expressions of rebellious indignation and revolutionary intent. When cautioned by Simeon Halliday against acting violently out of the heat of his "young blood," George responds that he would "attack no man" but would fight to the death to prevent the recapture of his wife and son. And, while Phineas agrees with Simeon that the "temptation" of armed resistance is best avoided, he adds, "if we are tempted too much, – why, let them look out, that's all." In response to Phineas's readiness to use force to protect the Harris family, Simeon says, "It's quite plain thee wasn't born a Friend . . . The old nature hath its way in thee pretty strong as yet" (163–64). These divergent impulses manifest on a larger scale the tension between submission and self-assertion seen in *The Wide, Wide World* and *The Lamplighter*, and these different responses to the same moral crisis do not cohere any more comfortably in *Uncle Tom's Cabin* than they do in Warner's and Cummins's novels. Indeed, the Quaker community's relative isolation, the homogeneity of its members, and the uniformity of the members' emotional moral responses suggests a fear on Stowe's part that the good-hearted rule of sympathy may be impracticable in the face of social diversity.

In the Quaker community the unity of sentiment obviates the need for resolving conflict through negotiation, debate, and compromise. Such tools of consensus formation are rendered unnecessary because Stowe's Quakers simply obey the same inner voice, a shared voice that defines the members as fundamentally homogeneous or like each other.[8] If the measure of the equity of any society's political and legal system is gauged by how it deals with a diverse population with divergent interests and viewpoints, then the Quaker model of sentiment offered by Stowe would seem decidedly inadequate to the task of achieving justice. The sameness of her Quaker exemplars also seems to reflect Stowe's apprehension that the possibility of a racially heterogeneous citizenry raised by the abolitionist campaign might fracture the homogeneity that makes a governing moral consensus possible in the first place. As many readers have noted, Stowe does not imagine her two black heroes as living happily ever after in the United States. By the end of the novel, George Harris is in Liberia, and Uncle Tom has been martyred.

The way that sameness, an uncanny similarity of emotional and moral response, largely replaces debate and compromise in the Quaker community also points to certain problems or limitations in Stowe's attempt to connect the moral inspiration of sympathetic emotions with the often messy processes of creating a new political or social consensus. Does the Quaker consensus represent the agreement of people from different walks of life and diverse backgrounds, independently and voluntarily arriving at certain shared values? Or to what extent are the members' shared beliefs produced by the fact that they are members of the sect? By telling Phineas Fletcher that his divergent opinions make it clear he was not "born" a Quaker, Simeon Halliday would seem to suggest that some part of the sect's moral consensus follows from the status of being born a Quaker. To put this problem another way, does the spontaneous eruption of sympathy for the fugitive slave automatically result in a new social and legal consensus? If not, what will the ensuing discussion, debate, and compromise look like? What effects will differences in religious affiliation or racial, class, and gender status have on the establishment of a new social compact? At times, Stowe seems to think that the onrush of sentiment and fellow feeling can overcome such differences in background and social status. At other moments, the reformist potential of sentiment to create a new consensus seems limited by Stowe's deference to notions of inherent racial or gender roles prescribed by God or nature. In *Uncle Tom's Cabin*, Stowe sometimes imagines human relations as determined or governed by status (e.g., one's being born a Quaker, a woman, or a black man). Sometimes, she entertains the notion that they may be based on contract – the voluntary agreement of individuals regardless of status. Her vacillation between status and contract as principles properly structuring human association can be seen by comparing a pair of scenes from *Uncle Tom's Cabin*: the debate between Mr. and Mrs. Bird and the colloquy between George Harris and Mr. Wilson.[9]

The Birds' cozy home provides the setting for the first of these scenes. Worn out by the "tiresome business" of legislating, Senator Bird has returned for some "good, home living," distinguishing the worries and concerns of his public career from the harmony of his private, domestic life. However, Senator Bird's vision of domestic tranquility is interrupted by his wife's query "what have they been doing in the Senate?" (67). While she does not normally "trouble her head" about the affairs of state, the moral issues raised by the passage of the Fugitive Slave Act of 1850 compel Mary Bird to interrogate her husband. Senator Bird replies, "Your feelings are all quite right, dear . . . I love you for them; but . . . we mustn't suffer our feelings to run away with our judgment; you must consider it's not a matter of private feeling, – there are great public interests involved." In response to her husband's argument separating private feeling from public discourse and his suggestion that, as a woman, Mrs. Bird has stepped outside of her area of expertise, Mrs. Bird replies, "I don't know anything about politics, but I can read my Bible; and there I see that I must feed the hungry, clothe the naked and comfort the desolate" (69).

In their conversation, each assumes his or her conventional role (the male lawmaker and the female homemaker). However, to accept these conventional roles as delineating antithetical concerns or areas of expertise – law and morality or head and heart – is to ignore the legal significance of Mrs. Bird's moral challenge to the Fugitive Slave Act and the symbolic value of the couple's legal–moral intercourse. Spontaneous sympathetic feelings corresponding to the teachings of Christ clearly indicate to Mrs. Bird that the deference normally given to law does not apply in this case. Mrs. Bird's argument is disingenuous to the extent that it seems to separate the moral and legal areas of expertise.[10] And Mr. Bird's invocation of the public–private distinction to suggest that amateurs, such as Mrs. Bird, have no role in setting public policy is alien to Mrs. Bird's religious and moral convictions ("Obeying God never brings on public evils"), which do not stop at the threshold of her home (69). Indeed, in its positing of self-evident moral truths, Mary's objection to the Fugitive Slave Act accords with the Founding Fathers' belief in a legal system grounded in virtue and sanctioned by the citizenry's moral sense.

Ultimately, Mrs. Bird's argument and the couple's joint decision to violate the Fugitive Slave Act are decisively advanced by Eliza Harris's appearance:

> A young and slender woman, with garments torn and frozen, with one shoe gone, and the stocking torn away from the cut and bleeding foot, was laid back in a deadly swoon upon two chairs. There was the impress of the despised race on her face, yet none could help feeling its mournful and pathetic beauty, while its stony sharpness, its cold, fixed, deathly aspect, struck a solemn chill over him.    (70)

For Stowe and other anti-slavery advocates, such as William Lloyd Garrison and Senator William H. Seward, the image of the shivering fugitive appealing for aid can work a kind of "magic" on an audience, arousing powerful emotions and galvanizing the political will to end the wicked institution of slavery (Crane *Race* 12–18, 60). Confronted with "the real presence of distress," Mr. Bird, the lawmaker, acts upon the sentiment ably urged by his wife as the foundation for all legitimate law and public policy (77). Far from representing an opposition of head and heart, law and moral feeling, the Birds' dialogue embodies the process of inspiration and conversation through which the public conscience is animated and revised. The Birds' joint efforts to aid Eliza and her son represent a new consensus, holding the Fugitive Slave Law to be ethically invalid.

The Birds' discussion and formation of a new jointly held position is, however, hedged or limited by the fact that their negotiation and debate of this issue runs in the channels provided by their respective gender and spousal roles. Senator Bird brings his worldly experience and rationalist argument to bear on the topic of the Fugitive Slave Law, and Mrs. Bird responds with the moral intuition and sympathy native to women. The happy outcome of their discussion depends in part on each performing his or her role. Mrs. Bird's moral intuition, which is transparently a part of her proper role as wife and mother, must inform Mr. Bird's worldly experience and professional expertise for the latter to be legitimate. The sheer typicality of Mr. and Mrs. Bird makes it hard to envision them expanding their discussion to include Eliza in their debate on the propriety of the Fugitive Slave Law. And as the archetype of the

shivering fugitive, Eliza's very appearance – a frail and desperate mother need-
ing protection – obviates the necessity of seeking her approval for the next leg
of her escape, which the Birds plan without her counsel or consent, despite the
substantial evidence of Eliza's agency as the author of her own bold escape. As
a woman and a supplicant, she must take what they will give. The transparency
and legibility of Stowe's characters as types seems to limit the degree to which
feelings of sympathy and human connection might inspire a new ethical and
political consensus.

In a subsequent scene depicting a conversation between George Harris and a
well-intentioned white acquaintance, Mr. Wilson, Stowe goes somewhat further
in removing the limitations of type or status from the consensual processes of
mutual sympathy and rational debate. Harris and Wilson meet in a tavern,
a place of business and politics (a few pages earlier we witness the tavern
negotiations between Haley, the slave trader, and Tom Loker, the slave hunter).
In their discussion, Harris and Wilson seek to persuade each other of the
propriety or impropriety of Harris's plan of escape. Harris begins with the
tools of logical argument. He offers Mr. Wilson an analogy: "I wonder, Mr.
Wilson, if the Indians should come and take you a prisoner away from your
wife and children, . . . if you'd think it your duty to abide in the condition in
which you were called" (95). Harris suggests an imagined reversal of positions,
but analogy is not Wilson's strong suit (in a neat reversal of racial types). When
Wilson responds that Harris's desperate state of mind drives him to break "the
laws of your country," Harris sounds a theme taken up by Douglass in his
"What to the Slave is the Fourth of July?" address:

> My country again! Mr. Wilson, you have a country; but what country
> have I, or any one like me, born of slave mothers? What laws are there
> for us? We don't make them, – we don't consent to them, – we have
> nothing to do with them; all they do for us is to crush us, and keep us
> down. Haven't I heard your Fourth-of-July speeches? Don't you tell us
> all, once a year, that governments derive their just power from the
> consent of the governed?   (95–96)

Harris's conclusion is inescapable: by the founders' own principles, the duty to
obey is predicated on the right to participate. The nullity of the latter voids the
former. To make his argument effective in inspiring a new sense of duty and
obligation in Mr. Wilson, Harris speaks to Wilson's heart, reducing the latter to
tears with a vivid portrait of the cruelties inflicted on his family by the system
of slavery.

As with the Birds' debate, when argument is infused with sentiment, a
new consensus becomes possible, but here it is a different kind of consensus.

Separated by racial and legal status as well as differing views of religion and civic duty, Harris and Wilson manage to come to terms, and the two men become, in effect, co-conspirators defying the Fugitive Slave Act. Even though Harris's independence and intelligence – his competence to enter into contract – are figured as an inheritance from his white father, this scene comes close to suggesting that people of disparate backgrounds may be able through debate and shared moral feeling to decide what is right rather than simply referring moral questions to the prescriptions of traditional status and role. At the end of their debate, Mr. Wilson notes, "George, something has brought you out wonderfully. You hold up your head, and speak and move like another man" (98). In his revolutionary ardor, George would seem to be an icon for the way powerful feelings can inspire a dramatic and positive transformation, and his mutability is a hopeful sign of a broader social mutability. In connecting the new consensus between Harris and Wilson to George Harris's new manner of being, Stowe's novel suggests not only that our principles may shift or receive new impressions but also that transformation may itself be a gauge of ethical and aesthetic value.

In celebrating the end of slavery after the war, Stowe overtly connects personal development to legal and societal transformation – in both cases, mutability is a sign of moral vitality. The very possibility of personal transformation functions as a measure of the virtue of the American legal system: "It is the pride and the boast of truly republican institutions that they give to every human being an opportunity of thus demonstrating what is in him. If a man is a man, no matter in what rank of society he is born, no matter how tied down and weighted by poverty and all its attendant disadvantages, there is nothing in our American institutions to prevent his rising to the very highest offices in the gift of the country" (*Men of Our Times* 380–81). Citizens, such as Frederick Douglass, who fully embody this process of personal transformation, best represent the nation's values:

> Now if we think it a great thing that [Henry] Wilson and Lincoln raised themselves from a state of comparatively early disadvantage to high places in the land, what shall we think of one who started from this immeasurable gulf below them? Frederick Douglass had as far to climb to get to the spot where the poorest free white boy is born, as that white boy has to climb to be president of this nation, and take rank with kings and judges of the earth.    (*Men of Our Times* 381–82)

Stowe similarly locates the Constitution's ethical value in its "progressive character," commending Charles Sumner for demonstrating that the Constitution is not graven in stone but is and was intended by the framers to be revisable so as "to suit new exigencies and new conditions of feeling" (*Men of Our Times* 223).

A fairly persuasive argument can be made that Stowe's fiction played an important role in pushing the nation in the direction of the eradication of slavery and the recognition of black Americans as citizens. Of course, it is hard, if not impossible, to measure the effect of a novel on the course of public policy and national consensus, yet a few facts suggestive of the impact of Stowe's novel jump out. When published in book form (March 1852), it sold 10,000 copies within a few days. In the first year of publication, 300,000 copies of the novel were sold in the United States. Lending libraries could not keep enough copies to satisfy their patrons (Gossett 164–65). Many newspapers and journals in both North and South saw *Uncle Tom's Cabin* as a turning point in the mobilization of anti-slavery feeling in the North. Legislative debates on the issues of slavery, race, and citizenship bear many signs of the shift in the nation's political discourse toward an approach imbued with the language of sympathy and sentiment, a shift that Stowe's very popular anti-slavery fiction helped to underwrite. Ohio Representative John Bingham (the prosecutor in Andrew Jackson's impeachment trial and primary drafter of the 14th Amendment) clearly alluded to one of the most dramatic moments in *Uncle Tom's Cabin* in objecting to an amendment of the 1850 Fugitive Slave Law proposed in 1860 as a part of an eleventh-hour union-saving compromise:

> that the amendment proposed ... does not relieve the American people from the unjust obligations imposed upon them by the act of 1850, by which, at the beck of the marshal, they are compelled to join in the hunt – to make hue and cry on the track of a fugitive slave woman who is fleeing, with her babe lashed upon her breast, from the house of bondage. I will not perform that service, and I ask any man on that side whether he will? (Bingham 183)

Given the fact that in 1860 the Fugitive Slave Law was still the law of the land with no legal precedent qualifying or terminating its obligations, Bingham's comments derive their compelling emotional force from the image of the fugitive mother and her babe made famous by Stowe's vivid rendering of Eliza Harris's escape. Bingham and other Republicans repeatedly pointed to this scene as the key test of the illegitimacy of the Fugitive Slave Law.

The sentimental images and tropes so charismatically adduced against slavery in *Uncle Tom's Cabin* form a prominent rhetorical aspect of Senator Charles Sumner's anti-slavery advocacy. In "Freedom National, Slavery Sectional," his first great address as a senator, Sumner introduces himself not as a politician but as a disinterested friend of human rights and democracy who speaks "from the heart" and who attacks an evil institution "which . . . palpitates in every heart and burns on every tongue." Like Stowe, Sumner uses the image of the "shivering fugitive" seeking aid to force his audience to confront the immorality of the Fugitive Slave Law:

> The good citizen, who sees before him the shivering fugitive, guilty of no crime, pursued, hunted down like a beast, while praying for Christian help and deliverance, and then reads the requirements of this Act, is filled with horror . . . Not rashly would I set myself against any requirement of law . . . But here the path of duty is clear. By the Supreme Law, which commands me to do no injustice, by the comprehensive Christian Law of Brotherhood, by the Constitution, which I have sworn to support, I AM BOUND TO DISOBEY THIS ACT. ("Freedom National" 194)

Sumner's arguments against slavery and race proscription also often emphasize the disruption of the domestic scene as the quintessential moment of moral outrage. An anti-slavery address Sumner gave in 1855, "The Antislavery Enterprise," climaxed its condemnation of the law of slavery with the observation that this law gave slave holders the power "to separate families, to unclasp the infant from a mother's breast, and the wife from a husband's arms" ("Antislavery Enterprise" 15).

Stowe's influence on "Freedom National, Slavery Sectional" can be felt in Sumner's trope of tears as the outward manifestation of the moral sense: "Not a case occurs [under the Fugitive Slave Act] which does not harrow the souls of good men, bringing tears of sympathy to the eyes, and those other noble tears which 'patriots shed o'er dying laws.'" Sympathy, for Sumner as for Stowe, properly governs human behavior and reveals the course of justice. He counts on its arousal in the public on behalf of the fugitive: "But the great heart of the people recoils from this enactment. It palpitates for the fugitive, and rejoices in his escape" ("Freedom National" 181). Sumner singles literature out as an apt tutor of the nation's sympathies and moral sense, praising Stowe in particular:

> Sir, I am telling you facts. The literature of the age is all on [the slave's] side. Songs, more potent than laws, are for him. Poets, with voices of melody, sing for Freedom. Who could tune for Slavery? They who make the permanent opinion of the country, who mould our youth, whose words, dropped into the soul, are the germs of character, supplicate for the Slave. And now, Sir, behold a new and heavenly ally. A woman, inspired by Christian genius, enters the lists, like another Joan of Arc, and with marvellous power sweeps the popular heart. Now melting to tears, and now inspiring to rage, her work everywhere touches the conscience, and makes the Slave-Hunter more

hateful. In a brief period, nearly one hundred thousand copies of "Uncle Tom's Cabin" have been already circulated. But this extraordinary and sudden success, surpassing all other instances in the records of literature, cannot be regarded as but the triumph of genius. Better far, it is the testimony of the people, by an unprecedented act, against the Fugitive Slave Bill.   ("Freedom National" 181–82)

Whether we might find such a claim considerably exaggerated (or implausible because it assumes literature is somehow not molded by precisely the same cultural context producing the politics of the moment), the fact that Charles Sumner, a politician who as much as anybody moved the nation toward a revision of its fundamental charter and basic notions of citizenship, found it plausible is concrete evidence of the political influence of Stowe's emotionally redolent images.

## Sentiment and the argument against reform: *The Planter's Northern Bride*

The South was by no means blind to the influence of Stowe's novel. In a review of George Fitzhugh's proslavery tract *Cannibals All!*, the Richmond *Enquirer* lamented the fact that, though "In every mode of argument the champions of the South excel," "they have produced no romance quite equal to 'Uncle Tom's Cabin'" (23 January 1857). A number of anti-Tom novels were inspired by the perception that the South needed fiction defending the Southern way of life and turning the figures and themes of sentiment against abolitionism. When Caroline Lee Hentz, a New Englander transplanted to the South, wrote *The Planter's Northern Bride* (1854), she could draw upon the well-established pattern of the plantation romance (e.g., John Pendleton Kennedy's *Swallow Barn* [1832]). Typically, these novels feature loyal black servants, good-natured plantation owners, Southern belles, dashing young gentlemen, and Northern visitors who are won over to Southern ways.

The *Planter's Northern Bride* begins with Moreland, the noble plantation owner, traveling to the North in search of a respite from his disastrous first marriage to Claudia, which has ended in divorce (16). Early in the novel, Moreland's soulful response to church music gives the reader a clear signal of his fundamentally good character (34–35). During this service, he first hears the angelic voice and sees the beautiful figure of "Miss Eulalia Hastings," the daughter of the abolitionist editor of the "*Emancipator*" (39). Eulalia is predisposed to like Moreland because she has heard of his charitable aid to one of the poor women in her community (45). Clearly symbolizing sectional reconciliation, Moreland's successful courtship of Eulalia illustrates how the best elements of the two sections can come together and be united in mutual affection and respect. To achieve this goal, Moreland must convince Eulalia that her "opinions [regarding the South and slavery] are erroneous, and that though we have a dark spot in our social system, like every other cloud, 'it turns its silver lining to the light'" (55). Moreland has a personal blemish in the form of his prior marriage to Claudia. Dark, beautiful, and gypsy-like, Claudia recalls Rochester's mad Creole wife, Bertha, in *Jane Eyre* (1847), which was very popular in the antebellum era. Eventually, Claudia becomes the mad, Gothic specter of a destructive passion from the past, haunting Moreland's better union with Eulalia (315–16, 359). Moreland's child by Claudia, little Effie, must be reclaimed from wildness (like Stowe's Topsy) by the loving discipline of a surrogate parent (Eulalia) in a continuation of the sentimental novel's emphasis on discipline as the concomitant of genuine parental love (214, 216). By submitting to Eulalia's loving discipline, Effie becomes more loveable and more human (216–17). The villain of the novel is the abolitionist, Thomas Brainard, who deceives the Morelands into welcoming him into their home only to attempt to urge their good-hearted but not terribly bright slaves to the project of bloody insurrection. Changeable and hard to read, Brainard can write with either hand, a symbol of his uncanny and unwholesome nature (414–16, 523). He is particularly dangerous because the black imagination he skillfully exhorts is very powerful once aroused and hard to bring back to reason (447–48, 450). Ultimately, however, Brainard's slave revolt is discovered and thwarted, and paternalistic harmony is restored to the Moreland plantation.

Hentz's proslavery version of the sentimental novel seeks to rebut *Uncle Tom's Cabin* by means of a series of carefully staged parallels or juxtapositions. Instead of the intrepid slave mother attempting to keep her child, Hentz's fugitive slave, Crissy, is conned into running away only to find that freedom in the North is far worse than slavery in the South (270–71). Crissy is a "passive tool in the soft, insinuating hands" of the corrupting Mr. and Mrs. Softly who commit the moral outrage of breaking up the extended "family" of the plantation, rending "asunder the bonds of affection and gratitude which united this faithful heart to the master and mistress she so fondly loved" (271, 280). Instead of Northerners compassionately aiding fugitive slaves, the Southern slave holder, Moreland, compassionately cares for the poor, sick, and discarded worker of the North, Nancy. At a minimum, these parallels are intended to make us doubt that compassionate feeling condemns slavery and endorses the North's "free" labor system. The tearful death scene of poor Nancy, including the ritual of cutting locks of her hair as keepsakes (something Stowe's little Eva does on her own deathbed) is a testimony against the cruelties of capitalist labor. The dying woman asks, "why should I wish to live? I've struggled with poverty all my life, and it has been a bitter warfare" (160). In Hentz's novel, the moist eye and throbbing heart expose abolitionism to be founded on prejudice and ignorance, and they reveal that slavery is more compassionate than capitalism, which has no respect for the great mass of laboring individuals it consumes and casts off.

Closely resembling the autocratic but benevolent authority of parents over children and husbands over wives, slavery is based on the ubiquitous and inevitable fact of inequality. The "great commanding truth" guiding More-land and his creator, Hentz, is that "wherever civilized man exists, there is the dividing line of the high and the low, the rich and the poor, the thinking and the labouring" (32). If one accepts that inequality is permanent and ubiquitous (at least in "civilized" societies), then the only realistic ethical question in Hentz's view is not how to erase what is indelible but what is the best and most compassionate form of authority for regulating an unavoidably hierarchical society. Instead of a society torn apart by the constant competition and destructive individualism of capitalism, Southern society is, in Hentz's view, "the affectionate community" (149).

By yoking sentiment to inequality, Hentz redefines it as the benevolent feeling of the strong for the weak. One powerful effect of Hentz's overt recasting of sentiment as paternalistic compassion is that it illuminates the degree to which anti-slavery notions of sympathy depend on the benefactor's awareness of his/her power and the beneficiary's weakness and need. Despite the fact that, unlike Hentz's Crissy, Eliza Harris is intelligent and courageous, the shape and nature of the Birds' sympathetic response is determined by their sense of her distress and misery and their power to make things better. They offer Eliza charity not collaboration or partnership. In addition, if the reader can be as moved by the plight of the discarded Northern worker as by that of the abused slave, then the reader's confidence that sentiment cuts in one particular political direction may well be shaken. The fact that sentiment can push for and against reform, for and against principles of freedom and equality, for and against breaking down racial barriers, tends to undermine the sentimental novel's assumption that a powerful emotional experience offers clear and authoritative moral guidance. Unlike the workings of rational analysis, which require and even thrive on doubt, sentiment, as an intuitive, divinely sent guide to proper behavior and public policy, deteriorates when doubted.

While Hentz would convert good-hearted Northerners from their anti-Southern and anti-slavery prejudices, she does not conceive of her project as bringing her audience to the fever pitch of emotion required for reform. Instead, her version of sentiment works in the opposite direction to soothe the sectional animus aroused by abolitionism and to conserve the status quo. In her preface, Hentz suggests that the proslavery perspective is really common sense and that an overwrought public needs to recover "from the effects of transient inebriation" (implicitly caused in part by Stowe's novel) (3). Defending the South's hierarchical social system from fanatical reform is not only wise and humane, but is also, Hentz indicates, the outcome of a racial instinct instilled by God in humankind as a stabilizing principle:

> My dear Eulalia, God never intended that you and I should live on equal
> terms with the African. He has created a barrier between his race and
> ours, which no one can pass over without incurring the ban of
> society . . . This is the result of an inherent principle of the human
> breast, entwined, like conscience, with our vitality, and inseparable from
> it. The most ultra Northern philanthropist dare not contradict this
> truth. He may advocate amalgamation with his lips, but in his heart, he
> recoils from it with horror. He would sooner see a son or daughter
> perish beneath the stroke of the assassin than wedded to the African,
> whom he professes to look upon as his equal and his friend. Nature has
> marked a dividing line, as distinct as that which separates the beasts of
> the field, the birds of the air, and the fishes of the sea. And why should
> any one wish to violate this great law of nature, – this principle of
> homogeneousness? The negro feels the attraction of his kind, and forms,
> like ourselves, congenial ties.   (202–03)

The opposite of balance, stability, and order, amalgamation is the incarnation of chaos, a defiance of the racial instinct, potentially unleashing a monstrous social metamorphosis. Despite his admission that the racial divide may be crossed and racial hybrids produced thereby, Moreland holds racial difference up as an immutable principle of social stability (84–85). Moreland's comments reflect Hentz's notion of nature as divided into impenetrable categories (an idea contested by Darwin's account of evolution). Hentz's novel draws our attention to the ways in which the slavery debate raised important and elemental questions about whether the law of nature is stasis or fluidity, categorical purity or hybridity, homogeneity or heterogeneity.

For Hentz, the idealist values of purity and stasis, which, as we have seen, animate such sentimental novels as *The Wide, Wide World* and *Uncle Tom's Cabin*, are threatened by freedom. By encouraging people to deviate from the roles given them by virtue of their race, gender, or other "natural" category, freedom leads to degeneration. Hence, free blacks are considerably more degraded than slaves (202). The corrupting influence of freedom as a value derives in part from its assumption of an open-ended, developmental model of existence in which one is continually growing and changing. Hentz illustrates the ungovernable chaos of free society in her description of a Cincinnati boardinghouse's kitchen. The free kitchen workers are in continual "discord" because they are "constantly changing" positions and employers, leaving "[f]or the slightest cause of dissatisfaction" (259–60). By contrast, slavery is a system of order and stability – there is a place for everyone and everyone is in his or her place. Hentz's notion of a preordained social ladder assumes a high degree of transparency. One's proper place and role are clearly signaled by one's appearance, background, or other external factors. Despite certain obvious problems with racial identification (e.g., the nominally "black" person who can pass as white), race is, for Hentz, an instantly recognizable indicator of social role. Thus, "Free" Judy finds confirmation that black people were not made for freedom in the visible signs of racial difference,

> Look a' me, black as de chimney back, – dey, white as snow; what great, big, thick, ugly lips I got, – dere's look jist like roses. Den dis black sheep head, what de Lord make dat for? Dey got putey, soft, long hair, jist like de silk ribbons . . . I do wonder what the Lord made us nigger for? (265)

Intuitively, the black servant discontented with freedom understands that racial differences signify social function – "what the Lord made us . . . for?"

Violating such obvious signs produces misery and chaos. The aspiration of free laborers to exceed their predetermined roles creates instability and lowers the overall quality of life (e.g., you cannot obtain a good meal in a Northern hotel because the kitchen staff is always in flux). Like George Fitzhugh, Hentz deems a stable social hierarchy to be not merely the byproduct of civilization but the very fundament of civilization, which cannot exist or reach its highest forms without it. For Hentz, Crissy's desire for freedom is nothing more than a vulgar yearning for luxury and self-indulgence (270). If, however, we read Crissy's "fine ladyism" as a desire for the possibility of real transformation – not to impersonate a fine lady but to become a fine lady – then the emotional and moral valence of her escape from slavery and aspiration shifts. The tokens of economic success that Hentz reads as a crass and superficial materialism become signs of self-ownership and creative agency (271).

## Sentiment, upward mobility, and the African American novel

Hentz's desire to sever sentiment from social mobility makes for an illuminating contrast with sentimental novels connecting sympathy and the intuitive sense of right and wrong with the project of self-improvement or uplift. As we have seen, such sentimental fiction as Cummins's *The Lamplighter* asserts eternal and unchanging ideals *and* recommends the project of bettering one's condition in life through education, thrift, and hard work. Cummins is plainly comfortable with the idea that the Gerty Flints of the world may rise and become members of middle-class society. Hentz, by contrast, fears that the social changes endorsed by such fiction will wind up undermining the sentimental novel's foundational values of compassion and moral responsibility. Suggesting that absolute values naturally produce a static social system, Hentz finds in the plantation system of the South a static society mirroring a divinely ordained hierarchy. As we have noted, the equity and appropriateness of this social structure requires considerable transparency of character. The individual's proper place and role must be somehow plain or unmistakable. The sentimental novels of uplift and social mobility, particularly those taking up racial issues, seek to revise or complicate such notions of social legibility, arguing that people can be misread or overlooked, especially when class or race prejudice is present. As a result, even if one accepts Hentz's notion that there is a divinely or naturally ordained place for each person, the status quo still requires revision to the extent that it is based on misapprehension of individuals and groups.

Horatio Alger's children's novel *Ragged Dick* (1867) offers a telling example of how individuals can be misplaced in society and how, once they are read aright, their upward movement is natural and beneficial to society. This popular novel famously preaches the Franklinian values of pluck, luck, thrift, hard work, and education as a formula for rising from poverty, but Alger does not tout the accumulation of wealth as an end in itself. For the acquisition of material success to have moral validity, it must be connected to the good character of the person climbing the social ladder. Indeed, the social and economic success of Alger's hero, Dick Hunter, is extraneous to what really matters – Dick's innate sympathy, generosity, honesty, and bravery. As in most sentimental novels, the characters in *Ragged Dick* are morally transparent and unambiguous. Even in his most degraded state, Dick "was above doing anything mean or dishonorable." Dick does not require book learning or clean clothes to sympathize with the suffering of another orphan (43–44, 46). Similarly, Dick's metamorphosis into a literate, well-dressed young lad has nothing to do with his bravery in rescuing a child from drowning in the East River (208–10). Though his better deportment and new literacy are essential to his material progress, enabling him to take advantage of the employment opportunity offered to him by the father of the saved child (Dick couldn't take on the job of clerk if he hadn't learned to read), his educational advances are not material to the heroic act itself or Dick's innate character (215). While still in his "ragged" state, Dick

shares his meager earnings as a bootblack with a hungry child and protects
a young boy from a bully. In effect, Dick's transformation moves toward not
away from the coherence that Hentz's novel argues for – the coherence of inner
character and social role. By improving himself, Dick does not become a different kind of person; he becomes more fully, more transparently, the person
he already is and will always be. As a result, his quick mind and good heart
are better placed to benefit society. The inherent nature of Dick's intellectual
abilities and fundamental decency checks any (Hentz-like) alarm one might
feel at his transformation.

The connection between moral character and social uplift becomes particularly provocative when race is involved. Arguably, the era's most striking
representations of social progress are to be found in African American novels,
such as Frank Webb's *The Garies and Their Friends* (1857), Frances Harper's
*Iola Leroy* (1892), and Charles Chesnutt's *The Marrow of Tradition* (1901).
These novels attempt to liberate the social, economic, and political aspirations
of black Americans (e.g., Crissy's "fine ladyism") from the imprisoning scorn
of Hentz and others. Like Alger, but with the added obstacle of racial bias,
these authors distinguish between one's innate moral character and one's original social position, arguing for the radical improvement of the latter without
necessarily calling into question the permanence and fixity of the former. The
project of making black uplift seem intuitively natural and right to the sympathetic reader requires that these writers recalibrate the sentimental novel's logic
of transparency, either so that visual racial differences do not enter the assess-
ment of proper social role or so that they do not signify moral or intellectual
debility.

Early in her novel of the Civil War and Reconstruction, *Iola Leroy*, Frances
Harper describes in classic sentimental fashion the death of Tom Anderson,
a noble, if uneducated, black soldier. Tom is ministered to by Iola Leroy, a
beautiful nurse: "Iola laid her hand gently in the rough palm of the dying man,
and, with a tremulous voice, sang the parting hymns. Tenderly she wiped the
death damps from his dusky brow, and imprinted upon it a farewell kiss" (54).
This scene is observed by Dr. Gresham, a white physician from an aristocratic
background. Dr. Gresham is "mystified" by Iola's behavior, most particularly
her kissing of Tom. What is a refined, ladylike woman such as Iola doing
exhibiting such familiarity with "colored people"? (56–57). Dr. Gresham then
is astounded to learn that Iola is "black," being the daughter of a white man
and a very light-skinned black woman. The doctor responds, "What you tell
me changes the whole complexion of affairs" (58). Harper's wry joke here is
that complexion is the one thing that has not changed. The revelation of Iola's
racial background hasn't wrought a sudden change in her character or her
appearance. She is still the same kind-hearted, brave, and honest woman, and

Tom, the dying soldier, is no less noble and brave for being black than he is for being unlettered and rough in his manners. The white doctor has misread the significance of race.

Harper's novel tells the story of a community of black Americans of various complexions (and bloodlines) who are bound by a shared history of oppression. Their various features and skin colors do not signify differences in moral character. Very dark characters, such as Tom, Lucille Delany, and Dr. Carmicle, are just as noble as Iola. As Harper's characters observe, "Every person of unmixed blood who succeeds in any department of literature, art or science is a living argument for the capability which is in the race" and works to correct "one of the great mistakes of our civilization[,] that which makes color, and not character, a social test" (199, 84). *Iola Leroy* does not interrupt or challenge the sentimental novel's assumption that one's fundamental moral nature is fixed and transparent. The inherent goodness of dark-skinned characters, such as Lucille Delany and Dr. Carmicle, is utterly plain and unambiguous and should, in the sentimental novel's moral logic, make their quest for advancement seem natural and proper. Harper objects to the assumption that all visible marks or extrinsic traits bear the same moral significance.

In *The Garies and Their Friends*, Frank Webb provocatively illustrates the innateness, relative immutability, and nonracial aspect of moral character by imagining a racist white family with one member who inexplicably resists prejudice. The wicked George Stevens and his hateful wife have two children: a boy who resembles his parents, and a girl who does not. Little Lizzie Stevens persists in wanting to play with mixed-race children living next door despite the injunction of her parents (152). Lizzie's very presence in the Stevens family makes moral character, whether good or malign, seem a thing of nature not nurture, but differentiates this moral nature from Lizzie's whiteness. Her essentially good temperament is no more subject to revision than are the ideals expressed by that temperament and no more a matter of complexion than is Tom Anderson's good heart in *Iola Leroy*.

With character as a given, education, deportment, and better social position become a kind of language that one can master, enabling public discourse among people of very different backgrounds and with highly divergent domestic arrangements and practices.[11] The friendship of two doctors, one black and one white, in Chesnutt's *The Marrow of Tradition*, is just one example of the social fluidity facilitated by shared education and social conventions (Crane *Race* 209–16). In the same novel, Lee Ellis, the middle-class Southern Quaker's son who proves to be the better suitor for the aristocratic Clara Pemberton, provides another example of the beneficial movement created through an acceptance of shared ethical principles and deportment in lieu of inherited status as the basis for social connection. In their depictions of deportment as a means of social mobility, these narratives have tended to trouble certain 20th- and 21st-century critics and scholars, who are embarrassed by what they see as a distasteful capitulation to the cultural standards of the white middle class. Earlier critics such as Sterling Brown, Arthur Davis, Ulysses Lee, and Addison Gayle dismissed such narratives as cravenly assimilationist (Harper xii–xiii, Tate 78–83). More recently, Richard Brodhead takes Chesnutt to task for his taste for "high-cultural" literature and bourgeois life (189, 194–95). One can feel similar aversions in Robert Reid-Pharr's introduction to Webb's novel. Citing Addison Gayle, Robert Reid-Pharr finds in Webb's novel an argument for "the nonviability of interracialism" and the creation of a "space that, however hemmed in by whiteness, remains purely black" (Webb xii–xiii). According to Reid-Pharr, Webb's novel endorses his black characters' economic and social mobility but simultaneously posits that their racial identity remains fixed and pure (Webb viii). It is hard, however, to square Reid-Pharr's "nonviability of interracialism" with the mutually loving and respectful interracial marriages in Webb's novel. And, like other sentimental novels, Webb's narrative valorizes the purity and fixity of moral character rather than racial identity.

*The Garies and Their Friends* revolves around the intertwined fate of three families: the Garie, Ellis, and Stevens families. Clarence Garie, a wealthy Southern planter, buys Emily, a light-skinned black woman. After falling in love, they live as man and wife and soon have two beautiful children who are light enough to pass as white. Fearing for the fate of these children, Emily persuades her husband to move North, to Philadelphia, where they will be able to marry and where their children will be beyond the grip of slavery. The Ellis family is a hard-working, respectable free black family living in Philadelphia, attempting to improve their circumstances. While their children, Esther, Charlie, and Caddy, differ in temperament, each has his/her own particular gifts and all of them have good characters. The Stevens family is led by George Sr., a greedy and unscrupulous Philadelphia attorney. His children George Jr. and Lizzie are very different in temperament. George Jr. shares his father's bad character while Lizzie stands out as a loving and open-minded little girl. By coincidence, Stevens learns from a piece of long-lost correspondence that he is Clarence Garie's first cousin, and that he will inherit the Garie estate should Garie die and no will be found. He engineers a race riot as cover for his murder of Garie. This racial violence results in the brutal maiming of Mr. Ellis as well as the deaths of Emily and Clarence Garie and their prematurely born baby. The surviving Garie children are separated. Clarence Jr. goes north to school, passing as white – a decision which later proves disastrous when his racial heritage is exposed. Little Emily stays in Philadelphia to be brought up by the Ellis family. She happily marries Charlie Ellis. The other important player in this drama is

Mr. Walters, a successful black real estate investor who protects and cares for the Ellis family after the riot.

The novel expressly mocks the notion of racial purity and natural racial aversion touted by Caroline Hentz and others. Clarence Garie enjoys the thought of George Winston, a black man light enough to pass as white, escorting a "Fifth-avenue belle" (3). The humor is particularly rich because the belle's father, Mr. Priestly, is an ardent white supremacist who "prides himself on being able to detect evidences of the least drop of African blood in any one; and makes long speeches about the natural antipathy of the Anglo-Saxon to anything with a drop of negro blood in its veins" (4). Such notions of innate racial aversion are contradicted by Clarence and Emily Garie's love for each other. Similarly, Clarence Jr. and his "Little Birdie"'s love for each other is thwarted not by an insuperable, natural barrier of racial difference but by the cruel artifice of racist social conventions frowning on miscegenation.

Webb adds the element of race to the Horatio Alger story of the impoverished boy who overcomes long odds to become a success. Like Frederick Douglass, the dignified and cultured George Winston is a living argument against slavery and racial caste:

> Mr. Winston had been a slave. Yes! that fine-looking gentleman seated near Mr. Garie and losing nothing by the comparison that their proximity would suggest, had been fifteen years before sold on the auction-block in the neighbouring town of Savanah – had been made to jump, show his teeth, shout to test his lungs, and had been handled and examined by professed negro traders and amateur buyers, with less gentleness and commiseration than every humane man would feel for a horse or an ox. Now do not doubt me – I mean that very gentleman, whose polished manners and irreproachable appearance might have led you to suppose him descended from a long line of illustrious ancestors. Yes – he was the offspring of a mulatto field-hand by her master. He who was now clothed in fine linen, had once rejoiced in a tow shirt that scarcely covered his nakedness, and had sustained life on a peck of corn a week, receiving the while kicks and curses from a tyrannical overseer. (8)

This passage traces a reversal of fortunes not unlike Ragged Dick's, Benjamin Franklin's, or Oliver Twist's, but that reversal is made more dramatic and more impressive by the greater depth of suffering and hardship overcome by Winston. Also, by overcoming the preconceptions of racial type, Winston's story casts doubt on the idea of a fixed racial identity, challenging the superficial assumption that outward signs of a degraded status accurately represent a person's inner character. Ultimately, George Winston leaves the United States to go to some country "where, if he must struggle for success in life, he might do it without the additional embarrassments that would be thrown in his way in his native land, solely because he belonged to an oppressed race" (14). In other words, were it not for his native land's race prejudice, George Winston could be a rising young man and a representative instance of the American success story.

In charting Charlie Ellis's uplift narrative, Webb draws upon the conventions of sentimental fiction, depicting how identification leads to sympathy and aid, when a white woman, imagining how she would feel if her son were denied employment on the basis of race and not character or ability, lobbies her husband to find Charlie the employment he needs to support his family (302, 307). Like other sentimental protagonists, young Charlie has much to learn, including a measure of self-control, yet he also manifests a good and engaging character from the outset, including his youthful bravery ("manfully" enduring the setting of his broken arm), his capacity and enthusiasm for learning, and his spirited objection to his employment as the servant to a vain wealthy white woman (90, 36, 67, 75–82). Charlie's capacity for self-sacrifice comes to the fore when he returns to Philadelphia after the bloody race violence to help his family. Over the course of the novel, Charlie progresses substantially in manners and education, but, as is the case with Alger's Dick Hunter, the emotional, moral, and psychological fundaments of his character are relatively stable.

But Webb's novel goes even further in endorsing the uplift project. Webb describes upward mobility as a moral imperative for black Americans. On hearing the argument of a white character that children of the black working class should be prepared for their inevitable role in life as servants, the successful Mr. Walters responds:

> A great many white people think that we are only fit for servants, and I must confess we do much to strengthen the opinion by permitting our children to occupy such situations when we are not in circumstances to compel us to do so. Mrs. Thomas may tell you that they respect their old servant Robberts as much as they do your husband; but they don't, nevertheless – I don't believe a word of it. (63)

It is one thing to do manual labor and service with dignity if one is forced to by circumstances, but it is another and worse thing to accept it as fate for all black people. Through Walters, Webb seeks to impress on his audience that it is "a shame to make a servant of a bright clever boy" like Charlie (62).

Harriet Wilson's 1859 novel, *Our Nig*, subjects the sentimental novel's modeling of personal transformation and upward mobility to intense scrutiny and implicit skepticism. While in many ways Wilson's novel fits the sentimental template, it ultimately casts doubt on both the efficacy of sympathy and the prospect of social mobility and personal transformation. A combination of autobiography and fiction, *Our Nig* was forgotten for almost 120 years, until rediscovered by Henry Louis Gates, Jr. in the 1980s. The first novel written by an African American woman, it tells the story of Frado, a bright and spirited six-year-old girl, abandoned after the death of her black father by her poor white mother on the doorstep of a prosperous New Hampshire family, the Bellmonts. Frado's life in this prosperous New England home proves to be every bit as fraught and tortured as that of a slave in the deep South. She suffers endless hard labor and cruel and violent punishment from her mistress Mrs. Bellmont. Frado finds some degree of sympathy in Mr. Bellmont, his son, and an invalid sister, but these glimmers of humane feeling are largely ineffectual in ameliorating Frado's plight. Throughout the harrowing and unrelenting round of toil and punishment, Frado continues to fight for survival and to improve herself. After twelve years, Frado comes of age, completing the term of her servitude, but her physical resources have been largely broken by the years of harsh treatment and labor. She meets and marries a fugitive slave, and they have a son. When Frado and her son are abandoned, the young, poor, and sickly mother desperately turns to writing to support herself and her son, reminding us of Fern's *Ruth Hall*, but with the notable difference that there is no providential intercession on Frado's behalf and no apparent escape from an ongoing cycle of poverty and oppression. Frado and the author's intertwined stories do not come to a conclusion. Instead, the novel ends with a plea for support.

The central tug-of-war in *Our Nig* is between forces attempting to confine Frado within a life-denying servitude and Frado's efforts, with some help, to assert her humanity and agency. Mrs. Bellmont and her unsympathetic daughter, Mary, think of Frado as "our nig," a label signaling the practical equivalence of Frado's position in this Northern household with that of a slave child. Mrs. Bellmont even forbids Frado to display her emotions, such as her sadness at her mother's failure to return for her. Frado, however, finds ways of asserting her humanity. She is permitted to go to school (after a heated dispute within the Bellmont family – one of the few triumphs of the more sympathetic members of the family), and Frado makes as much as she can of this opportunity, ever "striving to enrich her mind. Her school-books were her constant companions, and every leisure moment was applied to them" (115). Frado's efforts in the vein of self-improvement suggest a belief that even in the most oppressive of circumstances human character remains capable of growth and development. Frado also finds religion under the kind instruction and example of James Bellmont, and her new faith offers a spiritual refuge from the cruelties of her daily existence. In such moments, Frado's tale would seem to fit the template of the sentimental novel.

However, *Our Nig* differs from the sentimental novel in at least two marked and revealing aspects. First, Wilson would seem much more disposed to sanction Frado's willful mischief than to see it as requiring a rigorous program of discipline. In her predilection for pranks, Frado resembles Topsy, but in this novel such pranks become signs of Frado's humanity, her resistance to being objectified, rather than a symptom of degradation. The fact that her playfulness persists despite the incessant round of toil and cruel punishments is an expression not only of her resilient nature, but also of her rebellious opposition to the hateful order of Mrs. Bellmont. Frado's pranks are also a kind of agency, a subversive interjection of will, desire, and imagination into the system and setting that proscribe it. Frado eventually learns that she can abate, even avoid some beatings by signaling her intent not to work again if she is struck. Second, Wilson unflinchingly represents the uncertainties of Frado's fate. Will Frado survive, find a way to make a living and support her son? Will she continue to grow ("[e]very leisure moment was carefully applied to self-improvement" [115–16])? Ending in uncertainty for Frado, her alter ego, and a plea for assistance for herself, Wilson's narrative breaks down the distinction between autobiography and fiction, creating a striking overlap between the fictional story controlled by the author and the unpredictable life lived by the narrator. In effect, the documentary aspect of Wilson's novel looks forward to realism while the fictional aspect looks back to the sentimental tradition. The reality of Wilson's life overshadows the sentimental conventions of the novel. Frado's long-suffering endurance and progress against the odds is not rewarded with a happy, prosperous marriage or her ascension to a heavenly reward. Instead, at the tale's end, Frado's fate is utterly doubtful. Wilson's frank portrayal of the uncertainty and unrelenting difficulty of Frado's life undermines the sentimental template, making it seem too neat, too confident. Even as it calls for sympathetic aid, *Our Nig* calls into question the assumption that the hand of a benign Providence directs human affairs, ensuring that each character receives his or her just deserts, either in this world or the next.

## Moving toward realism: Rebecca Harding Davis and Elizabeth Stoddard

In undertaking any comparison of sentimental fiction and realism, a fictional mode flourishing after the Civil War, it is important to avoid the mistake of assuming that one genre comes along and replaces the other. Sentiment no more disappears from American fiction than romance does. However, to understand and situate realist fiction, we should note that the realists expressly sought to distance their work from the sentimental novel. Among other things, the sentimental novel was, to their minds, too polite, too reluctant to engage the rawer realities of life, and it was far too confident in a providential view of existence. By contrast, realist novels self-consciously strive for an unvarnished, more accurate representation of everyday life, speech, and manners and move away from religious certitude and toward a more skeptical and secular point of view. Indeed, the distinction between sentimental and realist fiction could well be redrawn as a contrast between religious and secular fiction. The need for realism, so to speak, can be felt in sentimental novels in which the form's conventions seem inadequate for the task of addressing the lives and experiences the novelist wants to depict. The uncertain fate of Frado in *Our Nig*, for example, does not fit neatly within the providential framework of typical sentimental fiction.

The drift of sentimental fiction toward realism is strikingly apparent in Rebecca Harding Davis's *Life in the Iron-Mills* (1861) and Elizabeth Stoddards's *The Morgesons* (1862). Rebecca Harding Davis's vivid images of the hellish lives of mill workers in *Life in the Iron-Mills* push for reform of industrial capitalism by provoking the reader's sympathies for its victims. The tale is straightforward: Hugh Wolfe is a Welsh immigrant iron worker and Deborah is his cousin. Deborah is deformed, and both cousins are crushed by the harsh circumstances of their lives in the shadow of a West Virginia iron mill. Hugh has some artistic talent as a sculptor, which is noted by some upper-class visitors to the mill who happen to see Hugh's Korl woman, a sculpture of a woman carved out of the slag or refuse of the iron mill. Appreciating Hugh's talent, a doctor in the group of visitors urges Hugh that he has the "right" to improve himself, but the depth of Hugh's poverty renders this "right" a mocking delusion. Deborah picks up some money that has fallen out of the pocket of one of the visitors. She gives the money to Hugh whom she loves. Hugh initially shrinks from taking the money but weakens as he considers the daydream of leaving this hellish existence behind. The denouement is predictable – he and Deb are arrested for theft; he is sentenced to nineteen years hard labor, and Deb receives a sentence of three years. Hugh kills himself in jail, and, after jail, Deb is rescued by a Quaker woman who reclaims her to a somber, penitent, but happy life among the Friends.

Davis compares the mills to a scene from Dante's *Inferno* (50), and Davis's description reminds one of the infernal symbolism of the "Try-Works" chapter of *Moby-Dick*, Hawthorne's lime kilns in "Ethan Brand," and Stowe's initial description of Legree's plantation:

> The mills for rolling iron are simply immense tent-like roofs, covering
> acres of ground, open on every side. Beneath these roofs Deborah
> looked in on a city of fires, that burned hot and fiercely in the night. Fire
> in every horrible form: pits of flame waving in the wind; liquid
> metal-flames writhing in tortuous streams through the sand; wide
> caldrons filled with boiling fire, over which bent ghastly wretches
> stirring the strange brewing; and through all, crowds of half-clad men,
> looking like revengeful ghosts in the red light, hurried, throwing masses
> of glittering fire. It was like a street in Hell.   (45)

Davis's description of the workers and their squalid living conditions foreshad-
ows similar images in Jacob Riis's muckraking classic *How the Other Half Lives*
(1890):

> [The Wolfe dwelling] was low, damp, – the earthen floor covered with a
> green, slimy moss, – a fetid air smothering the breath. Old Wolfe lay
> asleep on a heap of straw, wrapped in a torn horse-blanket. He was a
> pale, meek little man, with a white face and red rabbit-eyes. The woman
> Deborah was like him; only her face was even more ghastly, her lips bluer,
> her eyes more watery. She wore a faded cotton gown and a slouching
> bonnet. When she walked, one could see that she was deformed, almost
> a hunchback. She trod softly, so as not to waken him, and went through
> into the room beyond. There she found by the half-extinguished fire an
> iron saucepan filled with cold boiled potatoes, which she put upon a
> broken chair with a pint-cup of ale. Placing the old candlestick beside
> this dainty repast, she untied her bonnet, which hung limp and wet over
> her face, and prepared to eat her supper. It was the first food that had
> touched her lips since morning.   (*Life in the Iron-Mills* 43)

One can see affiliations between these descriptions and other earlier scenes of
destitution in sentimental fiction such as in *The Lamplighter* or *Uncle Tom's
Cabin*, but there would seem to be a difference here. The unrelenting quality of
Davis's descriptions of the bleak conditions of these lives gives one a feeling of
hopelessness. Deborah will ultimately be reclaimed by a good-hearted Quaker
woman who represents the possibility of regeneration by sympathy and faith
shared by all of the sentimental novels, but the number of pages devoted to
her life before and after this rescue is such that the feeling of darkness and
despair preponderates. While as in other sentimental writing Davis's characters
generally conform to type (e.g., Deborah is "a type of her class"), Davis's portrait
of Hugh Wolfe, at least partially, moves away from type (46). His "thirst for
beauty" marks him as different from the typical mill worker and gives his story
its tragic pathos (48). The rough muscularity of Hugh's sculpture, the Korl
woman, dispenses with idealized notions of beauty. Instead, the strength of the

piece, its very living quality, seems to come from its alloy of strength, yearning, and suffering (52–53). This is certainly not beauty of a conventional sort, but its moving blend of strength and suffering would seem an uncanny anticipation of such sculptures as Rodin's *Crouching Woman* (1880–82) and William Rimmer's *Dying Centaur* (1869).

When a visiting doctor tells Hugh "Make your self what you will. It is your right," Hugh responds, "I know . . . Will you help me?" The doctor flatly rejects this plea even as he endorses it, citing his lack of economic resources for the project of raising Hugh up (56). This scene is designed to expose the hypocrisy of a nominally sympathetic but ultimately selfish middle class, signaling the impotence of such cheap pieties as "A man may make himself anything he chooses" (56). The doctor's refusal of aid and Hugh's fate do not conform to the sentimental formula – there is no sympathetic rescue. Hugh does not have an opportunity to better himself through self-discipline, faith, and hard work. His death by suicide is not redemptive. For Davis and Harriet Wilson (as well as for Elizabeth Stuart Phelps, whose comparable novel of industrial privation and upper-class privilege, *The Silent Partner* [1871], embodies a similar tension between its realist and sentimental elements), the sentimental formula seems inadequate to the task of representing such lives as Hugh's or Frado's.[12] When the sentimental formula reappears at the end of Davis's novel in the form of the Quaker woman's reclamation of Deborah and a reassertion of God's oversight of human existence, it coheres uneasily with Davis's more "realistic" awareness of the torturous difficulty faced by Hugh and Deborah Wolfe, leading some critics to discount the novel's sentimental elements and class it with realism.

Elizabeth Stoddard's novel, *The Morgesons* (1862), breaks with the conventions of sentimental fiction in a very different manner. While the novel centers on the conventional domestic subject matter of the sentimental novel – concerning a young woman's growth and struggle to make her way in the world – it does not attempt to engage the reader's tearful sympathies, and it is wholly, even startlingly, secular in tone and perspective. Instead of sympathy, piety, and a program for self-improvement, Stoddard gives her readers irony and characters of considerable psychological depth and complexity. Instead of the self-sacrificing and essentially angelic female protagonist typical in sentimental fiction, Cassandra Morgeson is driven by passion and a hunger for beauty and self-fulfillment. In personality and range of feeling, Cassandra's predecessor is not Ellen Montgomery or Gerty Flint, but Hester Prynne. But it is important that Stoddard takes this personality type and makes it central to the domestic setting so typical of sentimental fiction. She would seem by this gesture to be intent on upending the genre.

Unlike most sentimental fiction, *The Morgesons* is written in the first person and its narrative structure is somewhat more complex, beginning in the present, looking back to the past, then proceeding. Like Melville, Stoddard has a taste for contradiction at the level of the phrase or term. Her prose makes use of oxymorons, such as "humbly proud" or "bashfully arrogant" and double negatives, such as "not unpicturesque" (23, 29). These devices make her prose more dense, more difficult to translate or paraphrase, calling attention to the difficulties of comprehension, not to thwart such understanding but to make the reader less confident that the ultimate significance of any detail will prove to be transparent or knowable. But the novel's most striking stylistic difference from sentimental fiction is its application of an ironic, irreverent tone to descriptions of the domestic scene. A child's rudeness or defiance is not attended by a disciplinary project of moral and spiritual reform. When Cassandra or Cassy tells her mother, "I hate good stories," she is not brought around by her mother or anyone else to a more docile and tractable attitude (6). No one undertakes to reform or discipline Cassandra's singularity, her willfulness, or her honesty. She is not punished for refusing to say "good morning" to her grandfather or for accounting for this rudeness by saying "I am not fond of my grandfather" (10). Instead of collecting flowers to make her home more beautiful or bring joy to her mother, Cassandra pulls up dandelions to see them crushed in the road (11). The degree of frankness in Stoddard's portrait of children is striking in comparison to the fictional portraits of childhood in sentimental fiction.

Not much happens in *The Morgesons*. Cassandra goes away from home three times. She falls in love, first with a married kinsman (Charles Morgeson), a dark Byronic figure, who dies after a carriage crash in which Cassandra is injured and scarred, and second with Desmond, the brooding brother of the man who will marry her sister, Veronica. Cassandra's mother dies. After his business fails, Cassandra's father marries Charles Morgeson's widow. The novel closes with the death of Veronica's husband, Ben, and Cassandra's marriage to Desmond. Instead of action, Stoddard gives us a close look at the maturation and development of a singular young woman, the course of her passions and desires, and this development is figured more as a matter of aesthetic values than religious principles, as when Veronica's piano playing puts Cassandra into "a dream, chaotic, but not tumultuous, beautiful, but inharmonious" (53). Cassandra's life, like her aesthetic experience, values both the beautiful and the discordant.

During her residence with her kinsman Charles Morgeson and his family in Rosville, Cassandra opens up to change. Charles represents power and transformation. He is the new model of the successful American. Instead of being bound to the land, like a genteel republican farmer or plantation owner of the revolutionary generation, Charles sells the family farm to become a capitalist and factory owner (76). He moves into town, where he is respected, feared, but not accepted by the town's old wealth (77). Thrust into this family on the move, a family which lives "fast," Cassandra readily adapts:

> I found that I was more elastic than before, and more susceptible to sudden impressions; I was conscious of the ebb and flow of the blood through my heart, felt it when it eddied up into my face and touched my brain with its flame-colored wave . . . I missed nothing that the present unrolled for me, but looked neither to the past nor to the future. In truth there was little that was elevated in me.   (77)

Unlike the heroine of the sentimental novel, such as Ellen Montgomery, who seeks a heavenly stasis, Cassandra seeks change, movement, continuing rupture with the past without concern for the future. Stoddard has a very keen sense of the fleeting and quixotic nature of her characters' psychological states and their relations with others. She describes, for instance, how Cassandra's sudden impulse to tell her father about her passionate feelings for Charles ("an overpowering impulse seized me to speak to him of Charles") is killed by his off-hand comment ("You are faded a little. Your face has lost its firmness" [101]).

Ultimately, Cassandra finds "that Love, like Theology, if examined, makes one skeptical" (137). The skepticism here works against the idealist pretense that we can know the overarching significance, meaning, or direction of our lives. Without the supposed absolute certainties of romantic love or religion, Cassandra turns away from grand schemas of meaning toward the present moment:

> A habit grew upon me of consulting the sea as soon as I rose in the morning. Its aspect decided how my day would be spent. I watched it, studying its changes, seeking to understand its effect, ever attracted by an awful materiality and its easy power to drown me. By the shore at night the vague tumultuous sphere, swayed by an influence mightier than itself, gave voice, which drew my soul to utter speech for speech.   (143)

In a striking anticipation of Wallace Stevens's "Idea of Order at Key West," Stoddard comes up with an overwhelmingly fluid image of life lived in the moment, creating meaning out of the material reality before it, without the benefit of a second story of perfect ideals to guide it, with nothing more than human responsiveness and imagination. In this approach to life, transition or movement is appreciated not because it leads toward some complete and ideal vision of existence, but more simply as an immanent fact of life, which, like the ocean, is always in movement, always swayed by influences beyond our comprehension.

*Chapter 3*

# The realist novel

## What is American literary realism?

At the outset, we should distinguish American literary realism from the notion of verisimilitude – the fictive illusion that the reader is vicariously entering a world elsewhere. This effect, which is common to fantasies, sentimental novels, Gothic tales, and historical romances as well as realist texts, requires that the characters, actions, and settings be imagined with a sufficient degree of plausibility so that the reader feels as though he or she were watching events unfold in the world and time of the tale. Reflecting on the different sorts of writing he read during his youth, Benjamin Franklin singles out the fictive illusion as the defining aspect of fictional narrative: "Honest John [Bunyan] was the first that I know of who mix'd narration and dialogue; a method of writing very engaging to the reader, who in the most interesting parts finds himself, as it were, brought into the company and present at the conversation" (17). That feeling of vicarious presence at the events being described is to fiction what malt is to beer and sugar to candy. It is the sine qua non of most fiction from Cervantes to the present. While the feature Franklin enjoyed can be found in the body of texts we think of as exemplifying realism, it does not define that mode of fiction, neither its particular formal nor its thematic qualities.

The term "realism" as it is used here should not be thought of as an attribute of fiction in general but rather as a specific literary historical phenomenon. It is a rubric under which we can gather a wide variety of novels written in the late nineteenth century, from the vernacular fictions of Mark Twain and Sarah Orne Jewett to the cosmopolitan novels of Henry James and the determinist fictions of Frank Norris. Despite certain obvious and marked differences between them, these novelists share a general conception of fiction as a detailed and accurate representation of historically specific characters and settings – their manners, ways of dress, speech patterns, social habits, main concerns, and topics of conversation. While it may strike readers as being unsystematic and not wholly coherent, the realist trend in fiction of the late nineteenth century is palpable. In survey classes, having just finished sentimental novels by Harriet Beecher Stowe and Susan Warner, students are quick to comment on the less stagy and melodramatic aspects of realist fiction. Characters in realist fiction behave and speak more naturally, and the realist author does not overtly instruct us how to feel about the novel's events. Such contrasts furnish a revealing perspective on the loose and baggy form of realism. Noting the errors and problems the realists saw themselves as avoiding or correcting can help to sharpen our sense of the features defining realism.

American realists were particularly pointed in their criticism of the emotional excesses and implausibilities of sentimental fiction and the historical romance. Mark Twain, for instance, enjoyed mocking the inaccuracy of James Fenimore Cooper's woodsmen and the historical romance's excessive notions of honor and chivalry. William Dean Howells and Kate Chopin were similarly critical of the excesses of sentimental fiction. In Howells's *The Rise of Silas Lapham* (1885), a young female reader re-titles the latest popular sentimental novel from *Tears, Idle Tears* to *Slop, Silly Slop*. In Chopin's *At Fault*, Fanny Hosmer reads "the latest novel of one of those prolific female writers who turn out their unwholesome intellectual sweets so tirelessly, to be devoured by girls and women of the age" (78). For the realist, sentimental fiction, at its worst, substituted the ready gush of feeling aroused by pathetic images or romantic misadventure for a more thoughtful engagement with individual needs and social problems. In his account of an effort to reform Pap Finn, Twain bluntly ridicules the facile assumption that warm feelings will result in real change (we might here think of T. S. Arthur's *Ten Nights in a Bar-Room*, which is discussed in the chapter on the sentimental novel). After reaching Pap through "sympathy" and persuading him to forego strong drink, Pap's reformers, a judge and his wife, share tears of joy with Pap, as the reprobate pledges that he will "turn over a new leaf." The judge says "it was the holiest time on record" and invites Pap to stay with them. While his hosts sleep, Pap slips out, gets drunk, returns, and leaves their spare room in such a condition that "they had to take soundings before they could navigate it." In view of Pap's precipitous fall from the wagon, the judge concludes, in Huck's words, that "a body could reform the ole man with a shot-gun, maybe, but he didn't know no other way" (*Huckleberry Finn* 23).

It would be a mistake, however, to see the realists' criticism or mockery of sentiment as indicating a wholesale rejection of the value of sympathy or the affective register used by the sentimental novelists. Twain and Stowe, for instance, shared many political and ethical values, and Twain's greatest novel, *Huckleberry Finn* (1884), has moments clearly designed to produce in the reader an affective response similar to that sought by Stowe, such as the scene in which Jim rebukes Huck for tricking him into thinking Huck was lost or dead. But one of the distinctive aspects of realism lies in the realists' efforts to prevent their versions of sentiment from becoming mawkish or lapsing into facile melodrama by the use of carefully layered descriptions of local detail, including affective gestures that seem authentic to the characters, and by the use of irony, indicating a canny awareness of the manipulability and frequent hollowness of such feeling.

The realists were also critical of what they saw as the previous generation's squeamishness when it came to depicting the more common, harsh, or even vulgar aspects of life, such as adultery, crime, alcoholism, racial violence, labor strife, and political corruption. Refusing to let notions of propriety prevent them from engaging controversial or "low" topics, realists depicted the excesses of capitalism, the plight of the poor, and the narrow or straitened circumstances of women, black Americans, and immigrants. People hostile to the realists' frankness in addressing such issues were, in Theodore Dreiser's view, worried about the maintenance of

> their own little theories concerning life, which in some cases may be nothing more than a quiet acceptance of things as they are without any regard to the well-being of the future. Life for them is made up of a variety of interesting but immutable forms and any attempt either to picture any of the wretched results of modern social conditions or to assail the critical defenders of the same is naturally looked upon with contempt or aversion.   ("True Art" 129)

Dreiser here allies realism's honesty with change and reform. Generally speaking, realist novels show a substantial democratic openness in choice of subject, applying their mode of detailed and unvarnished observation to marginal groups, such as black Americans (Charles Chesnutt), poor Midwestern farmers (Hamlin Garland), and Jewish immigrants (Abraham Cahan). Realists placed considerable emphasis on the cultural and religious conventions of the group being described. By virtue of the frankness of its depiction of such local details, the accessibility of its language, its everyday subject matter, and its mixture of the serious and the comic, realism, as George Levine has pointed out, reaches out to a wide audience and works against the distinction between high and low art (5–7).

Philosophically speaking, literary realism is generally empiricist in its orientation, privileging concrete examples of experience over totalizing systems of thought. Like pragmatism, its philosophical cousin, realism tends to move from the visible detail toward the invisible or more abstract realm of ideas and values rather than the other way around. To put it another way, realism and pragmatism seek truth not from the top down but from the bottom up, through an exploration of the here and now – the "multitudinous" and "tangled" "world of concrete personal experiences to which the street belongs," to borrow William James's description of pragmatism (*Pragmatism* 15). Resembling empirical science, realism is exploratory rather than definitive, inductive rather than deductive, experimental and open to uncertainty rather than claiming positivistic finality or certitude. Consequently, realism resists the use of allegorical forms, which depend on some version of the Platonic or idealist two-story universe, in which the particulars in the lower story more or less clearly emblematize the ideals or universals of the upper story. Not believing in the two-story schema or lacking confidence in the human capacity to ascertain the ideals of the second story, realists attempt to ferret out meaning and value from an ongoing engagement with the particulars of daily existence – a process too muddled and fluid for the purposes of allegory. Like the pragmatist, the realist dives into the "richest intimacy with facts," as William James puts it, in the faith that scrutinizing the complex web of details is in itself an ethical task worth performing, believing that grappling with factual complexity is the first step toward learning to accept ambiguity and working toward a just society (20).

To a certain extent or at least in certain writers, one can say that realism represents the effect of religious doubt on fiction. Consider for a moment a comment attributed to the great British realist, George Eliot: "God, immortality, duty . . . how inconceivable the first, how unbelievable the second, how peremptory and absolute the third" (Sutherland 4). The question posed by this point of view is plain. If one cannot turn with confidence to divine authority, how can one ascertain moral imperatives or find meaning and value in life? In response, the realist turns to daily life. Religious doubt does not prevent us from discovering in everyday existence a sense of connection with others and with the natural world we inhabit. Our growing awareness of these connections may become overwhelming and transcend our present state of rational understanding, filling us with a sense of moral significance and obligation that cannot be tied down to any particular religious orthodoxy. Huck's decision to "go to hell" in order to set Jim free is an example of a moral imperative emerging from friendship. Expressed as religious impiety to distinguish it from the religious, moral, or legal orthodoxies of his society, Huck's choice elevates a spontaneous, tangible, present connection with Jim over the imperatives of social milieu and tradition.

Acknowledging that our attempt to discover significance in the often chaotic and confusing details of daily life can be distorted by bias, ignorance, and self-interest, realists insist that we have no practical choice. Whether distorted or not, we compulsively read the bits and bobs of experience, like tea leaves, for signs of value. In *Middlemarch* (1870), George Eliot offers a wry and apt illustration of our compulsion to make meaning out of experience:

> An eminent philosopher among my friends, who can dignify even
> your ugly furniture by lifting it into the serene light of science, has
> shown me this pregnant little fact. Your pier-glass [large high mirror] or
> extensive surface of polished steel made to be rubbed by a housemaid,
> will be minutely and multitudinously scratched in all directions; but
> place now against it a lighted candle as a centre of illumination, and lo!
> the scratches will seem to arrange themselves in a fine series of
> concentric circles round that little sun. It is demonstrable that the
> scratches are going everywhere impartially, and it is only your candle
> which produces the flattering illusion of a concentric arrangement, its
> light falling with an exclusive optical selection. These things are a
> parable. The scratches are events, and the candle is the egoism of any
> person now absent. (251)

While we properly object to Rosamond Vincy's interpretation of her brother's illness as Providence's way of increasing her romantic contact with Dr. Tertius Lydgate and we doubt Nicholas Bulstrode's assumption that God has brought forward an associate from his past to punish him for his sins, nonetheless we are intended, I think, to see this very human activity, whether badly or nobly motivated, as a human necessity (with a very different image and set of references, Melville, as we have seen, makes a similar point in the "Whiteness of the Whale" chapter of *Moby-Dick*). To live, we need to find order and meaning in the random scratches, the events, of life. If that order and meaning do not come to us from on high, then we are compelled to discover it for ourselves in the facts and events before us.

In *Middlemarch*, the search for meaning is often precipitated by small and large moments of crisis. As in the following poetic moment, when Dorothea discovers a moral imperative by looking out beyond herself and her suffering (after seeing Will Ladislaw in the arms of Rosamond Lydgate):

> She opened her curtains, and looked out towards the bit of road that lay
> in view, with fields beyond, outside the entrance-gates. On the road
> there was a man with a bundle on his back and a woman carrying her
> baby; in the field she could see figures moving – perhaps the shepherd
> with his dog. Far off in the bending sky was the pearly light; and she felt

the largeness of the world and the manifold wakings of men to labour and endurance. She was a part of that involuntary, palpitating life, and could neither look out on it from her luxurious shelter as a mere spectator, nor hide her eyes in selfish complaining.  (751)

Here Dorothea's vision moves, as Eliot's novel does, from details to more abstract ruminations or reflections. The process of finding meaning and discovering duty is figured as a process of opening up, of allowing oneself to be penetrated by what is outside self. The humble vision of everyday people doing what must be done fills Dorothea with a sense of connection, which will inspire her to commit an act of generosity on behalf of Lydgate and Rosamond. The psychic and moral groundwork laid by Dorothea's abstract desire to do what is right, what is beneficial, what needs doing, causes her to open up to life, and life furnishes the necessary information about what needs to be done. As is the case with Huck Finn considering whether to turn Jim over to the authorities as a runaway slave, Dorothea's moral inspiration arises from the moment as her internal emotional crisis mixes with the texture of her immediate experience.

Discerning value in the details of everyday life without some higher authority or sacred text to act as a decoder involves a considerable degree of ambiguity and complexity. Events, people, and things often resist translation, and one's initial take on the significance of any particular encounter or event is often subject to substantial revision. In the interest of convincingly portraying and inculcating this process of grappling with the often slippery or elusive meanings of daily existence, the realist novel generally abandons the editorializing gesture of the sentimental novelists who occasionally step out from behind the stage curtain to tell the audience how to interpret or respond to certain events or characters (e.g., Stowe's famous injunction to her readers that "they see to it that they feel right" on the issue of slavery [*Uncle Tom's Cabin* 385]). Instead of contending for a particular response or arguing for a certain moral or political program, "realism," William Dean Howells writes, "is richly content with portraying human experiences" ("Introduction" viii). The realist models and recommends the process of closely studying the main actors, their context, and the intricacy of the problems facing them.

Something of the promise and limitations of this approach can be seen in Howells's greatest novel, *A Hazard of New Fortunes* (1890). The protagonist, Basil March, moves to New York to become editor of a new journal, a job much better suited to his literary gifts than working for an insurance company. In describing the March family's relocation to New York and the editor's search for a wide range of writers and picturesque materials, Howells paints a panoramic

portrait of urban life. His novel abounds in richly detailed descriptions of people representing the socio-economic spectrum, including recent immigrants,
transplanted Southerners, old money and the newly rich, artists and writers.
The points of view expressed by these characters include a property-is-theft
socialism, a conservative Gospel of Wealth capitalism, and a remnant of the
Old South's feudal aristocratic perspective. The crisis of Howells's novel, a
bloody riot, reflects the harsh inequities of capitalism in the late nineteenth
century and the class conflict simmering just below the surface of New York
society, but Howells's very dedication to the close observation giving the novel
its richness also blocks it from making a Stowe-like pitch for action. When violence comes in his novel, he is arrested by the spectacle like some horror-struck
but fascinated witness to a nasty accident.

Indeed, in its emphasis on observation, realism has been said to participate
in the rise of a spectator culture in which individuals conceive of themselves
as observers not actors (see, for instance, Carolyn Porter's *Seeing and Being*).
In this account, over the course of the nineteenth century, people increasingly
distinguished between their public and private selves, between the outward
self that acts in the public sphere and the inward (real and relatively stable)
self that observes the world and considers it from a private position separate
from if not immune to the world's affairs. Republican notions of belonging to
a community and serving the interests of that community disappear; instead,
people generally conceive of their identities and primary allegiances in personal
and private terms. The net effect of these changes is the creation of an individual
who reacts to the passing display of the world's events and changes as though he
or she had no connection with or no ability or duty to intervene in these events.
The reader, the narrator, even the main characters in realist fiction do not so
much act within the world as look at it and react in private, with occasional
forays into the world of action. According to this account, realism sold well
in part because of the appetite for observed "reality," marking or defining the
emergent observer culture.

Critics often subdivide American literary realism into the additional classi-
fications of regionalism and naturalism, but I find regionalism and naturalism
hard to distinguish from realism, at least on any recognizable formal basis. Typically, regionalism denominates the realist novels with rural settings, describing
Midwestern or New England communities or places relatively distant from the
urban centers of commerce and politics. Sometimes the term is used interchangeably with "local color" to name the novelists known for their portrayals
of particularly distinctive and disappearing local customs and peoples (e.g.,
Kate Chopin's accounts of life in New Orleans or Mary Wilkins Freeman's
detailed representations of rural New England). Perhaps because the Midwest

has always struck some as lacking color, Midwestern writers are not spoken of as local colorists but as regionalists. Looking at the roster of writers associated with regionalism or local color, it's hard to avoid the conclusion that one of the chief functions of such terms is to distinguish writers deemed minor from other more important realists. As I can find no substantive formal distinction between those denominated regionalists and those who are classed as realists, I do not emphasize the division.

The distinction between naturalism and realism is similar in that it does not represent a fundamental difference on the definitional level of novelistic form so much as a trend in the themes and subject matter. The naturalist and realist differ in that the realist insists to a greater degree on the importance of consent and human agency. Unlike naturalism, realism insists on the possibility that people can voluntarily structure their relations through agreements and mutual understanding. In *American Literary Realism and the Failed Promise of Contract*, Brook Thomas argues that realism can only be fully understood in relation to notions of consent and contract. From the contractual paradigm dominant in commerce and politics in the late nineteenth century, Mark Twain, William Dean Howells, and Henry James extract a utopian possibility of organizing society through an exchange of promises. This exchange of promises replaces status relations with consensual ones (e.g., Huck's promise not to play tricks on Jim during their raft trip reestablishes their relationship on the basis of "mutual benefit and trust" instead of their racial status) and replaces transcendental moral sanctions with "no higher sanction" than those created by the promises themselves (5, 135, 49). By recording the often determinative persistence of status in race, gender, and class relations, realist novels also expose the extent to which the potential of consent and its legal formulation as contract was unrealized.

The pivotal crisis of the realist text often involves a test of the protagonist's moral agency. Unlike the naturalist, the realist presumes that all people, including those in straitened circumstances, are endowed to some extent with moral agency. The realist focuses on the process of deliberation brought on by moments of crisis: Huck Finn's decision to "go to hell" so that Jim can go free, Silas Lapham's soul-searching as he considers a legal but unseemly stock deal as a means of saving his business, or Isabel Archer's ruminations on life and marriage before the dying embers of a fire. One paradox of these novels is that, while their claim to realism in part derives from the fact that the protagonist must grapple with important ethical questions in the absence of a clear guide, these struggles to extract meaning from life function for readers as a precedent of sorts, teaching us how to think about and respond to life. By modeling a process of moral judgment transcending the divergent social origins of such protagonists as Isabel Archer, Silas Lapham, and Huck Finn, realist fiction offers some comfort to a largely middle-class audience (all three of these realist heroes originally appeared in the pages of the middle-class periodicals – *Macmillan's Magazine*, the *Atlantic Monthly*, and *The Century Magazine*) made anxious by the apparent splits and tensions running through American society in the late nineteenth century (one thinks of xenophobic reactions to certain immigrants, the fear of labor unrest, or the common disapproval of women's suffrage).

By contrast, naturalism tends to portray agency and consent as illusory and to emphasize the determinative force of social divisions. In his or her actions, friendships, and other connections, the naturalist character is largely if not entirely controlled by forces and circumstances beyond his or her control, such as a biologically inherent predisposition to violence and/or an oppressive economic situation. Instead of creating a sense of identification between the reader and the character, naturalist novels often focus on lower-class or more marginal characters, such as Stephen Crane's Maggie or Frank Norris's McTeague, occupying a social position presumably inferior to that of the reader (who unlike the naturalist's protagonist can and does read such fiction). Indeed, part of the freakshow-like allure of these novels derives from the distance between the novel's middle-class readers and its lower-class protagonists. In the naturalists' fiction, the absence of a common ground of moral judgment is both a cause and effect of determinative differences of background, blood, and condition.

Indeed, if one juxtaposes descriptions of McTeague's or Maggie's mental processes with those of Isabel Archer or Silas Lapham, realism and naturalism can seem to occupy different universes. However, it is easy to overstate the clarity and simplicity of this distinction.[1] For instance, as we shall see, James shares with Norris and Crane a taste for excess and shock, and, like the realist, the naturalist finds meaning in experience not religious doctrine and eschews sentimental melodrama (if not sentimental values). In addition, we ought to ask whether the realist character's greater freedom isn't just a matter of degree. Doesn't Huck's apparently innate good nature drive his decision to help Jim to freedom, for instance? Silas Lapham's refusal of a dishonest stock deal seems similarly predictable given his innate character as a "good country" person. The deterministic aspects of moral and psychological character are even more expressly suggested in *A Hazard of New Fortunes*, where Howells's alter ego, Basil March, rejects the notion that external events, even profoundly disturbing events such as the death of a son, can "change us." Instead, March declares, we don't "change at all. We develop." When this internally driven "growth in one direction has stopped; it's begun in another; that's all. The man hasn't been changed by his son's death; it stunned, it benumbed him, but it couldn't change him" (422). How would we class Edna Pontellier's final act of apparent suicide in *The Awakening* (1899) – is it chosen or determined? And, conversely, is Theodore Drieser's Carrie Meeber really wholly without agency? *Sister Carrie* (1900) may prove, in fact, to be only somewhat more determinist than the texts we usually denominate as realist. Often the distinction between naturalist and realist texts boils down to varying degrees of determinism (but what quantum is necessary to make a novel naturalist is hard to determine; even a text such as *McTeague* [1899], often thought of as definitional of naturalism because of its apparently unrelieved determinism, does not seem to include the reader or the author in its vision of life without agency).

As the century draws to a close, individual moral agency seems more and more ephemeral or even illusory at least for people in certain circumstances, and, in its increasing determinism, realist fiction registers the era's waning confidence in human agency. This trend becomes apparent in a comparison of *Huckleberry Finn* and *Pudd'nhead Wilson* by Mark Twain. *Huckleberry Finn* holds out the hope that human relations, including those crossing racial boundaries, can be arranged consensually by individuals with some degree of moral agency – they know right from wrong and can act on that knowledge. As we shall see, *Pudd'nhead Wilson*, published a decade later, seems to foreclose the possibility of such ethical choice, with social relations and the fate of the individual largely determined by social forces beyond the individual's control.

## Realist technique and subject matter

The realists' style is defined by their careful depiction of details present in the scene being described – the dress, speech, and actions of characters as one would find them in their milieu, their neighborhood, jobs, and relationships. Examples abound of this kind of attention to local detail in realist fiction: Stephen Crane's opening description of a brawl among New York street urchins in *Maggie*, Hamlin Garland's portrait of fall plowing in "Under the Lion's Paw," Drieser's painting of Fitzgerald and Moy's saloon in *Sister Carrie*, Howells's description of apartment hunting in Manhattan in *A Hazard of New Fortunes*, and Sarah Orne Jewett's depiction of the New England farmhouse kitchen in *A Country Doctor*. Some of these portraits were lifelike enough for residents and locals to recognize the novel's people and places. For example, George Washington Cable's descriptions of particular homes in New Orleans in *Old Creole Days* (1879) were so accurate that Lafcadio Hearn could readily identify the particular houses described by Cable (*Grandissimes* vii).

Accurately rendering distinctive speech patterns and dialect was something of an obsession with such different writers as Mark Twain, Edward Eggleston, Sarah Orne Jewett, Kate Chopin, George Washington Cable, Thomas Nelson Page, and Charles Chesnutt. Thomas Nelson Page claims that one of his chief aims in writing the series of short stories collected in *Ole Virginia* (1895) was to reproduce the actual speech patterns and dialects of the South (vi). In prefatory material he wrote for the 1913 edition of *The Hoosier School-Master* (originally published in 1871), Edward Eggleston makes a similar claim, connecting his interest in dialect to the influence of Hippolyte Taine's conception of realism as the capturing of the local and particular: "in 1871 Taine's lectures on 'Art in the Netherlands,' or rather Mr. John Durand's translation of them, fell into my hands as a book for editorial review. These discourses are little else than an elucidation of the thesis that the artist of originality will work courageously with the materials he finds in his own environment" (7–8). The closely observed and believably rendered voice is Mark Twain's chief accomplishment in realist technique. Much in Twain, including his plots, is simply too outlandish and unbelievable to qualify as realism. But in the creation of Huck's voice Twain scores an undeniable realistic triumph (regardless of whether Huck's voice is based on black or poor white dialects Twain heard in his youth, which, in "The Negro-Art Hokum" [1926], George Schuyler would argue were virtually identical). To a remarkable degree audiences over the years have accepted Huck's speech patterns, the syntax, and the diction as the aural signs of a believable person. Like a vivid description that can make a pure invention such as a fantastic castle appear in the mind's eye, Twain's masterpiece seems great in proportion to its creation of that unmistakable voice.

In pursuing a detailed rendering of the scenes before them, realists were, to varying degrees, determined to examine subjects, images, or actions previously scorned by sentimental novelists and romancers as common, brutal, or even sordid. So in addition to portraying everyday events, such as ordering lunch for the first time in a Chicago café (*Sister Carrie*) or riding a street car in lower Manhattan (*A Hazard of New Fortunes*), they also described with striking frankness war, suicide, disease, crime, and poverty. John W. De Forest's *Miss Ravenel's Conversion from Secession to Loyalty* (1867) combined historical romance and sentimental melodrama with war scenes of considerable authenticity and honesty. Instead of gallant heroics and unambiguously moral results, De Forest gives his readers the confusion and chaos of battle, vivid depictions of the carnage of war including its haphazard quality and the frequent futility of the horrible sacrifices involved. Many critics have guessed that these scenes influenced Stephen Crane's war novel, *The Red Badge of Courage* (1895).[2]

While the bulk of Crane's earlier novel, *Maggie: A Girl of the Streets (A Story of New York)* (1893), would seem to depart from realism into the precincts of the phantasmagorical and sensationalist, the novel begins with a vivid description of a fight between gangs of boys. This scene was reportedly drawn from Crane's actual observation, and the prose has a pared-down, direct quality as Crane attempts to record what he saw and heard:

> A very little boy stood upon a heap of gravel for the honor of Rum Alley. He was throwing stones at howling urchins from Devil's Row who were circling madly about the heap and pelting at him.
> His infantile countenance was livid with fury. His small body was writhing in the delivery of great, crimson oaths. "Run, Jimmie, run! Dey'll get yehs," screamed a retreating Rum Alley child.
> "Naw," responded Jimmie with a valiant roar, "dese micks can't make me run." (36)

Despite its manifestations of Crane's appetite for the fantastic ("infantile countenance made livid with fury" and a "small body . . . writhing in the delivery of great, crimson oaths"), this scene economically captures the violence, the energy, the juvenile heroics, and the ethnic tensions of the great metropolis. The documentary quality of the portrait is enhanced by Crane's offhand observation, in passing, of people reflexively turning to look at the scuffle, a "curious woman" who leans out of a nearby apartment building, some laborers who pause "for a moment to look at the fight," and a tugboat engineer who lazily hangs from a railing and watches. Crane's raw depiction of the violence is far from squeamish: "A stone had smashed into Jimmie's mouth. Blood was bubbling over his chin and down upon his ragged shirt. Tears made furrows on his dirt-stained cheeks. His thin legs had begun to tremble and turn weak, causing his small body to reel" (37). While much of *Maggie* can be read as a kind of funhouse parody of Jacob Riis's muckraking classic *How the Other Half Lives* (1890), this opening scene feels like an homage to the kind of photographic realism Riis sought.

The realists brought this frank and close attention to detail to their portraits of the inner workings or psychologies of characters, including their sexual desires. A famous, even notorious example of this frankness is Frank Norris's blunt depiction of McTeague's animal lust for Trina ("the fury of a young bull in the heat of high summer") and Trina's "strange" desire for Mac to conquer and subdue her sexually or, as she puts it with considerable economy, to "love me *big*" (31, 180, 135, 186). Far subtler is Kate Chopin's depiction in *The Awakening* of the gradual evolution of Edna Pontellier's feelings and inner turmoil. Chopin convincingly dramatizes how an unnameable and relatively faint discontent grows into a very real emotional disturbance and eventually leads not only to actions and decisions contrary to established arrangements and social customs, but also to catastrophe and death. The initially understated feeling of marital oppression on the one hand and the taste for something better pushes Edna toward a more open-ended and romantic connection with Robert Lebrun, a sexual dalliance with Alcee Arobin, and a sense of her own artistic vocation through her contact with the pianist Mademoiselle Reisz. Throughout the novel Chopin gives the reader the sense that Edna is being continually moved by powerful, barely subterranean currents in her psyche. Famously, in Chapter 42 of *The Portrait of a Lady* (1881), Henry James describes the currents and cross-currents of Isabel Archer's thought as she struggles to comprehend and come to terms with her imprisoning marriage, her miscalculations of motivation and character, and the potential meaning of her marital mistake. Perhaps never before had the inner feelings and reflections of a character been made to seem so much like action, a dramatic and death-defying ballet of feelings and counter-feelings, thoughts and reflections. Reflecting on the novel in his preface to the 1908 edition, James describes Isabel's fireside meditations, her "motionlessly *seeing*," as an "act." His desire was "to make the mere still lucidity of her act as 'interesting' as the surprise of a caravan or the identification of a pirate" (15). Isabel is not only trying to make sense of how she arrived at her present situation, plumbing the mystery of her husband's character and motivation, but she is also trying to recover a sense of value and worth in her life in the wake of her bad mistake. In portraying Isabel's suffering as "an active condition," James brilliantly weaves in both the epistemological and ontological dimensions of her dilemma – she has misread people (Gilbert Osmond, Ralph Touchett, Madame Merle), and despite her mistakes she must still find a way to act and be in the world so as to endow both with meaning and significance (356).

Realist fiction responded to and participated in a period of sweeping and dramatic transformation following the nation's bloodiest war. Among other things, the post-war era included Reconstruction and its failure, the rise of Jim Crow, unprecedented population growth, revolutions in transportation and communications, a vast influx of immigrants and migration of rural Americans to cities, a turbulent economy characterized by a number of bankruptcies, depressions, and panics as well as by an equally staggering record of economic growth (by 1900, the United States produced 35 percent of the world's manufactured goods, more than the combined output of Germany, France, and Great Britain), presidential assassination, and political scandal. Some novels plainly criticize or lament certain aspects of this widespread transformation of American society. Both Howells's *The Rise of Silas Lapham* and *A Hazard of*

*New Fortunes* are built around the contrast between rural, familial values and urban, corporate values, a contrast that reflects the period's anxiety over the shift from comparatively close-knit communities bound by blood and shared tradition toward an urban world of strangers bound only by contracts. The lyric but melancholy stories of Sarah Orne Jewett's *Country of Pointed Firs* (1896) record the close-knit rural and seaside New England communities on the brink of extinction. Extolling the supposedly more authentic life of the small organic and rural community in contrast to an urban modernity overwhelmed by the gross tide of capitalism, industrialism, and immigration, realist novels by Howells, Jewett, Twain, and others reflect what Jackson Lears has described as an important cultural tendency toward anti-modernism at the end of the nineteenth century (57–58, 218). The famous mechanized massacre that ends Twain's *A Connecticut Yankee in King Arthur's Court* (1889) is both a giddy recognition of the triumph of industrialism as well as a bitter critique of its destructive force. Of course, rather than criticizing all efforts to "modernize" American society, some realist novels frankly mourn the fact that such changes have proved of little impact or are altogether illusory. Mark Twain's *Pudd'nhead Wilson* (1894) and Charles Chesnutt's *The Marrow of Tradition* (1901) both critically engage what these authors see as the lost opportunity of Reconstruction to push American society in a progressive direction.

Often, in realist fiction, broader concerns about social transformation take the form of the main character's roller-coaster career, the discovery of a hidden identity or creation of a new one, or the character's removal to completely different circumstances. In *The Rise of Silas Lapham* (one of many "rise of" fictions and biographies describing an upward reversal of fortunes), financial success radically transforms the Lapham family's situation, relocating them from rural Vermont to Boston. But Howells raises questions at the outset about whether the family can be changed in any essential way by this alteration of their circumstances and, if so, whether that change is positive. The Laphams have the money required for high society, but they don't know how to spend it. While Mrs. Lapham is generally good-natured and not envious or socially competitive, a cutting comment about the unfashionable neighborhood in which they live drives her to suggest to Silas that they move. Silas becomes consumed with questions of whether he can measure up to such high-society gentlemen as Bromfield Corey. The question posed by Howells's reversal-of-fortunes narrative is plain: has the Laphams' upward mobility, the revolution of their family's fortunes, been beneficial or harmful? Ultimately, we see that Howells has inverted the significance of the success narrative: Silas's financial success is a moral fall, and, conversely, his financial failure is his salvation. Twain was similarly fascinated by the strangeness of a rapidly changing society in which fortunes could be made and lost overnight, and his tales are pre-occupied with the wheel of fortune, a character's sudden rise or fall, which often depends on the success or failure of some hoax, fraud, stunt, or practical joke (one thinks here of the Duke and King in *Huckleberry Finn* or Hank Morgan in *Connecticut Yankee*). For Twain, the success of these manipulations raises questions as to whether people are generally capable of distinguishing truth and falsehood in the "gilded age," and whether permanent values can survive the volatility of the era. Realist novels are often both captivated and repelled by the prospect of indeterminate and shifting conceptions of meaning.

The fascination and ambivalence the realist feels for change can be felt in Crane's use of the figure of metamorphosis in *The Red Badge of Courage* – the metamorphosis of separate individuals into an army unit and the subsequent transformation of the unit of men into a machine or beast. One moment we are focused on Henry's particular concerns, the next moment we are confronted with an image of "the regiment . . . swinging off into the darkness. It was now like one of those moving monsters wending with many feet . . . There was an occasional flash and glimmer of steel from the backs of all these huge crawling reptiles" (126). In battle, Henry is a coward, a barbarian, a beast, a hero. He pursues the enemy "like a dog," an "infernal fool," "a war devil" (198–99). Henry's shapeshifting is radical enough to frustrate the attribution of any definite meaning to his actions. These abrupt changes tend to empty the conflict and the men's roles in it of any clear, transcendental significance. The combatants are turned into bits of meat: "We'll git swallowed" (204). In his moment of personal honor leading a charge, Henry runs not toward a goal but "*as* toward a goal" (205, my emphasis). The very notion that he is courageous is contradicted by his physiognomy: "His face was drawn hard and tight with the stress of his endeavor. His eyes were fixed in a lurid glare. And with his soiled and disordered dress, his red and inflamed features surmounted by the dingy rag with its spot of blood, his wildly swinging rifle and banging accouterments, he looked to be an insane soldier" (205). Such notions as bravery and personal honor seem highly improbable, even ludicrous, in the hectic chaos of war. The book's ending is similarly open to different interpretations. Like Henry's charge, Crane's novel moves "as toward a goal or end" rather than arriving at a definite conclusion.

The connection between realism and change is not accidental. Realism comes of age in an era influenced by Charles Darwin's conception of evolution and Herbert Spencer's application of that concept to human society. In "The Future of Fiction," Hamlin Garland, the Midwestern realist, connects realism (his term is "veritism") with the advent of evolutionary thought. Evolution, as announced by Darwin and Spencer, gives realism the possibility of looking into the future, extrapolating from the evolutionary past, what Garland terms a "prevision":

> Until men came to see system and progression, and endless but definite succession in art and literature as in geologic change, until the law of progress was enunciated, no conception of the future, and no reasonable history of the past, could be formulated. Once prove literature and art subject to social conditions, to environment and social conformation, and dominance of the epic in one age and the drama in another became as easy to understand and to infer as any other fact of a people's history. It has made the present the most critical and self-analytical of all ages known to us.  (515)

The fiction of the immediate past was romantic, says Garland, citing Hugo and Scott as examples, but the fiction of the future will be realistic, more democratic in outlook and impressionistic in style in the sense that it expresses the perception and experience of the viewer/witness/author. It will be more about character and less about language (which is somewhat paradoxical in that it is through language that these experiences and impressions are registered). In its honest and apt rendering of the local and particular nature of the texture of life, the realist novel will speak to the future about its own era. Garland's conception sees realism not only as commenting on the evolutionary processes of human existence but as participating in those processes as a kind of progressive manifestation of human evolution.

Whether viewed positively as progression or negatively as regression (e.g., McTeague's return to an animal level of existence after his brief upward mobility as a dentist) or whether the process proves real or illusory, the notion that human beings grow and develop over time furnishes the basic template for the realist's conception of character. *The Red Badge of Courage* repeatedly (if ironically) models the notion of development or growth as crucially important to the main character. Henry anticipates that his war experience will be characterized by gallant deeds and chivalric warriors (117). By the end of the novel, these imaginings have been shattered, and Henry is glad to shed them: "He found that he could look back upon the brass and bombast of his earlier gospels and see them truly. He was gleeful when he discovered that he now despised them" (230). Crane's irony prevents us from simply summing his novel up as a tale of disillusionment through which the main character has been stripped of his romantic pretensions and illusions and thrust into a more honest and accurate acceptance of reality – the tale of a boy becoming a man: "He had been to touch the great death, and found that, after all, it was but the great death. He was a man" (230). Henry's lack of agency, the way he is more acted upon than acting, obstructs this easy interpretation even as the narrative overtly insists upon it. We cannot buy, I think, the notion of development, because Henry does not seem capable of it. Yet Crane's setting up of his novel as a tale of growth, even if to criticize or cast doubt on the model, attests to the grip of the evolutionary framework on the fictive imagination of the era.

Many realist novels often denominated as local color or regionalist fiction address the massive social changes of the latter part of the nineteenth century through the figure of memory. These fictions often seem to recommend the impossible, a return to a pastoral moment before the onslaught of modernization. In *The Country of Pointed Firs* (1896), Sarah Orne Jewett records and mourns the passing of a simpler way of life – its particular accents, scents, knowledge, social customs, and flavors. Jewett and Mary Wilkins Freeman use the figure of the older women and men left behind by the migration of younger folk to the cities in pursuit of economic opportunity to personify the earlier and, in many ways, better time. Similarly wanting to recover a simpler, more natural and authentic manner of life, Edward Eggleston painstakingly recreates the speech patterns, manners, and customs of rural Midwesterners.[3] Of course, such novels depend for their appeal on change – local customs must be an endangered species for a novelist's description of them to have the values of rarity and nostalgia. The Civil War was, in effect, a defeat for the primacy of regional allegiance. The war represented an insistence by means of federal power that certain local practices (slavery) could be trumped by national norms (of course, what values and practices were perceived as "national" or "regional" in this case depended on one's point of view). The rise of the federal government's power after the war was attended by the growing dominance of the idea of national identity, which in turn made peculiar traits of particular groups and locales seem more valuable. Paradoxically, local-color or regionalist celebrations of the particular identities, manners, speech, and customs of particular groups or parts of the nation depended for their commercial success on the very mechanisms of modern transportation and communication (e.g., the interconnection of the nation by a web of railroad and telegraph lines) dooming such piquant and distinctive ways of life and unifying the nation. While the local-color or regionalist novel sets up a contrast between a nostalgic "then" and a modern "now," these portraits of dying customs and speech are oddly timeless, as though the fast-fading customs, practices, and particular societies could somehow be lifted out of time. Eggleston contends that, despite the inevitable extinction of such local traits, we define our national character by reference to these obsolescent customs, paradoxically looking to what we've lost to define what we are (7).

Memory as a marker of both loss and preservation takes on a particular significance in the South, where it is associated with the defeat of a way of life. This defeat – the overturning of an entire social, economic, and political system, and self-conception – constitutes, as C. Vann Woodward has compellingly argued, the distinctive burden of Southern history. Many novels and stories of the realist period (by both Southern and Northern writers) take up that seismic shift by recalling a more genteel antebellum era. For instance, Thomas Nelson Page's collection of stories, *In Ole Virginia,* portrays the antebellum South as a society connected by feelings of affection and loyalty more honorable than the marketplace values animating America in the late nineteenth century. Some of the prominent novelists taking up the subject of the transformation of the South were Northerners such as John W. De Forest and Albion Tourgee. De Forest's novel *Miss Ravenel's Conversion from Secession to Loyalty* (1867) mixes elements of the historical romance and the sentimental novel with realism. For De Forest, slavery and the arrested society built upon it had to be cleared away to make room for progress: "It must make room for something more consonant with the railroad, electric-telegraph, printing-press, inductive philosophy, and practical Christianity" (49). The resolution of the novel's standard romantic triangle, told in conventional sentimental and melodramatic terms, symbolizes the post-bellum sectional reunion hoped for by De Forest and many others. In *A Fool's Errand* (1879), Albion Tourgee, a Northern lawyer who participated in the "Reconstruction" of North Carolina, portrayed the ideology of white supremacy as a remnant of slavery retarding progress in the South. Black writers, such as Frances Harper and Charles Chesnutt, also described the South after the war in both hopeful and despairing terms as the promises of Reconstruction faded to failure.

For many realists, the central storyline of nineteenth-century history was the shift toward more consensual modes of human association – the rise of consent and decline of status as principles structuring society. From this perspective, the Civil War was fought over the primacy of consent to American law and society. As Abraham Lincoln framed the issue, "No man is good enough to govern another without that other's consent. I say this is the leading principle – the sheet-anchor – of American republicanism" (266). In opposition to this line of reasoning, George Fitzhugh contended that slavery was justified precisely because consent cannot properly be adopted as an organizing principle for individuals and society. Anything can be consented to, Fitzhugh warned, including such horrors as polygamy and interracial marriage (Crane *Race* 43–46). Many realists were sympathetic to Lincoln's reasoning. And many felt that consent was practically speaking the only possible means of creating social bonds given the massive social transformations of the late nineteenth century.

Other models of social connection, such as a shared cultural heritage and tradition, seemed increasingly remote in the face of the cultural diversity brought
about by immigration of foreign nationals and migration of rural Americans
to cities. Realists, such as William Dean Howells and Charles Chesnutt, hoped
that consent would not only prove capable of providing social cohesion and
coherence, but that it would be superior to allowing the dead hand of the past
in the form of tradition or blood to shape our lives and our relations with
others.

Before undertaking a more detailed examination of the realists' notions of
consent, we need to pause and acknowledge the importance of this principle to the marketplace. Like its cousin, the newspaper, the nineteenth-century
novel was a creature of mass production and consumption, depending for its
very existence on some insight into what, by common consent, would qualify as a worthwhile or engaging fictional entertainment. Whether sympathetic
or skeptical, fictional depictions of consent by such novelists as Kate Chopin,
Charles Chesnutt, William Dean Howells, Mark Twain, and Henry James con-
spicuously try to shape the popular taste that creates a market for their works.
For these writers, the novel, as both a creature and creator of consensus, has a
form of cultural authority, which they variously conceive in social, religious,
philosophical, political, or aesthetic terms. Even as they attempt to influence
the popular consensus about fictional entertainments, these novelists, in deal-
ing with such controversial issues as race relations and divorce, also invoke the
potential of consent to transform society.

In *The Marrow of Tradition* (1901), Charles Chesnutt makes consent and
contract central to his exploration of the failure of Reconstruction and his
recommendation for the future of race relations. Chesnutt embraced the notion
that American citizenship is fundamentally grounded on "the ideal of volitional
allegiance," as James Kettner puts it (197). Similarly, for reformers, such as
Booker T. Washington, Elizabeth Cady Stanton, and Susan B. Anthony, contract
was both the mode and sign of just human relations. Booker T. Washington, for
example, made the mechanism of commercial contract central to his program
for racial uplift. If equipped to compete, Washington urged, black Americans
would be able to find security and freedom transcending race in economic
partnership with white America. For feminists, such as Elizabeth Cady Stanton,
Susan B. Anthony, and Victoria Woodhull, the symbol of free and equal contract
illuminated the way marriage was mired in anti-consensual notions of gender
status and role. Stanton and others felt that making marriage more genuinely
contractual would strike a blow for all women.[4]

These reformers were hardly alone in using the language of contract. In 1861,
Sir Henry Maine famously observed that the history of progressive societies was

characterized by a shift "from Status to Contract," and many eighteenth- and nineteenth-century intellectuals considered contract to be the appropriate and inevitable means of structuring human association (182). For Adam Smith, Jeremy Bentham, and John Stuart Mill, contractual freedom was "the fundamental and indispensable requisite of progress" (Williston 365–66). William Graham Sumner, the Yale sociologist famous for his laissez-faire and social-Darwinist approach, expressed the prevailing turn-of-the-century appreciation that contract promotes a free and changing community and untrammeled individual development:

> In our modern state, and in the United States more than anywhere else, the social structure is based on contract, and status is of the least importance . . . [i]t seems impossible that anyone who has studied the matter should doubt that we have gained immeasurably [through the shift from status to contract], and that our farther gains lie in going forward, not in going backward. The feudal ties can never be restored. If they could be restored they would bring back personal caprice, favoritism, sycophancy, and intrigue. A society based on contract is a society of free and independent men, who form ties without favor or obligation, and co-operate without cringing or intrigue. A society based on contract, therefore, gives the utmost room and chance for individual development, and for all the self-reliance and dignity of a free man.[5]   (*What the Social Classes Owe* 15–16)

A conservative judiciary echoed these sentiments, using the concept of liberty of contract to symbolize certain ethical limits to the power of democratic majorities. While, early in the nation's legal history, bench and bar increasingly tended to characterize law as solely an expression of political power, higher law, the notion that law must be grounded in a transcendent morality, began a second life in such liberty of contract cases as *Calder* v. *Bull* (1798) and *Dartmouth College* (1819). These cases suggested that, in certain circumstances, the judiciary would check the legislature's power to interfere with private contracts (Crane *Race* 36–40). When reduced to its essential contours as a voluntary and reciprocal exchange, the contractual quid pro quo conjured for John Marshall and many others a primary scene of free and consensual relations among peers that was antecedent to all law.[6]

Early in *The Marrow of Tradition*, Chesnutt stages a confrontation between two black domestic employees of a Southern family with aristocratic pretensions to illustrate the importance of consent and contract to the ongoing transformation of American society. The novel is particularly concerned with the transition from interracial relations based on status to those formed by consent.[7] Mammy Jane's fond and respectful deference to the Carterets, her employers, is a remnant of a time when "society was dependent, throughout all its details, on status" and exemplifies the sentimental and quasi-familial relationship thought by Southerners, such as Fitzhugh, Page, Pendleton, and Simms, to be the antithesis of the modern relation of contract (Sumner *What the Social Classes Owe* 16). By contrast, the Carteret's young nurse typifies the contractual form of relation. Her arrangement with the Carterets is "purely a matter of business; she sold her time for their money" (Chesnutt *Marrow* 42). Her identity and place in society are in flux, and contract furnishes the means by which she structures her rights and duties within that society, not personal affection or sentimental reverence for an old social order. Negroes of the old school, such as Mammy Jane and her grandson Jerry, are stuck – their identities, roles, and forms of social connection are fixed. However, the "new negroes" despised by Mammy Jane as well as the Carterets are in motion, using contract to climb "the ladder of life" (42). As the encounter between Mammy Jane and the young nurse suggests, defining oneself by contract (for example, identifying the young nurse by profession, not by status-driven titles such as Major, Aunt, Uncle, or Mammy), implicitly allows for identity to shift as one changes positions or forms new contracts, new connections, new consensual relations.

The young nurse may be at the "chip on the shoulder stage," blocking the kind of emotional connection that enriches human association, but Chesnutt's point is that it is a *stage*, a step in the direction of a truly consensual and equal exchange that then can form the basis of a redeemed intimacy. Chesnutt does not drive a wedge between contract and affective relations, such as family ties, but connects them, arguing not for cold, economically driven connections but ultimately for relations in which affect is tied to consent and reciprocity. Thus, Chesnutt contrasts Mammy Jane's connection to the Carterets with the "old-fashioned" yet genuinely reciprocal bond of mutual affection characterizing Mr. Delamere's relation with Sandy Jenkins – a bond that does not prove counterfeit as Mr. Delamere saves Sandy, his friend, at the expense of his grandson, Tom, his blood relation (26, 206–09, 222–25).

Even *The Marrow of Tradition*'s most dramatic evocation of family relations frames kinship and moral duty within a contractual pattern of offer and counteroffer. In the novel's climax, the estranged half-sisters of different races, Janet Miller and Olivia Carteret, finally face each other. Janet's only child has been killed in a race riot incited by white supremacists, including Major Carteret, seeking political power. Ironically, the riot has put the Carteret's only child in desperate need of the medical expertise of Janet's husband, a black doctor. Olivia Carteret comes to plead with the Millers for help. Despite her own loss, Janet sends her husband to aid the Carteret baby. In its renunciation of the "strict justice" or fair trade of a son for a son, Janet's compassion at first glance might seem to transcend or reject contract. However, Chesnutt stages this scene as a confrontation and negotiation between equals, between sisters. Janet's compassion is presented as a counteroffer to Olivia's offer of familial recognition and money in return for medical care for her son. Responding "that you may know that a woman may be foully wronged, and yet may have a heart to feel, even for one who has injured her, you may have your child's life, if my husband can save it," Janet prominently terms her gesture of unmerited and incommensurable compassion as an act that is to be perceived and understood by another – "that you may know." And, though Janet's comment is ostensibly intended as the final word between the sisters, it inevitably summons an acknowledgment by Olivia – "God will bless you for a noble woman!" As a result, Olivia declares that their communications are not at an end but at a beginning (329). By imagining Janet's compassion as part of an exchange, Chesnutt suggests that ethical obligation and even sacrifice are a part of the communication that arrives at consensual relations. The sense of justice impels one to conversation, broadly conceived as including action as well as speech, and that conversation has the potential to create the ethical consensus and reciprocity required for any worthy interpersonal bond. Whether Janet and Olivia will have future consensual relations grounded in mutual respect is left open, as Chesnutt's realistic acknowledgment of the uncertain future of American race relations and insistence on some measure of individual agency in charting the course of those relations.

In *A Modern Instance* (1882), William Dean Howells uses a disagreement between a lawyer, Atherton, and his friend Halleck to argue against a slavish deference to tradition and for a more consensual or contractual notion of marriage. Halleck is in love with Marcia Hubbard, a married woman who has been deserted by her cynical journalist husband, Bartley Hubbard. Halleck wants Marcia to divorce Bartley so that he can marry her. Atherton is thoroughly repulsed by this course of action, asking whether Halleck really proposes "to give your father's honest name, and the example of a man of your own blameless life, in support of conditions that tempt people to marry with a mental reservation, and that weaken every marriage bond with the guilty hope of escape whenever a fickle mind, or secret lust, or wicked will may dictate?" (354). Atherton plainly fears the advent of uncertainty and experimentalism such an approach to marriage would entail. Halleck responds, "I will take my chance with the men and women who have been honest enough to own their mistake, and to try to repair it." He declares he will "preach by my life that marriage has no sanctity but what love gives it, and that, when love ceases, marriage ceases, before heaven. If the laws have come to recognize that, by whatever fiction, so much the better for the laws!" (355). The argument between Halleck and Atherton vividly reveals the stakes involved in favoring consent over tradition. Atherton fears that Halleck's endorsement of consent as the sole basis and justification of marriage will destabilize society, as people can dissolve their connections at whim. By contrast, Halleck's approach to marriage, like realist fiction itself, is frankly experimental, open-ended, and tolerant of change. It allows for mistakes and the possibility that such errors might be corrected by dissolving marriages and trying again. Also, Halleck's vision is decidedly not transcendent. Marriage, in Halleck's view, is a human-made arrangement authorized and governed by no higher authority than the consent of the parties. The reference to heaven suggests that God does not so much want human beings to make life decisions in simplistic adherence to clear rules laid down from on high but to adjust their relations in accordance with their own insights and conclusions. By being willing to "take [his] chance" with this more experimental and consensual approach, Halleck accepts that his way does not entail the comfort of certainty. What will happen remains a question.

The disagreement between Atherton and Halleck should, I think, be read against the backdrop of the conflict over slavery leading to the Civil War. Halleck adopts Lincoln's theme of consent, and Atherton takes up Fitzhugh's warning about the monstrosities human consent can produce. And, at least in one way, Howells's novel proves Fitzhugh's point: that adopting consent as a legitimating principle opens American society to experiments, including the revision of one of the most basic and fundamental of social relations. Marriage, after all, is not only arguably the most fundamental contract in the establishment of society, but it is also a unique form of contract, magically converting consent to blood in the supposed unity of the husband and wife. Liberalizing divorce would turn the marriage contract into a mere pact, something that can be dismantled as well as constructed, making it a matter of human law, not divine sanction. Like the pragmatists, Howells endorses an experimental and instrumentalist approach to social arrangements, asking what will work rather than what is proper. As William James puts it, the "pragmatist talks about truths in the plural, about their utility and satisfactoriness, about the success with which they work" (*Pragmatism* 34). A few years later, in *At Fault* (1890), Kate Chopin similarly argues for a more liberal approach to divorce, and her novel recasts marital dissolution as more natural than a rigid adherence to traditional notions of the sanctity of marriage. The fluidity of human relations symbolized by divorce mirrors the volatility of the Cane River which dominates the landscape of *At Fault* and corresponds to the dynamic and changing social context of the lives of the people who live along its banks.

## Tensions, divergences, and extremes within realism

While realist novels share much in the way of technique and subject matter, as we noted at the outset, this fiction is also characterized by a set of tensions or divergences. For instance, while both Howells and James, like George Eliot, are drawn to the idea that value and meaning must be wrested from experience, their portraits of that process differ in important ways. Howells's portraits of the determinative moral crisis tend toward a kind of transparency, and the problems posed by his narrative are resolved by the preexisting good nature of the character, a moral essence which like sacred text trumps or clarifies experience. James, by contrast, refuses both character type and transparency, plunging the reader into the complex and dense web of relations and facts tethering his main characters. The idea of moral agency also divides realism. Some lean toward free will, others toward determinism. And while some seem to conceive of realism as a literary program enacting a form of balanced reason and insight, others want to use realism as a platform for jumping off into sensation and a passion for the extremes. The following discussion traces some of the important rifts and trends in realism.

### Degrees of transparency: Howells and James

To varying degrees, Howells and James embraced an idea of moral insight as less a form of obedience to a preexisting script and more a process of trial and error. They resisted the kind of conventional and static equivalences between characters/events and significances/values one finds in the sentimental novel and the historical romance (e.g., in *Uncle Tom's Cabin* [1852] and *The Last of the Mohicans* [1826], respectively, Simon Legree's and Magua's appearances offer unambiguous signs of their moral depravity). However, some of James's comments about Howells give us a revealing (if slanted) view of the degree to which Howells accepts symbolically transparent characters and events, while James wants something more elusive, less conventional, and more representative of the experiential tangle from which we attempt to extract a sense of some meaning and worth. In these comments, James tends to associate Howells's brand of realism with a focus on the externals, the observable details of life: "[Howells] seems to have resolved himself, however, into one who can write solely of what his fleshly eyes have seen." James complains that Howells lacks "a really *grasping* imagination" (Anesko 15). "[G]rasping" here suggests a degree of imaginative agency that is absent in Howells. In another letter James humorously but critically noted his appreciation of Howells: "Through thick and thin I continue to enjoy him or rather thro' thinner and thinner" (Anesko

16). The opposite of Howells's superficiality, his thinness, would be a "thickness" – a term suggestive of opacity, complexity, and difficulty. The thinness or transparency of Howells's fiction goes hand in glove with what James sees as his greater conventionality, his willingness "to insist more upon the restrictions & limitations, the *a priori* formulas & interdictions, of our common art, than upon that priceless freedom which is to me *the* thing that makes it worth practising" (Anesko 266). James implies that Howells's conventionality results in a prose that is too easily paraphrased to be able to give nuance and complexity and depth to the characters and scenes depicted. Because the events and characters are too readily translatable, they mislead by failing to engage the reader in the arduous process of making meaning out of experience.

We can flesh out this distinction by comparing the main characters and central moral crises in Howells's *The Rise of Silas Lapham* and James's *The Portrait of a Lady*. The comparison will implicitly ask how one addresses ethical problems, to what extent a preexisting morality or inherent moral nature determines the outcome of the crisis, whether the outcome is predictable, and whether that predictability indicates an allegorical approach to representing moral issues. As we shall see, Howells's characters are less fluid, less obscure than James's, bearing a resemblance to Harriet Beecher Stowe's or Maria Cummins's fiction and connecting Howells's version of realism to the sentimental fiction he would supplant.

*The Rise of Silas Lapham* opens with an interview of the title character by Bartley Hubbard (the caddish husband of *A Modern Instance*). In the course of the interview, Hubbard reveals that he sees and will portray Lapham by means of a shorthand of cultural stereotypes and narrative conventions: "Worked in the fields in the summers and went to school winters: regulation thing? . . . Parents poor, of course" (4). Hubbard categorizes Lapham's life by means of such standard narratives as the return of the prodigal son (8). When Lapham signals his discomfort with this reductive approach to his life story, Hubbard assures Lapham that his portrait will "come out all right," and, we are told, "in fact it did so." Hubbard's account of Lapham's "early life, its poverty and its hardships" and his "devoted" and "unpretentious" parents turns out to be apt (4–5). In other words, Bartley's use of types and conventions to describe Lapham's parents as good country people and his subject's upbringing as hard but wholesome captures something Lapham would see as true (5). Though cynical, Hubbard has mastered certain narrative categories and gestures that Lapham and Howells's readers will see as useful for the classification of human facts. The aptness of Hubbard's portrait is confirmed by Lapham's wife's comment that she and Lapham are "both country people" stuck in their "country ways" (25).

Howells is, of course, doing something far more complex in his novel than Hubbard is doing in his profile. After all, the novelist distances us from both the journalist's cynical invocation of cultural stereotypes and Lapham's inarticulate discomfort with the reductive portrait. This distance suggests a superior perspective capable of seeing how Hubbard's types work or don't work to capture Silas who, as we see, exceeds easy types of the crude journalistic stripe. Though generally and essentially true, such characterizations cannot adequately account for the Laphams' lives in Boston. Silas and Persis Lapham are not entirely immune to or unchanged by Silas's financial success. In the country, Persis would not have fretted over comments regarding the neighborhood in which she lives, and Silas wouldn't have been subject to the kinds of compulsive desire for social advancement that afflict him in Boston. In addition, Silas's deeply personal attachment to his mineral paint business has, as Persis recognizes, a kind of "poetry" to it: "his paint was more than a business to him" (40–41). Silas's passion for the paint, his complete belief in its inherent superiority, transforms his feelings about his business into a kind of religious fervor that leads to the wrongful termination of his partnership with Milton Rogers. In Silas's feelings for his business, we see a complex mix of symbolism, emotion, history, and faith. This transformative passion cannot be encompassed by Hubbard's cynical use of narrative types and conventions to describe Silas. A form of psychological excess, defying Hubbard's expectations, Silas's passion exceeds type and complicates Silas's own self-conception (manifest in his ultimate approval of Hubbard's portrait).

The resolution of the novel's central moral crisis, however, evacuates such complications, reaffirming Silas's identity as a good country person. Though Silas goes back and forth confusedly wondering what to do to get out of his increasingly dire financial straits, we know that he won't sell worthless stock to strangers as his former partner Rogers suggests. To ease Silas's conscience, Rogers introduces an additional transactional layer in the form of some Englishmen who will buy Silas's stock, knowing its true value. Silas then, Rogers argues, will be innocent of any subsequent sale of the stock. In addition, baffled by the complexity of these transactions, Persis, who has played the role of wifely conscience for Silas, is incapable of advising him in this matter. Yet, even as Silas wrestles unaided with the complexities of the transaction, his great and growing financial need, and his conscience, the reader is never really in doubt about the outcome (262–72). At bottom, Silas's values are as clear as his essential self is, though the social and economic circumstances as well as mixed human feelings may confuse matters. Silas's salvation (the irony of the title is that his financial fall is his moral rise) is his ability to return to a better, truer self – his country self – a return suggesting in its very possibility that Silas was essentially unchanged by his success and relocation to Boston all along and that the needed moral norms for solving his moral dilemma were always present in the form of his inherently good nature.

Through Hubbard's interview at the opening of the novel, Howells raises the question of the adequacy of such types to represent human character – do they tell us who and what Silas really is? The novel ends up ratifying their adequacy and to that extent insists that human character is transparent, readily interpreted and understood, and predictable in the face of moral crisis. Howells's portrait of Silas suggests a faith in the notion of a fundamentally fixed and essential character – the real, deep-down person – and an empirical confidence that we can fully know others' essential selves as well as our own. In effect, Howells seems to be caught between psychological models. He is apparently willing to entertain a more mutable sense of character as formed and reformed in response to changes in environment (e.g., the Laphams's move to Boston) and complex emotional factors (e.g., Silas's desire to identify with yet distinguish himself from his long-suffering parents), but, to provide an emotionally satisfying resolution of his main character's crisis, he falls back on the moral sense psychology of the eighteenth and early nineteenth centuries, which supposes that human beings are implanted with an innate and permanent emotional register of right and wrong. This natural or divinely given moral compass is what Stowe expressly appeals to in *Uncle Tom's Cabin* when she urges that we see to our feelings on the issue of slavery.[8]

In *The Portrait of a Lady*, James gives us a far more open-ended and complex sense of character as something much harder to know and predict as well as a more ambiguous and uncertain conception of moral insight and action. Early in the novel we are told that Isabel Archer strikes Ralph Touchett as "natural," and as being "some one in particular" (48, 47). These descriptive terms have the interesting narrative value of giving the reader the beginnings of an impression without defining or limiting that impression. Ralph finds Isabel to be "not insipid" (46). James's use of the double negative or litotes works as it does in Melville's "Benito Cereno" by simultaneously putting in our minds two opposed concepts – insipidity and lack of insipidity. Though it gives us an idea of what Ralph values, the phrase "not insipid" does not really tell us what she is. Instead it holds us in suspense as to the nature of her character, and, as we discover, this is a suspense that carries through to the end of the novel. We never arrive at a final resolution of Isabel's character into a certain or essential self. Unlike that of Silas, Isabel's identity is less an inherent essence than an outcome of whatever course of action she embarks upon.

If we take Ralph's approach, we appreciate Isabel for her potential, despite or even because of the fact that we don't know the direction that potential will take. Isabel is capable of real change, as her friend Henrietta Stackpole worryingly observes: "She's taking different views, a different colour, and turning away from her old ideals" (109). Isabel is capable of genuine surprises, such as turning down Lord Warburton's marriage proposal. In the interest of seeing something more of the direction Isabel's as yet unformed capacities might take, Ralph asks his father "to put a little wind in her sails" by leaving her a fortune (160). The simple figure of wind and sails, of course, puts us in mind of movement and change. When his father wonders whether it isn't "immoral" to make "everything so easy" for Isabel, Ralph suggests that their generous act will be redeemed by Isabel's "execution" of her "good impulses" (162). Yet, given the briefness of his acquaintance with Isabel and her youth, Ralph's gesture is more a roll of the dice than a considered judgment about a fully formed and stable character. Indeed, when viewed from the perspective of someone who conceives of moral improvement as the result of rational plans, there is something vaguely oxymoronic about the phrase "good impulses." In Ralph's gamble and his appreciation of the creative potential of Isabel's impulsive nature, we see James's esteem for risk and the inchoate desire or drive. Isabel's "goodness," rather than a given like Silas's character as a good country person, is a potential for action, surprise, and the uncovering of unforeseen value and moral connection. She will not resolve her moral crisis by reference to a moral script or by a return to some prior better self but by improvisation and a discovery of value in experience.

Like her creator, Isabel is "fond of the unexpected" and has a taste for the richness and density of "thick detail" (133, 114). Her attraction to Osmond derives in part from the fact that he is hard to read, hard to place; the absence of the usual markers of identity and social role makes him a kind of pure potentiality of signification: he could be anything. Isabel's error of judgment or interpretation is to see in Osmond a kindred soul of open-ended possibility, but, as it turns out, "she had not read him right." He is not going anywhere. He is not a poor lonely but beautiful soul waiting for someone to put wind in his sails to "launch his boat for him" (357). He is fixed, terminal, contemptuous, willfully not interested in change or development but obsessed with the possession of others as well as of himself. He is bent on controlling and arranging people and things in scenes (such as the perfect drawing-room conversation with just the right sort of characters and beautiful objects staged in impeccable taste) which will have the static quality of a still life. Indeed, Osmond comes to despise Isabel for her potentiality, her many ideas, her propensity to throw off his domestic designs. He tells "her one day that she had too many ideas and that she must get rid of them" (359). To Osmond, Isabel would be better as a beautiful exterior emptied of the passions, intuitions, and insights that propel people to act (359). When Isabel's eyes are finally opened to the rigidity of Osmond's character as well as the pettiness of his ambition, he suffers a vertiginous drop in her estimation: "He was going down – down; the vision of such a fall made her almost giddy" (402).

To arrive at this clarity or insight is no simple matter in James's novel. People here resist easy translation. Generally, they don't conform to type, or type is depicted in gradations of nuance – both Ralph and Osmond to some extent fit the type of the dandy or aesthete yet they are crucially different from each other and, in their heterogeneity, tend to expand or destabilize the type. Over time and through many ordinary or unremarkable details, the characters and their relationships come into fuller view. The nature of the relation between Madame Merle and Osmond emerges from a series of impressions. In the key moment, Isabel walks through the house to put into water the flowers she has gathered with Pansy, her stepdaughter:

> Just beyond the threshold of the drawing-room she stopped short, the reason for her doing so being that she had received an impression. The impression had, in strictness, nothing unprecedented; but she felt it as something new, and the soundlessness of her step gave her time to take in the scene before she interrupted it. Madame Merle was there in her bonnet, and Gilbert Osmond was talking to her; for a minute they were unaware she had come in. Isabel had often seen that before, certainly; but what she had not seen, or at least not noticed, was that their colloquy had for the moment converted itself into a sort of familiar silence, from which she instantly perceived that her entrance would startle them. Madame Merle was standing on the rug, a little way from the fire; Osmond was in a deep chair, leaning back and looking at her. Her head was erect, as usual, but her eyes were bent on his. What struck Isabel first was that he was sitting while Madame Merle stood; there was an anomaly in this that arrested her. Then she perceived that they had arrived at a desultory pause in their exchange of ideas and were musing, face to face, with the freedom of old friends who sometimes exchange ideas without uttering them. There was nothing to shock in this; they were old friends in fact. But the thing made an image, lasting only a moment, like a sudden flicker of light. Their relative positions, their absorbed mutual gaze, struck her as something detected. But it was all over by the time she had fairly seen it. Madame Merle had seen her and had welcomed her without moving; her husband, on the other hand, had instantly jumped up. He presently murmured something about wanting a walk and, after having asked their visitor to excuse him, left the room. (342–43)

In this crucial passage, we move from quotidian, everyday detail – the walk with Pansy, the need to put the flowers in water, moving through the house – to seeing Osmond with Madame Merle (by itself, not a remarkable event). As the scene progresses, the ordinary details become extraordinary; a familiar occurrence – Madame Merle and Osmond talking together – becomes infused with some obscure but important significance which can be sensed if not fully understood by the perceptive observer whose unsystematic but considerable volume of experiences and impressions pushes toward some new idea.

Perception is stressed throughout the passage: what the characters are aware of, have seen or not seen, noticed or not noticed – Isabel's step is "soundless," Osmond and Merle are "unaware" that Isabel had come in, and Isabel "instantly perceived that her entrance would startle them." The scene is fairly vivid and precise visually. Wearing her bonnet, Madame Merle stands on a rug a small distance from the fire, and Osmond sits in a deep chair looking at her. But despite the clarity of these observations, the scene remains somehow obscure, freighted with meaning the exact nature of which is not announced. This would appear to be James's view of how we use human perception and inference to navigate through life, finding our bearings in the stream of alternatively definite and indefinite impressions. Certain details appear to have symbolic weight – the posture and position of Merle and Osmond. And these details "strike" Isabel in waves – she registers the impression as something new, something she had not noticed. She is first "struck" by their posture, then by their "musing, face to face." The effect of these details is "a sudden flicker of light," a sense of "something detected." But what has Isabel detected? She senses a degree of intimacy complexly symbolized in the scene's subtleties, something that the capacious imagination and internal computation of lived experience detects without knowing how it does so. In sum, the scene slowly unfolds the latent significance of these details, not pushing to an immediate and starkly clear-cut conclusion, as would be the case in the discovery of illicit lovers *in flagrante delicto*, but leading bit by bit into a feeling of association, intimacy, the final or blunt nature of which is not stated.

This passage emphasizes the elusiveness and opacity of the events we need to interpret to move forward. I would argue that we are a long way here from the kind of automatic and crystal-clear significance of characters and actions that one finds in Stowe and Howells. The details of the scene have no allegorical meaning; they don't stand for anything necessarily. The scene's significance is not discovered by reference to a second story of universal significance or ideals but is actively created by characters and readers who, with the right accumulation of observations and experiences, reach a tentative interpretation. Like Melville and Hawthorne and unlike Stowe and Howells, James cherishes the

ambiguities present in the interpretive exercise. He does not rush to translate experience into clear forms of signification; he lingers in the muddle,
the baffling and maze-like nature of perception and cognition. I think this is
because, for James as for Hawthorne and Melville, muddle characterizes our
experience, and uncertainty is a given in the modern world. For James, the
uncertainties of experience are more aesthetically and emotionally powerful
than fixed forms of symbolic association (e.g., Tom = Christ) and typification
(e.g., Silas = good country people). This is neither a necessarily anti-religious
point of view, nor is it an anti-spiritual point of view, but it does reject the
decoder-ring allegorical certainties of particular forms of symbol making and
reading.

Isabel's working through the obscurities of experience toward new knowledge resembles the way she comes to find sources of emotional value and moral
commitment in her life. James illustrates this process in Isabel's intuition that
Pansy presents an opportunity for an affective relation and sense of responsibility and duty, though the exact form and nature of that relation and duty are
somewhat obscure, lying outside of prescribed roles and categories:

> She had said to herself that we must take our duty where we find it, and
> that we must look for it as much as possible. Pansy's sympathy was a
> direct admonition; it seemed to say that here was an opportunity, not
> eminent perhaps, but unmistakeable. Yet an opportunity for what Isabel
> could hardly have said; in general, to be more for the child than the child
> was able to be for herself. Isabel could have smiled, in these days, to
> remember that her little companion had once been ambiguous, for she
> now perceived that Pansy's ambiguities were simply her own grossness
> of vision. She had been unable to believe any one could care so much –
> so extraordinarily much – to please. But since then she had seen this
> delicate faculty in operation, and now she knew what to think of it. It
> was the whole creature – it was a sort of genius.   (341)

In Pansy, Isabel senses an opportunity for connection and responsibility, but
she cannot yet fully recognize the nature and extent of the bond. Not only does
Isabel have to overcome a certain "grossness of vision" to understand Pansy,
but she also has no template for this kind of relation, which does not fit the
usual script. The ostensible source of Isabel's connection to Pansy, the marriage with Osmond, is based on a fraud, and that deception vitiates Isabel's
consent. Isabel is bound to Pansy neither by blood nor by the fraudulent marital contract. Instead their emotional ties and moral responsibilities are part
of an unexpectedly arising human connection, and this connection does not
come with any rule book. Isabel cannot wholly sort out or lucidly conclude

her dilemma. There are too many unknown and unknowable aspects of it, but she must act nonetheless. So by default, she acts in a provisional fashion, feeling her way toward some tentative outline of her obligations to and relationship with Pansy. James's description emphasizes that Isabel's mind and emotions are not passive or inert; her thoughts, feelings, and intuitions are presented as forms of action that properly and inevitably respond to new facts and unforeseen events, such as the emergence of an emotional tie with Osmond's daughter.[9]

Instead of readily translatable characters and events, James insists on the opacity of experience, its complexity and uncertain significance. He plunges the reader (like his characters) into events that may ultimately prove difficult or even impossible to decipher. This aesthetic of immersion is perhaps the biggest and most important distinction in nineteenth-century fiction. The desire to plunge the reader into experiences that will exceed his or her expectations and habitual frames of reference connects James's fiction to the teasing enigmas of Poe, Hawthorne, and Melville (one thinks of Pip's disorienting plunge and Melville's appreciation of those who dive beneath the surface of things), the contradictory, ironic, and difficult aphorisms of Emerson, the riddling poetry of Dickinson, and the wild poetic juxtapositions of Walt Whitman. And, by way of contrast, it reveals a commonality running through the sentimental fiction of Stowe, the romances of Cooper, and the realism of Howells. Another way to understand this important distinction running through the era's fiction is to see it as ranged along a continuum, as Edward Eigner puts it, from more mimetic novels describing the effect of experience (e.g., Howells) to those more metaphysical fictions exploring the nature of the experience itself (e.g., James) (2–3). At one end of the spectrum, the fiction becomes more transparent, more sure of its moral truths, and more confident in our intuitive and cognitive powers to sort problems out. At the other end, the fiction becomes increasingly opaque and skeptical, not of human inventiveness or imaginative power, but of the power of the rational mind to arrive at certain knowledge and ultimate truths.

## From agency to determinism – a sliding scale

"Free will" stands for the capacity of rational beings to weigh and choose among various courses of action. The notion of free will comes into play when we think about personal forms of association and values such as friendship and love. Philosophers accepting this notion have argued that human activity is differentiated from that of animals by the human ability to mull over conflicting or different desires and beliefs and reach a conclusion about which is best (Frankfurt 11–25). Love without volition would hardly seem to deserve the name: hence, one's humorous impatience with the pet whose signs of affection are so clearly merely a mechanical behavior repeated over and over to obtain food, water, or a walk. The concept of free will is often tied to notions of moral responsibility. American law, for instance, commonly deems free will the prerequisite for the imposition of civil or criminal penalties because it seems unjust and pointless to impose a duty on one without agency. So, for example, children below a certain age or people with certain mental limitations are traditionally not held to the same legal standard. When justifying the American Revolution, the framers of the Declaration of Independence and the Constitution claimed an inherent ability to distinguish just from unjust forms of government and the agency to act on that judgment.

If one views each human being as an independent agent potentially capable of free will, then the necessity of insuring that each individual has a considerable measure of autonomy in order to develop and exercise his/her agency follows as a matter of course. Liberalism is founded on the connection between free will and human development, and liberals, such as the British philosopher John Stuart Mill, used the notion of free will to contend both that the state should intervene to liberate individuals from prejudice, ignorance, and poverty, which impede the development of moral agency, and that state power should be limited so that the individual's agency is not unduly obstructed.

Mill's views on free will are particularly useful for the student of nineteenth-century realist fiction because he both posits the possibility of agency and acknowledges the influence of external circumstances on the thought and behavior of individuals. Describing a decisive mental crisis in his *Autobiography*, Mill writes that

> during the later returns of my dejection, the doctrine of what is called Philosophical Necessity weighed on my existence like an incubus . . . I pondered painfully on the subject, till gradually I saw light through it. I perceived, that the word Necessity, as a name for the doctrine of Cause and Effect applied to human action, carried with it a misleading association; and that this association was the operative force in the depressing and paralysing influence which I had experienced: I saw that though our character is formed by circumstances, our own desires can do much to shape those circumstances; and that what is really inspiriting and ennobling in the doctrine of free-will, is the conviction that we have real power over the formation of our own character; that our will, by influencing some of our circumstances, can modify our future habits or capabilities of willing. All this was entirely consistent with the doctrine of circumstances, or rather, was that doctrine itself, properly understood. From that time I drew in my own mind, a clear distinction between the doctrine of circumstances, and Fatalism; discarding altogether the misleading word Necessity. (97–98)

While our circumstances clearly influence our behavior, thoughts, and desires, character is not merely a mechanical reflection or outcome of such influences. In moments of free will, we can influence those circumstances, reshape our outlooks and beliefs, and redirect our actions. William James similarly found in the notion of free will a way out of dejection, finding hope in the possibility of choosing one line of thought over others: "My first act of free will shall be to believe in free will" (qtd. Kloppenberg 81). As James puts it in *Pragmatism* (which is dedicated to Mill "from whom I first learned the pragmatic openness of mind"), free will means that "the future may not identically repeat and imitate the past" (55). Individuals, if genuinely free to consider and choose, would, Mill and James believed, generally opt for moral development over more stagnant and less productive states of being, even if that moral development entailed considerable difficulty and discomfort.

However, as the century drew to a close, this vision of ethical autonomy became less and less credible. To the extent that free will depended on or assumed models of economic independence (e.g., it is relatively easy to imagine the society of yeoman farmers and the small business owners as having a high degree of individual agency), it was, by the turn of the century, an endangered or even obsolete concept, as were William James's notions of pioneer individualism and distrust of all "big" things (Thayer 441–42). By 1900, the American nation had been rapidly transformed from a decentralized aggregation of rural, agricultural regions into a centralized, industrial behemoth, with a massive circulation system of railroads and telephone and telegraph wires. The nation's economic future seemed to be tied to industry not agriculture, and industry required thousands of workers and an abundance of capital. Business grew ever bigger, and wave after wave of immigrants from abroad and migrants from within the nation came to urban centers to fill the ranks of the laboring classes needed to operate factories and mills. The widening gulf between poor and rich, labor and capital, made class violence appear inevitable. The growth of state and federal governments roughly kept pace with the growth of business, and, as government got bigger, it seemed increasingly to be the pawn of big business. The sheer size of businesses and governments making policy on federal and state levels made the idea of an individual's free will appear more and more remote. As the nation became more urban, less rural, more industrial, less agricultural, more diverse, less homogeneous, the republican faith in the commonweal as meaningfully joined by a general consensus regarding fundamental values became hard to maintain.

Determinism, a word entering the lexicon in 1846 (according to the *Oxford English Dictionary*), denoted the idea that our lives are determined by forces beyond our control. Nineteenth-century scientific investigations, such as Georges Cuvier's paleontology, Sir Charles Lyell's geology, and most radically

Charles Darwin's natural history – in particular his 1859 theory of natural selection and evolution – gave determinism a new kind of intellectual authority, far more compelling for the era than religious notions of predestination. It became plausible that we might eventually be able to chart all such causes and influences, arriving at a complete understanding of the web of circumstances driving and controlling human behavior. After Darwin, we might be able to pinpoint the exact manner in which individuals were defined and driven by heredity and environment (Kern 31–37). William James's major philosophical antagonist, Herbert Spencer, applied evolutionary notions to human society and was widely influential in America in the late nineteenth century. Coining the phrase "survival of the fittest," Spencer and his followers argued against governmental intervention in broader economic struggles to survive. The evolution of society through this struggle would, the social Darwinists admitted, necessarily entail certain short-term inequities and suffering, but these costs were a part of the necessary progress of the human species, in which the unfit elements would be purged, leaving only the fittest members of society and their progeny.

In the fiction of the late nineteenth century, we find a corresponding shift in emphasis from the liberal's conditioned but still free individual to the individual who is either incapable of agency or whose moments of autonomous intellectual and moral judgment are largely impotent. Realist characters of a slightly earlier vintage, such as Huck, Isabel, and Silas, embody the possibility of free will, while later characters, such as Crane's Maggie Johnson, Dreiser's Carrie Meeber, and Norris's McTeague seem to contradict the very notion of independent agency. As free will comes to seem increasingly unreal in the face of economic and social realities and current scientific theory, realism becomes more fatalistic: independent thought as well as moral and intellectual development seem more and more alien to its protagonists. Comparing *Sister Carrie* and *The Adventures of Huckleberry Finn*, for instance, the most striking contrast may be the relative absence of independent thought and moral development in Dreiser's novel. In the more fatalist versions of realism, as Richard Poirier puts it, "Environmental force is made altogether more articulate than are any of the characters" (239). When the conditioned but free individual of liberalism does make an appearance in the more fatalistic novel, he or she has little power to reshape or influence the direction of the determining factors of circumstance. As we shall see, this is what distinguishes *Pudd'nhead Wilson* from *Huckleberry Finn*. Free will has not disappeared from Twain's later novel – Wilson has autonomous judgment – but the social context is determinative of the narrative's chain of events and conclusion. Wilson's independence proves powerless to alter or change that context. Fatalism doesn't require an utter rejection of free will; it can derive from freedom's relative impotence to make any substantial difference to society or the individual.

A wrinkle or nuance in the deterministic perspective of these later novels becomes clear when we recall that such authors as Dreiser and Norris do not ask us to identify with their main characters. Instead, they encourage the reader to view the novel's protagonist as not only different but somewhat inferior. The distance between the reader and McTeague is bluntly signaled by Norris's description of the dentist as "too hopelessly stupid to get much benefit from [books]" (3). Dreiser similarly creates a gulf between the reader and Carrie by noting at the outset that "[b]ooks were beyond her interest" (2). By virtue of being readers, the audience is exempt, at least to some extent, from the determinism described by these novels. In its opposition to the determined and limited lives of these characters, reading stands for independent cognition. The consequent separation of the reader and fictional character, in effect, puts the reader and the author in the position of scientists studying a phenomenon from the outside – poking, prodding, dissecting, and observing from a detached and intellectually superior position (the question of whether or not the scientific endeavor is itself determined is largely ignored). Yet, as we shall see, the tone of these novels is rarely if ever detached or scientific. Their authors (and readers) are not only fascinated by but drawn to the lurid and excessive aspects of the utterly determined lives being described. This is the paradox of the more deterministic fiction of the era – we are simultaneously separated from the lives of the main characters by some intellectual qualification and presumably greater independence of thought and agency, yet attracted to the compulsions, excesses, and grotesqueries of life without agency.[10]

### Jewett's A Country Doctor – free will with limits

Even those realists insisting on the possibility of free will were not blind to the influence of circumstance on the lives and actions of their characters. Acknowledging the historical and material conditions limiting a character's agency, they portray the continuing potential for free will in characters who defy conventions or expectations. The heroine of Sarah Orne Jewett's *A Country Doctor* (1884), Nan Prince is an embodiment of the conditioned but free individual, and her progress toward a professional vocation as a medical doctor represents the kind of growth called for and promised by the liberal project of self-development. The question driving *A Country Doctor* is whether Nan Prince will choose marriage to an attractive and eligible young man or a vocation as a country doctor. Like *A Modern Instance* or *The Marrow of Tradition*, Jewett's novel takes up one of the central conflicts of the era: the rights and role of women in American society – in particular, the propriety of women undertaking professional careers. In passing, it should be noted that this drama has a distinctly middle-class dimension to it. When *A Country Doctor* appeared in 1884, women from the lower economic classes of society had been working for quite some time without any outcry. Nan's choice of a professional career is provocative because she does not have to work. She could marry a man who would be able to provide for her.[11]

Yet, even here, where a choice in defiance of the determining influence of context is central to the drama of the novel, Jewett hedges or moderates her representation of Nan's agency by emphasizing the "natural" aspect of Nan's medical vocation. Nan's inclination for medicine and science flows from her apparently innate love of and curiosity about nature. From an early age her sympathy for nature is frequently observed by the adults in her rural community: "she belongs with wild creatur's, I do believe, – just the same nature." One of the quietly unconventional aspects of Jewett's novel is its description of the rustic countryside as more open to Nan's unconventional but natural vocation than the city where she would be far more greatly hemmed in by social conventions, an openness captured by the farmer Martin Dyer's comment that he believes "in young folks makin' all they can o' theirselves" (19). For Dr. Leslie, Nan's mentor and surrogate father, she is the model of natural development: "I believe she has grown up as naturally as a plant grows, not having been clipped back or forced in any unnatural direction. If ever a human being were untrammeled and left alone to see what will come of it, it is this child" (77–78). From this perspective, Nan is conditioned by her natural gifts and inclinations but sufficiently free of the constraints of social conventions to become what she will. She is both unique and natural. And it is the paradoxical association of the uniqueness and naturalness of her medical vocation that will ultimately justify her breaking with tradition. The readers worried that Jewett's novel will undermine the institution of marriage should be somewhat reassured by the fact that Nan is unique, yet other readers chaffing at the restrictions of social tradition can find hope in Nan's embodiment of a developmental model not imprisoned in convention.

Nan comes to see her own development as a matter of both free will and determinism:

> it seemed to her as if she had taken every step of her life straight toward this choice of a profession. So many things she had never understood before, now became perfectly clear and evident proofs that, outside her own preferences and choices, a wise purpose had been at work with her and for her. So it all appeared natural every day, and while she knew that the excitement and formality of the first very uncomfortable day or two had proved her freedom of choice, it seemed the more impossible that she should have shirked this great commission and trust for which nature had fitted her. (136)

Nan has been led by forces beyond her control, "a wise purpose," to this "great commission." Nan's gifts as a doctor are "God-given," yet her role as doctor is not readily recognized in or plainly endorsed by religious text or tradition (138). As a result, Dr. Leslie and Nan have to experiment and interpret experience without the determining guidance of tradition to figure out the best course of action. God or some notion of a transcendent good becomes the starting point and goal of their experiments. Another way of understanding the apparently interchangeable references to "God-given" and natural gifts and purposes is to put the pair of terms into the form of a question: what happens when we shift to a more secular diction in speaking about what "nature" intends for us instead of what "God" intends for us? By having Nan and Dr. Leslie focus more on the work "for which nature had fitted" Nan, Jewett signals a movement away from a direct and immediate communication with God toward a messier and less certain process of inferring what is right and good from experience and a process of trial and error. The association of this more experimental approach to life and openness to change is represented in Dr. Leslie's willingness to take (for him) extraordinary measures for the sake of Nan's unconventional medical vocation. Though he is an older bachelor well settled into a solitary and rural way of life, in order to foster Nan's career he plunges back into professional associations long ago abandoned (141).

In her vocational role, Nan represents a certain degree of novelty. Jewett dramatizes this novelty in a neat reversal of roles when Nan's suitor, George Gerry, feels "weak and womanish" at the "noise the returning bone made" as Nan expertly resets a dislocated shoulder. When this emergency arises, it is Nan, not George, who is quick to act and who acts with confidence and capability (197–99). The scene pleases the reader in proportion to the reader's taste for people and performances that exceed or defy expectations based on identity and conventional roles. The scene speaks to our desire to set at odds the expectations of type and our openness to innovation and surprise. But while she would free Nan from the constrictions of identity and predetermined role, Jewett is careful to limit that freedom, never suggesting that her heroine could pursue both her profession and a marriage (212).

## From Huckleberry Finn *to* Pudd'nhead Wilson – *Twain's increasing fatalism*

*Huckleberry Finn* (1884) contemplates the possibility that individuals may have, at least in certain circumstances, the ability to defy social and legal conventions in the interest of choosing something better. Huck can, despite training and legal prescription to the contrary, do the "wrong" thing and aid his friend's escape from slavery. Early in the novel, Twain uses a prank to prepare us for Huck's defining crisis of conscience and free will. At one point in their raft trip, Huck decides to amuse himself by pretending to Jim that their actual separation in a dense fog was nothing but an apparition in a dream. Jim chastises Huck with a touching description of his grief at the boy's apparent loss and his joy at Huck's safe return. Jim emerges from the objectification of Huck's joke and the infantilization of his minstrel-like characterization as a responsible adult sensitively and successfully reprimanding a mischievous but good-hearted child. Huck responds: "I didn't do him no more mean tricks, and I wouldn't done that one if I'd knowed it would make him feel that way" (72). "With Huck's apology," as Brook Thomas notes, "their relationship promises to be one of free and equal individuals bound together by mutual benefit and trust" (5). As long as Huck and Jim remain on the raft, separated from a political and social context animated by racism and power, their connection can be governed by an interracial moral consensus rather than force.

At the novel's famous climax in Chapter 31, Huck worries that his moral commitment to Jim is a breach of both divine law and the customs of his slaveholding community. He shudders at the thought of divine scrutiny:

> Providence slapping me in the face and letting me know my wickedness was being watched all the time from up there in heaven, whilst I was stealing a poor old woman's nigger that hadn't ever done me no harm, and now was showing me there's One that's always on the lookout, and ain't agoing to allow no such miserable doings to go only just so fur and no further.

In Huck's case, moral inspiration does not come in the form of the clear-cut obligations arising from social convention or divine instruction, but rather emerges from reflection, internal debate, and conversation. Instead of a straightforward recognition of divine absolutes, Twain's moral insight is a horizontal and uncertain matter of mutable human experience and connection. Because Huck and Jim have created a relation based on and governed by their moral consensus, Huck can only say "obedience"; he cannot "do the right thing":

> Somehow I couldn't seem to strike no places to harden me against him, but only the other kind. I'd see him standing my watch on top of his'n, stead of calling me, so I could go on sleeping; and see him how glad he was when I come back out of the fog.

Huck tears up the letter he had written revealing Jim's whereabouts, deciding to conform his words to his actions and his feelings: "All right then, I'll go to hell" (168–69). While Huck's agency is mooted by the fact that Miss Watson has already freed Jim, his crisis of conscience holds out the possibility of a moral reason capable of judgment independent of social and legal conventions. Huck's rebellion is a distant echo of the themes of the Declaration of Independence and an affirmation of the liberal notion of agency.

The hedged but also hopeful quality of Twain's depiction of agency in *Huckleberry Finn* is shared by George Washington Cable's novel *The Grandissimes* (1879–80). The burden of history is omnipresent in Cable's novel, which like *Huckleberry Finn* looks back to the South before the War. History attends every action, movement, or comment. The idea that Southern society inflexibly requires submission to its customs is the recurrent theme of conversations between the outsider, Joseph Frowenfeld, who has moved to Louisiana, and one of the region's favored sons, Honoré Grandissime. Honoré sympathetically counsels Frowenfeld, "You cannot afford to be *entirely* different to the community in which you live; is that not so? ... You must get acclimated ... not in body only ... but in mind – in taste – in conversation – and in convictions too." Honoré predicts that Frowenfeld will take the shape given him by his new society, "My-de'-seh, the water must expect to take the shape of the bucket." "They all do it – all who come. They hold out for a little while – a very little; then they open their stores on Sunday, they import cargoes of Africans, they bribe the officials, they smuggle goods, they have colored housekeepers" (37). And to a certain extent, Honoré is right. Frowenfeld does change, becoming wiser and more judicious about how to behave and speak in this society, but Frowenfeld's demurrer, "One need not be water!," also proves prophetic (37).

Honoré is more changed by Frowenfeld than the other way around. Frowenfeld will help to inspire Honoré to attempt to right the wrongs of the past despite the considerable weight of family obligation, history, and social custom and prejudice. Land taken by the Grandissimes from the Nancanou family will be returned to Aurore and Clotilde; Honoré's half-brother, an octaroon also named Honoré Grandissime, will be acknowledged and brought into the family business as a partner (though, as the white Honoré ruefully acknowledges to himself, this gesture is hardly altruistic given the considerable wealth his darker brother brings into the business).

By 1894, however, both Twain and Cable had come to doubt that individuals or groups could escape the determining hand of history and the will of the majority. Cable's novel *John March, Southerner* (1894), published the same year as *Pudd'nhead Wilson*, exhibits this change in its bleak tone and racist language. A decade earlier in 1884, Cable was so sensitive to the use of the term "nigger" that he convinced Mark Twain to change the title of one of his readings from "You Can't Teach a Nigger to Argue" to "How Come a Frenchman Doan' Talk Like a Man?" (Butcher 117–25). Ten years later, in *John March*, Cable uses "nigger" frequently as well as racist caricatures of black appearance. In Cornelius Leggett's ungrammatical and foolish paraphrase of Cable's own essay "The Freedman's Case in Equity," Cable portrays the civil rights advocate as a minstrel buffoon (*John March* 122–23, Cardwell 105).

Pudd'nhead Wilson is Twain's pessimistic rejoinder to his own suggestion in *Huckleberry Finn* that individuals could model their behavior and frame the terms of their lives together by means of a free agency undetermined by the pressures of history, the traditions of slavery and racism, and the positivist workings of majority will. In *Pudd'nhead Wilson*, Twain uses the "Prince and Pauper" trick of exchanged identities to play with notions of free will and determinism in the form of questions of nature and nurture. Roxy, a slave, substitutes her own very light-skinned baby boy for her master's son, and in the sequel a set of questions arise involving nature and nurture. Is Tom's criminality the result of his black blood or is it the product of his being the pampered and spoiled heir of one of the town's most prominent families? Roxy's bravery would seem to challenge the idea that blood or nature determines identity and moral character; however, she herself attributes her bravery to a noble lineage. As Eric Sundquist and others have pointed out, Twain so entangles the questions of nature and nurture in this tale as to render them inseparable – we cannot parse whether Tom's cowardice, laziness, dishonesty, and other flaws are the product of bad blood, racial heritage, or curable moral deficiencies (Sundquist *To Wake the Nations* 240–41). And to a far greater degree than *Huckleberry Finn*, *Pudd'nhead Wilson* questions whether we can effectively act outside of or in contravention of the operative norms of our context.

The climax of *Pudd'nhead Wilson* comes with the criminal trial of the Italian twins for the murder of Judge Driscoll. As foreigners with a recent history of conflict with Judge Driscoll and his putative nephew Tom, they are the most likely suspects. The key player in this climactic scene and the one person in this community with the best chance of exercising some degree of agency is David "Pudd'nhead" Wilson, the twins' lawyer. Wilson is a transplanted Northerner of Scottish background, and his status as an outsider would seem to give him the greatest chance of acting independently of the determinations of Southern history and the continuing effect of racist customs and law. The derisive nickname given to him by townspeople who are too dim to understand a joke he makes at the beginning of the novel is in part a marker of his independence from the Dawson's Landing community, an independence best exemplified by his intelligence, sense of irony, and scientific curiosity – all of which come into play in his exoneration of the Italian twins. In particular, it is Wilson's interest in fingerprints that saves the twins. For years, he has been collecting the fingerprints of the residents of Dawson's Landing, and this hobby has added to his reputation for foolishness. (In fact, Twain's fictional hero is in advance of law enforcement's use of fingerprints by more than a decade [Friedman 358].) Twain sets Wilson up as the kind of independent thinker who, by standing outside the customs and prejudices of his community, might be able to challenge or alter the determining influence of the majority's expectations and conventions. But the denouement of the tale, the solution to the riddle offered by Wilson, that the slave woman Roxy's very light-skinned son has been impersonating the Judge's nephew and has killed the Judge, exactly fits the racist expectations of the townspeople.

The climactic trial is conducted as a relatively informal dialogue between the attorneys and the community. Almost no formal legal procedure stands between the story-telling lawyers and their audience – which prominently includes the gallery of townspeople as well as the jury. There are no evidentiary objections, motions, or other legal procedures to obscure the emotional impact of the attorneys' tales. Each lawyer casually testifies to certain facts without being sworn, taking the stand, or justifying to the court the necessity of such an irregular procedure. By emphasizing the centrality of the gallery's response to the attorneys' tales and eliminating legal procedure, Twain creates an emphatic vision of adjudication as theater, and legal judgment as audience approval. In his magic show ("black magic" as Tom and Roxy call it), Wilson deploys the carny trick of fingerprint identification as a kind of entertainer casting a "spell upon the house" –

> "Upon this haft stands the assassin's natal autograph, written in the blood of that helpless and unoffending old man who loved you and whom you loved. There is but one man in the whole earth whose hand can duplicate that crimson sign" – he paused and raised his eyes to the pendulum swinging back and forth – "and please God we will produce that man in this room before the clock strikes noon!" Stunned, distraught, unconscious of its own movement, the house half rose, as if expecting to see the murderer appear at the door, and a breeze of muttered ejaculations swept the place.   (217, 218–19)

Wilson's performance becomes even more theatrical when he asks people in the gallery to participate in testing his magical skill in recognizing fingerprints. At each demonstration of this uncanny ability, the gallery responds with "A deafening explosion of applause." Even the Judge confesses his amazement at Wilson's hocus pocus ("This certainly approaches the miraculous"), turning a white man black and a black man white: "'A was put into B's cradle in the nursery; B was transferred to the kitchen and became a negro and a slave' – (Sensation – confusion of angry ejaculations) – 'but within a quarter of an hour he will stand before you white and free'" (221). Through the trial's overtly theatrical quality, Twain suggests the futility of scientific, legal, or moral action that does not play to the crowd. Omnipresent and ultimately determinative, context overwhelms and moots agency in *Pudd'nhead Wilson.*

## Freedom from thought – life without agency

We recognize that we have arrived at a fully fledged determinism when a novel's main characters not only lack the capacity to push against the tide of whatever societal forces are in play but don't even seem to have independent rational judgment. In novels such as *Sister Carrie, The Red Badge of Courage,* and *McTeague,* the main characters seem mentally imprisoned. The workings of their minds do not rise to the level of independent thought. They seem incapable of either breaking an issue down into its component parts or seeing how their own actions may represent what they dislike or condemn in others. Their mental processes are hemmed in by the dictates of their environment, heredity, and ungovernable desires. They cannot be said to have free will, and, in the absence of such agency, the idea of moral character so important to realists, such as Howells, and sentimental writers, such as Harriet Beecher Stowe or Frances Harper, becomes decidedly problematic.

Without moral agency, the liberal's notion of reform is impossible. In hopes of inspiring landlord-tenant reform, Jacob Riis's famous documentary of tenement life *How the Other Half Lives* (1890) offers graphic portrayals of lives distorted, mangled, and unfairly balked by poverty. The payoff of Riis's proposed reform project is represented by the "readiness with which the tenants respond to intelligent efforts in their behalf . . . The moral effect is as great as the improvement of their physical health." Riis's poor and downtrodden are able to recognize a more wholesome way of life, and that insight, if "properly cultivated," can effect their "rescue" and improvement (218). Crane's *Maggie* similarly focuses our attention on the brutally determinative impact of environment on the lives of the poor, but, unlike Riis's text, Crane's novel does not plausibly argue for reform. The emptiness of the characters, their relative lack of psychological depth, their very oddity, make notions of reform seem alien and inapt. If the novel is to inspire reform, the reader has to recognize Crane's slum dwellers as capable of the kind of improvement Riis describes, but Crane's novel fights this recognition. His characters are an entirely different and fantastic order of beings – grotesques, freaks – incapable of critical thought and progress. Vowing revenge on Pete, Maggie's seducer, her brother Jimmie cannot see that, having committed similar acts, he is in exactly the same moral position as Pete (76). And in her ludicrously inappropriate moralizing, Maggie's mother, Mary Johnson, is powerless to perceive that her home is a cause of, not an obstacle to, Maggie's sexual misconduct (75).

Crane's characters react to external forces they can neither understand nor control. In *The Red Badge of Courage*, Henry Fleming is at one moment "carried along by a mob" and full of fear and resentment of his powerlessness: "He had not enlisted of his free will" (133). At another moment, he is a fearless, even joyous cog in the war machine, happy to be a part of a vast mechanism raining destruction down on the enemy. In neither case does he seem to have agency or self-control. In Crane's war novel, heroism becomes a kind of reflexive reaction to great stress and a variety of other causal factors and coincidences. The hero of Crane's story "A Mystery of Heroism" acts with apparent disregard for his personal safety, not as the result of a conscious decision that the effort is worth the risk to life and limb, but in an automatic or mechanical fashion as the result of being teased at a certain moment. Whatever nobility might be superimposed on his fetching of a bucket of water under fire in terrifically dangerous circumstances is undermined by the closing fact that bickering officers spill the bucket. The hero's accomplishment and his moral capacity for bravery prove to be literally empty, without significance. Yet the random quality of who is saved and who isn't, who proves "brave" at one moment and who doesn't, does not stop us from trying to attribute meaning to experience. Hence at the end of "The Open Boat," when the strongest has drowned and the weakest has survived, "the white waves paced to and fro in the moonlight, and the wind brought the sound of the great sea's voice to the men on the shore, and they felt that they could then be interpreters" (*"Red Badge" and Other Writings* 242, 245, 313). But these tales do not lend any authority to any interpretation. Existence in Crane seems too much governed by chance to be susceptible of meaning.

In *McTeague: A Story of San Francisco* (1899), Frank Norris attributes his central characters' lack of agency and reason less to random cosmic forces than to their innate animal-like natures. Under stress or in states of desire, the animal inside each character proves irresistible. As, for instance, when Marcus Schouler bites McTeague's ear during a wrestling match,

> The brute that in McTeague lay so close to the surface leaped instantly to life, monstrous, not to be resisted. He sprang to his feet with a shrill and meaningless clamor, totally unlike the ordinary bass of his speaking tones. It was a hideous yelling of a hurt beast, the squealing of a wounded elephant. He framed no words; in the rush of high-pitched

> sound that issued from his wide-open mouth there was nothing
> articulate. It was something no longer human; it was rather an echo
> from the jungle. (234)

The exaggerated grotesqueness of Norris's descriptions of his characters in inhuman or nonhuman terms at times becomes comedic. For example, the light doesn't simply shine through McTeague's ears, it "shone pink through the gristle of his enormous ears" (178).[12] Norris's depiction of human beings driven by forces beyond their control evidences the influence of one of his Berkeley professors, Joseph Le Conte, who conceived of the battle between ethical and evolutionary forces in human behavior (which included the possibility of de-evolution back to animalism) as the central drama of human existence, and of Emile Zola, whose fiction, Norris argued, amounted to a scientific observation of how heredity and environment played out in the social and psychological processes of the working and lower classes.

The brute force that distinguishes and drives McTeague's character embodies a "foul stream of hereditary evil" which runs through him "like a sewer" and taints him with the "vices and sins of his father and of his father's father" (32). This hereditary evil would seem, given the dearth of evidence Norris provides about his hero's particular parentage (his father is an alcoholic and his mother, "an overworked drudge" [2]), to be a general inheritance – more a matter of his being human than of his being a McTeague. Contrary to those who find in Norris a replication of the idea of inherited criminality made famous by Cesare Lombroso, I would argue that the human evil portrayed in this novel crosses lines of heredity in an equal-opportunity fashion (Kern 33). Quite a range of ethnicities and national origins are represented by the dramatis personae of this novel – McTeague, Trina, Marcus, Maria Macapa, and Old Zerkow. Yet all of them are variously described as being overpowered by inner compulsions and greed.

In distinction to the irresistible compulsions driving Norris's characters, Dreiser's characters in *Sister Carrie* are caught in a kind of fruitless oscillation between impulses and fears. Juxtapositions of the things one has and those one doesn't spontaneously arise, creating desire.[13] In turn, desire propels the back-and-forth movement between longing and anxiety, which, like the movement of Carrie's famous rocking chair, goes nowhere because it is not thought or analysis but something decidedly less, something incapable of reasoned conclusion or judgment (369).[14] Dreiser's characters live by habit until their routine is unsettled by some contrast between what they have and don't have into a new pattern of desire and pursuit. When Hurstwood comes into her life, Carrie is loosed from her mooring to Drouet and begins drifting toward a relation with Hurstwood. Hurstwood's contrastive presence signals the existence of a better option, making Carrie unsatisfied with her present alliance. Hurstwood similarly doesn't "trouble" himself with reflection and self-examination. He doesn't inquire into the quality of his life, its meaning, its correspondence with certain aspirations or ambitions. He simply proceeds, comfortable in his existence, unless and until something "better [is] immediately and sharply contrasted" (66).

In Dreiser's novel, the disruptive and compulsive principle of desire drives a marketplace approach to people and things.[15] We can see this process at work in Carrie's success in an amateur theatrical. Having been recommended by Drouet, Carrie performs in a production put on by the Elks. The novel describes how Hurstwood's desire is "heightened" "by the applause of the audience." She is more attractive both for being what he doesn't have and for being wanted by many in the audience: "He now thought she was beautiful. She had done something which was above his sphere" (135). Drouet's feelings are similarly kindled – here is a new Carrie, transformed by the audience's appreciation into a person different from the one he has known and possessed. His craving for her is proportional to this sense of her newness. Drouet's and Hurstwood's mutually reinforcing yearnings offer an apt illustration of René Girard's notion of triangular or mediated desire. The competition of desire not only produces conflict but elevates the object of desire into a figure for a desired state of being (10–11). Thus, the bond of casual friendship between Hurstwood and Drouet is replaced by the animosity of their competition not simply for Carrie but also for the elevation she now represents to each man. The force of these characters' cravings is proportional to the limitation of their understanding. Carrie, Drouet, and Hurstwood are compelled by desire in ways that the more critically aware and objective Ames cannot be. Introduced late in the narrative, Ames, the engineer, represents a more rational and consequently more human form of existence. The contrast between Ames and the other characters illuminates the reciprocal connection between the principle of desire and objecthood. The more like an object one is, the more one is driven by desire, and the more one is acted upon by desire, the more one resembles an object.[16]

Strikingly, in the amateur theatrical scene, the audience's desire does not rise to a determinative pitch until the desired person has become more like a thing. Once Carrie has really entered her role and begun to perform unselfconsciously, "[s]he turn[s] toward the audience without seeing." Carried away by her role and not really aware of the audience, Carrie becomes like an item in a store window – something looked at that does not look back (137). This is, of course, part of "the fascinating make-believe of the moment," but it is interesting that this one-way mirror effect of being seen by but not seeing the audience plays a role in the success of the theatrical make-believe – the living person before the audience must cease to see them and become, thereby, more purely an object of their imaginations and desires or aversions. When Carrie speaks the line, "Her beauty, her wit, her accomplishments, she may sell to you; but her love is the treasure without money and without price," Hurstwood suffers as if she had made "a personal appeal . . . he could hardly restrain the tears for sorrow over the hopeless, pathetic, and yet dainty and appealing woman whom he loved. Drouet also was beside himself. He was resolving that he would be to Carrie what he had never been before. He would marry her, by George! She was worth it" (139). Paradoxically, the intersubjective or interpersonal exchange of feelings, thoughts, and viewpoints that one might innocently presume to be the prerequisite of intimacy is unnecessary. Instead, the apparent antithesis of such exchange, objectification, is represented as the prerequisite for intimacy and marriage. Once she has been made into an object of their imaginations, the fiction of a person who sees them not, but upon whom they can look and fantasize, Carrie becomes especially attractive, even marriageable, to Drouet and Hurstwood.

In his depiction of Hurstwood's crime, Dreiser sets up the conundrum of action without agency. Hurstwood commits a theft of $10,000, but his act, if we can call it that, seems to lack the guilty state of mind we usually require before assigning moral and criminal responsibility. This moment in the novel is analogous to Huck's crisis of conscience, Isabel's fireside vigil, and Silas's long struggle with Rogers. As with Huck, Silas, and Isabel, Hurstwood is under pressure from at least two directions. He is drawn toward Carrie, and he is repelled by his wife, who is threatening to divorce him if he doesn't come to heel and comply with her wishes. But instead of making a decision, Hurstwood is pushed forward by an accident: on performing his habitual round of closing the fashionable saloon he manages, Hurstwood finds the safe not only open but full of money (190). Preoccupied with problems of his own, the cashier has failed, for the first time, to lock the safe. Viewing this scene with a prosecutorial eye, we are, I think, predisposed to find agency, to see Hurstwood as consciously acting, perhaps stupidly, out of an impulse he could and should govern by considering the consequences. After all, Hurstwood has motive, an unhappy marriage and a keen desire for another woman, and here is the opportunity to grab at something better, notwithstanding how idiotic the scheme may prove.

Dreiser, however, goes to great lengths to drain the scene of any form of agency. Hurstwood's initial look in the safe seems to lack motive or design: "'I'll look in here,' thought the manager, pulling out the money drawers. He did not know why he wished to look in there. It was quite a superfluous action, which another time might not have happened at all" (190). Like McTeague, who cannot explain to himself why he would take on the risks of Trina's complex dental problem – "Why he should pledge himself to this hazardous case McTeague was puzzled to know" – Hurstwood's crisis begins with an act that seems motiveless (*McTeague* 26). Once Hurstwood has taken the money drawers out, he splits into two beings – one directing, suggesting, and longing, and the other wondering at what he's doing, as though he could be a spectator to his own unconscious or unintended acts: "'Why don't I shut the safe?' his mind said to itself, lingering. 'What makes me pause here?' For answer there came the strangest words: 'Did you ever have ten thousand dollars in ready money?'" Like the reader, Hurstwood suspects that an illicit motive is somehow forming in his mind even though it hasn't been articulated or concretely formed. Consequently, he pulls the shades and takes care to move about quietly, suspicious but unsure: "What was this thing, making him suspicious? Why did he wish to move about so quietly" (191).

With a keen eye out for the moment of agency that will justify finding him culpable, we might well here expect Hurstwood to contemplate what he could do with the $10,000. But if Hurstwood, as a rational being, were capable of considering the benefits of taking the money, we would also expect him to consider the costs, and the costs are so obvious and so extreme that a rational person would put the money back and lock the safe. Instead, Hurstwood seems to reflect without thought: "He came back to the end of the counter *as if* to rest his arm and think . . . 'The safe is open,' said a voice. 'There is just the least little crack in it. The lock has not been sprung'" (191, emphasis added). To describe Hurstwood as thinking here is to speak metaphorically. Ultimately, he reaches no decision; instead, there is just an unexplained act and its consequences: "While the money was in his hand the lock clicked. It had sprung! Did he do it? He grabbed at the knob and pulled vigorously. It had closed. Heavens! he was in for it now, sure enough" (193). Hurstwood's feeling that he has made a "mistake" seems misplaced. He has not done anything, if doing something means acting consciously on one's choices. He calls it a "mistake" not out of a sense of moral responsibility but as a metaphor for the awful consequences now facing him. His regret is tantamount to wishing some catastrophe had not occurred to him, such as a lightning strike or trolley-car accident (194). Later in the novel, Carrie similarly feels she has made a "mistake" in going off with Hurstwood despite the fact that she is virtually kidnapped by Hurstwood, lured away under false pretenses (243). Given Hurstwood's and Carrie's relative lack of agency, questions about their moral judgment simply feel inappropriate or out of place.

One of Dreiser's considerable accomplishments in *Sister Carrie* is the novel's power to draw the reader into his representations of life as "mere sensation, without thought" (321). Dreiser's characters are compelling even in their lack of agency. The novel's imaginative grip would seem to be generated in large part by Dreiser's vividly detailed representations of Carrie and Hurstwood, their conflicts, defeats, and triumphs. The completeness of the fictive world he has created combines with graphically rendered but mentally limited characters so as to make them compelling objects of the reader's imagination. They are fascinating to observe. And it is at least possible that, like the audience at the amateur theatrical, we are drawn to them because of not despite their likeness to objects.

## The taste for excess – sensationalism redux

While Dreiser delineates the absence of agency with the same degree of care that James and Howells take in painting its presence, Norris and Crane turn their attention to the often violent drama of being swept away by forces that negate, or overwhelm, human agency. As William Cain observes, Norris is "transfixed by scenes of domination and power" (207). There is an appalling fascination in the image of McTeague tossing Marcus Schouler around as though he were "a bundle of clothes" (235). Crane is drawn to images of explosive energy – a bar-room brawl in *Maggie* that becomes a fantastic detonation of flying glass:

> High on the wall it burst like a bomb, shivering fragments flying in all directions. Then missiles came to every man's hand. The place had heretofore appeared free of things to throw, but suddenly glass and bottles went singing through the air. They were thrown point blank at bobbing heads. The pyramid of shimmering glasses, that had never been disturbed, changed to cascades as heavy bottles were flung into them. Mirrors splintered to nothing. (72)

In Henry Fleming's appetite for being part of a "thunderous, crushing blow" that "prostrate[s]" the enemy, Crane depicts the catharsis of giving oneself over to power, of being swept away by forces beyond one's control (224). In the face of such cataclysmic power, dramas of consent and agency seem not only tepid but fake.

The interest exhibited by writers such as Norris and Crane in images of irresistible power overlaps with a taste for excess running through nineteenth-century fiction from Charles Brockden Brown to Henry James. One gets a sense of this appetite in the many realist novels that flirt with moments of excess or shock only to pull back or hedge the effect. For instance, Jewett clearly enjoys confronting the reader with the startling and graphic spectacle of a woman ably snapping a dislocated shoulder back in place, but she is careful not to portray Nan Prince as "mannish" (120–21). And Nan expressly does not challenge the notion that it is improper for a married woman to engage in a profession (212). In *The Awakening*, Kate Chopin goes to some lengths to diminish the shock of Edna's apparent suicide. Edna's plunge into the Gulf water is warm and suggestive of a second birth, and there is a comforting symmetry in the fact that Edna's development begins and ends with swimming. Silas Lapham's return to the family farm and the rural values of his upbringing relegates such excesses as his drunkenness at a dinner party and his groveling apology to Tom Corey to the level of temporary aberrations. Symmetries of plot, such as the Laphams' return to rural life, conjure images of architectural balance and often suggest that life is subject to rational arrangement and control.

Some realist fiction, however, gives itself over to excess, sensation, and shock. A common detail may give rise to a flight of imaginative excess worthy of Poe (e.g., Henry Fleming's reaction to the babble of a wounded soldier). Or in its stripping away of the traditional sources of human dignity and worth (e.g., the ineluctable course of Hurstwood's degradation), the realist narrative may reach a kind of negative transcendence in which sensation without thought becomes definitional of human existence. Consider, for example, the following description of the grotesqueness of McTeague's physical being:

> The little stove was crammed with coke, the room was overheated, the air thick and foul with the odors of ether, of coke gas, of stale beer and cheap tobacco. The dentist sprawled his gigantic limbs over the worn velvet of the operating chair; his coat and vest and shoes were off, and his huge feet, in their thick gray socks, dangled over the edge of the foot-rest; his pipe, fallen from his half-open mouth, had spilled the ashes into his lap; while on the floor, at his side stood the half-empty pitcher of steam beer. His head had rolled limply upon one shoulder, his face was red with sleep, and from his open mouth came a terrific sound of snoring.   (184)

While each of these details is unremarkable, together they form an outrageous yet compelling image of the human being as a purely physical creature.

After its fairly reportorial opening, Crane's *Maggie* becomes phantasmagorical, taking us into a "dark region," where the horrible bits and events of life in the slum bob up to the narrative surface like submerged body parts. There are details but they are blurred, as though the "loads of babies," the "disordered dress," the "frantic quarrels," the "postures of submission" were coming at us in a rush (39). In this netherworld, doorways are "gruesome" (40) and seem to throb with the misery and degradation just beyond them.

The brutality of the street flows into the home. Maggie's father and mother battle each other and strike their children without hesitation. Mary Johnson's drunken moods swing from "a muddled mist of sentiment" to a demonic fury as "her brain burned in drunken heat" (42). The very figure of her brain burning in drunken heat catapults the narrative from any kind of straight-forward reportage into the creation of a fantastic realm where human beings metamorphose not regressively into beasts and animals as in *McTeague* but into nightmare beings and monsters: "'Good Gawd,' [Mary] howled. Her eyes glittered on her child with sudden hatred. The fervent red of her face turned almost to purple. The little boy ran to the halls, shrieking like a monk in an earthquake" (42).

At the novella's end, Maggie is nameless, a streetwalker seeking "dates," and her namelessness, the way we are not told but still know it is she, has that odd quality of recognition as if in a dream. The namelessness also suggests that this could be anybody, any girl. Crane's final image is horrific:

> When almost to the river the girl saw a great figure. On going forward she perceived it to be a huge fat man in torn and greasy garments. His grey hair straggled down over his forehead. His small, bleared eyes, sparkling from amidst great rolls of red fat, swept eagerly over the girl's upturned face. He laughed, his brown, disordered teeth gleaming under a grey, grizzled moustache from which beer-drops dripped. His whole body gently quivered and shook like that of a dead jelly fish. Chuckling and leering, he followed the girl of the crimson legions.
>
> At their feet the river appeared a deathly black hue. Some hidden factory sent up a yellow glare, that lit for a moment the waters lapping oilily against timbers. The varied sounds of life, made joyous by distance and seeming unapproachableness, came faintly and died away to a silence.   (89)

Maggie's last customer is a monstrous incarnation of the repulsiveness of the putrefying body that is physical existence for those trapped in the lower orders of society. The degraded lives Crane describes are rendered in such extreme terms as to make them seem a different species. Throwing reportorial restraint to the winds, Crane plunges the reader into a grotesquely comic impression of life in the slum that takes the real out of realism. This transmogrification of the real lends an almost metaphysical dimension to Crane's tale of the streets. Despite Crane's introductory note to *Maggie* suggesting that he seeks to promote social reform with his tale, the negative metaphysics of the world he depicts would seem to be far beyond the reach of progressive legislation – one cannot reform Hell.

When thinking about excess, it may seem counterintuitive to include Henry James. However, we can find in James a kindred interest in the onrush of sensation and a willingness to plunge into the muck and mire of life even though it is of a different magnitude and effect. Pulled by the polyglot "allure" of the New York street scene and the city's "dauntless power," James attempts in *The American Scene* (1907) to sustain both the "fine notes" and the "loud ones, the whole play of wealth and energy and untutored liberty, of the movement of a breathless civilization . . . the contrasts of prodigious flight and portentous stumble" (65, 59, 87). This taste for excess leads James to push against notions of refinement or "elegance." When his brother William warns him that his return trip to the US may "yield . . . little besides painful shocks," Henry replies that it is "absolutely *for* . . . the Shocks in general . . . that I nurse my infatuation" (qtd. Posnock 84). These shocks represent an opportunity to open the self to new possibilities, new connections, and new forms of value. James's appetite for such destabilizing sensation "represented a conscious attempt to cast off the burden of deliberation and to be 'led on and on,' subject at all times to the 'hazard of flânerie'" (Posnock 84–85).

Generic distinctions between such subcategories as realism and sensationalism or realism and naturalism can blind us to the overlapping impulses toward order and disorder driving much American fiction. While less graphic and overt, the taste for excess that James shares with writers such as Crane and Norris would seem to evidence some kind of cultural imperative or mutual reaction to the modern world.[17] The nature of this connection becomes clearer, I think, when we look back at the philosophical romances of Poe, Hawthorne, and Melville, the sensational novels of George Lippard, E. D. E. N. Southworth, George Thompson, and others, and the Gothic fiction of Charles Brockden Brown.[18] A taste for sensations that overpower rational processes and mix the high with the low, the pure with the impure, runs through all of this fiction, expressing a profound skepticism about notions of rationalist certainty and moral or aesthetic purity. Henry James's "rich passion . . . for extremes" is surely a part and parcel of his era, but it is also a culminating moment in a line of skeptical fiction stretching back to Charles Brockden Brown and looking forward to the modernists (*Art of the Novel* 31).

James's version of excess is distinctive. Where Crane and Norris distance the reader from their protagonists (as is often the case with sensational literature), a separation that makes their visions of excess in certain ways easier to handle despite their overt horrors and grotesqueries, James removes the distance between the reader and his protagonist. And while he doesn't indulge in the hideous or monstrous image, the shocking moments in his narratives may well prove more disconcerting because they cannot be relegated to the nightmare world of a distant species. *The Portrait of a Lady* offers a representative moment of excess. Isabel decides to leave Rome to see her dying cousin in defiance of her husband's wishes. Osmond, whose attention to the beauties of aesthetic and social form charmed Isabel during their courtship, now seems "malignant" in his desire for formal perfection. Monstrous in its abstraction and purity, his aestheticism is the product of calculation and a domineering rationality, seeking to erase the decay and disorder of life. In "the observance of a magnificent form," he would bar Isabel from visiting Ralph, sacrificing without a moment's hesitation his wife's emotional connection with her cousin (445, 446). But, without a clear foresight of what will follow from her rebellion, Isabel leaves Rome, and, by doing so, she accepts the uncertainty and potential for change that her husband seeks to eliminate. She opens herself to the shock of revelation.

This openness is epitomized in Isabel's embrace of her cousin's frail and diseased body. The contrast of the beautiful young woman and the dying man is stark, but it is the exact opposite of the images of diseased or gross flesh we find in *Maggie* or *McTeague*. The reader does not look down upon the scene from some detached and superior perspective, but is instead drawn into the merger of health and sickness, order and chaos represented by the cousins' embrace. The passion for extremes expressed here has different implications from the shocking moments of the sensationalist or naturalist text. Isabel's rebellion against the lifeless purity of Osmond's calculated formalism raises difficult questions about her marriage and her connection to Osmond's daughter Pansy. Like Isabel, the reader is uncertain as to the value and import of these relations and institutions. Should Isabel leave Osmond? Is her marriage utterly without value and undeserving of any deference? What about her connection to Pansy, which is real and valuable even if it is not the traditional or archetypal mother/daughter relation? James's pursuit of the disquieting experience intruding upon one's biases and habitual perspective is perhaps most fully captured by his novel's famous refusal of closure. James does not end Isabel's process of feeling her way into and through life. To render concrete the disruption of her preconceptions, James cannot end the novel with the kind of tidy closure that marks so many realist novels, including Eliot's masterpiece *Middlemarch*. James does not give Isabel or his readers resolution, and in that there is a kind of shock – the shock of the defiance of novelistic convention.

# Notes

## Introduction

1. Wanting a certain comprehensiveness of reference as well as depth of analysis, I have alternated in this study between passages surveying numerous texts and more detailed accounts of particular novels. The novels selected for more lengthy analysis strike me as usefully representative of certain important facets of the genre. Even when passing over many novels rather quickly, I have attempted to include enough information about the plots and characters so that the reader unfamiliar with these texts can follow the thread of my argument.

2. Citing Bakhtin's characterization of fiction "as a *subversive* literary form," Cathy Davidson finds that the novels of the early republic worked to subvert certain class notions of who should and should not be literate and of what is or is not a suitable literary subject matter and form and style (13). Davidson's account may make one wonder how the novel goes about nudging society in a certain direction (it's easy to see how the novel will inevitably reflect social change but a bit harder perhaps to see how it can be an agent of change). Do readers generally pick up and read novels because they look to fiction to subvert the dominant paradigm? If not, how does the novelistic entertainment work this bit of social alchemy? Critics such as Ian Watt and Larzer Ziff suggest an answer to this question when they view the novel's reader as being placed in the role of a juror or voter – someone with a decision to make, someone whose consent will be important, and whose choice will be based on bits of narrative evidence and the inferences derived from that evidence (Watt 31, Ziff 75–76). The reader is asked implicitly to reach a verdict about the characters and events related in the novel, and being put in that position by a piece of literature corresponds with the nation's democratic experiment in self-rule. Thus, as Cathy Davidson points out, the early American novel can be connected to the process historian Gordon Wood has called the "democratization of mind" (45).

3. Samuel Richardson's very influential novel, *Clarissa* (1748), is the prototype for the American seduction stories. Richardson's epistolary novel tells the story of Clarissa Harlowe, who is pursued by the handsome rake, Lovelace (whose name, "loveless," indicates his elemental flaw), with fatal results for both.

4. Legibility takes a racial cast in Jefferson's *Notes on the State of Virginia* (1785) when he describes "the real distinctions which nature has made" between black and white,

which bar the races from peaceful coexistence as equals in a republican society: "Are not the fine mixtures of red and white, the expressions of every passion by greater or less suffusions of colour in the one, preferable to that eternal monotony, which reigns in the countenances, that immoveable veil of black which covers all the emotions of the other race?" (138). Veiled emotionally by their complexion, black people, Jefferson suggests, cannot be read, and reading people aright clearly appears to be of critical importance to his conception of a democratic society. Important things, such as the character of our fellow citizens, their moral natures, must be legible in their features if we are to be able to judge for ourselves how to assess their schemes, proposals, and acts. The Revolution was partly driven by a confidence in each person's ability to derive fundamental principles, such as the "self-evident truths" of the Declaration, from individual experience. If people and their actions become unknowable or too fluid to ascertain, then what happens to the confidence in human reason underlying the democratic experiment?

5. As Jay Fliegelman has pointed out, the belief in contractual relations, by definition open to dissolution, was "[c]entral to the rationalist ideology of the American Revolution" (123).

6. Christopher Looby aptly describes the social break represented by the Revolution. Where other nations could plausibly posit "their coherence as a matter of racial and ethnic similarity, religious orthodoxy, population concentration, geographical definition, massive and dense structures of inherited customary practices," American notions of cohesion had to deal with radical diversity in terms of race, ethnicity, religion, population dispersal, and geographical mutability. These factors problematized if they did not "demolish" "traditional notions of nationality" (14). Instead, "[t]he new nationality that was being constructed in America was of a new kind: based on consent rather than descent" (250).

7. In her discussion of the "democratic personality," Nancy Ruttenburg astutely frames the ambivalence many authors felt about the common man in terms of the suspicion or anxiety that even the rudest and uncouth might have an access to truths that exceed or defy conventional social expectations of breeding and education (291).

8. In his Gothic novel, *The Asylum* (1811), Isaac Mitchell skips such gestures toward plausibility, surprising the reader with a castle in Connecticut.

9. The kind of romantic enthusiasm for social experiments and democratic reform that one finds in Gilbert Imlay's *The Emigrants* (1793) offers a revealing contrast to Brown's Gothic fiction. *The Emigrants* uses the frontier setting as the backdrop for a tale of romance and adventure, which, along the way, takes up legal and political questions, such as women's rights. As a guide to behavior and the proper structure for human relations, for Imlay, the individual's independent moral reason is clearly superior to social convention. As one of his characters says, the individual can independently discern "the eternal truths of morality" whereas traditional social convention is "nothing but the loud voice of foolish prejudice" and "has no more stability than the wind" (105). Imlay's argument in the novel for a more liberal approach to divorce reflects his apparent commitment to reciprocity and consent as

the governing principles of human relations. Reciprocity – the idea of fair exchange or quid pro quo – is perhaps the most emphasized concept in Imlay's novel, coming up over and over in the mouths of many characters and representing the standard of just human relations. The utopian community described at the end of the novel is presented as a model of democratic society, with each of the male members of the community owning equal parcels of land and being entitled to vote. The community's primary gathering place will be the hall of its democratically elected assembly rather than a church, suggesting the degree to which reason has displaced faith in Imlay's ideal community (233–34).

10. David S. Reynolds associates Brown's Gothic novels with the "visionary mode" of American fiction intent upon rebutting Enlightenment rationalism, and he observes how Brown "moved from the visionary to the secular, from an identification of religion with solitary communion to an interest in the workings of faith in human society" (*Faith in Fiction* 39, 43).

11. Jared Gardner finds in Brown's manipulations of the distinction between savage and civilized man a narrative of national identity: the identity at issue in Huntly is national as well as "(generally) human or (particularly) individual. Examining the novel in the context of the fiercely fought identity debates of the early national period, we are able to see the ways in which Brown's Indian adventure is not simply a shadowy progenitor of Cooper's nineteenth-century tales; for Brown the threat of the Indian has less to do with the questions of what it means to be civilized than with the question – newly urgent in the United States in 1799 – of what it means to be American" (53). Gardner's reading of *Edgar Huntly* corresponds with Christopher Looby's sense that Brown found "the rational-legal foundation of the United States" to be "dangerously inadequate by virtue of its neglect of the visceral need of citizens for more psychically compelling modes of attachment to their nation" (5). Rogers Smith's *Civic Ideals* presents an impressive array of historical evidence indicating the political necessity for emotionally powerful conceptions of national identity.

12. In sharp contrast to the nightmarish wild of Brown's *Edgar Huntly*, the wilderness in Imlay's *The Emigrants* is a place free from the taint and corruption of older, more established social systems. The natural processes of metamorphosis one finds in the wild are wholesome, life-affirming, and beautiful, and the human transformation that this landscape inspires is similarly beneficial. For instance, in describing the beauties of the wilderness, the hero and heroine of Imlay's tale, Captain Arl–ton and Caroline, observe that in contrast to London:

> here is a continual feast for the mind – every rock, every tree, every moss, from their novelty afford subject for contemplation and amusement. Look at yonder towering hills, (pointing at the same time at a rocky ridge considerably above the others,) whose summits appear to prop the heavens, and then view the various symbols which their chasms produce, and what sublime imagery does it afford? – What can more resemble the ruins of a great city? – That grand division which rises higher upon the right, has the form and figure of a superb mosque – the left and various other divisions, that of palaces, temples, churches, streets, and

squares, and you would suppose, if Pope had ever travelled this road, that he must have had the center division in his imagination, when he so beautifully described his temple of Fame. Caroline might have proceeded in this way to eternity, and I should not have interrupted her; for such was my astonishment at the fertility of her imagination, that I heard her with amazement, and gazed at her with the most ineffable transports!  (25)

The radical contrasts of the wild setting, suggestive of great forces acting upon the earth, inspires in Caroline a metamorphic string of associations, one morphing into the next, and this "fertility" of imagination, in turn, inspires Arl–ton. The aesthetics of the scene are clearly tied to notions of movement and transformation which are themselves symbols of energy and power – whether of the mind or of nature – the power to make and the power to become, to shift form and take on new and varied significance. Degeneration and waste are reserved for the city and "sophisticated" characters such as Caroline's brother who mocks her poetic response to nature (28). Even the dangers of the wilds, such as Indian kidnappers, do not obscure, for Imlay or his characters, the beauty and essential goodness of nature.

13. Brown's subtitle, The Transformation, as Jay Fliegelman has pointed out,

refers not only to the transformation of Wieland but to a broad historical trans-formation, the shift from a world that assumed stable forms and fixed relations between appearance and reality and between man and society to a world sen-sitive to shifting values, deceptive appearances, mixed motives and, most sig-nificantly, the tyranny of language over things, rhetoric over logic. A secure world has been made insecure and that, Brown announces, is the price of having become "free." By placing his novel in the decade before the American Revolu-tion, Brown suggests, by implication, that the great conflict for American indepen-dence, rather than merely being a result of that larger "transformation," decisively hastened it.  (240)

14. When rejecting the opportunity to inherit a vast fortune under the European laws of male primogeniture, Wieland sounds the republican themes of the Revolution: "What security had he [Pleyel] that in this change of place and condition, he should not degenerate into a tyrant and voluptuary? Power and riches were chiefly to be dreaded on account of their tendency to deprave the possessor" (42). Seeing the device as a means to prop up a corrupt "aristocracy of wealth," Thomas Jefferson was very proud of his work to abolish primogeniture in Virginia (Wood 182).

## 1  The romance

1. In *The American Novel and Its Tradition*, Richard Chase celebrated those qualities that distinguished the romance from the novel, including the romance's disconnec-tion from the probable and the usual. In romance, Chase explained, "'experience' has less to do with human beings as 'social creatures' than as individuals. Heroes, villains, victims, legendary types, confronting other individuals or confronting

mysterious or otherwise dire forces – this is what we meet in romances." The romancer was freed by his narrative form from being bound to descriptions of social mores, practices, and historical forces (38, 22, 39).

2. It should be noted that many aspects of the account of the rise of the novel offered by Ian Watt, Michael McKeon, and others have been challenged by Margaret Anne Doody. Among other things, Doody argues that the novel is not as new, as secular, or as English as Watt and McKeon say it is, and she demurs that the distinction between the novel and the romance is not as sharp or as important as she sees her adversaries as contending.

3. In "Georgia Theatrics," Longstreet's cultured narrator relishing the pastoral beauty of a bucolic countryside comes upon a rustic plowboy imitating a brutal fight in front of the local county courthouse. The fight ends when the imaginary opponent cries, "Enough! My eye's out!" Mistaking this reenactment for the event itself, Longstreet's narrator is appalled that "this heavenly retreat" should be disfigured by "such Pandaemonian riots" (4–5). The dark humor of the scene lies in the disruption of the narrator's romantic reverie. Sut Lovingood, George Washington Harris's malignly comic creation, contradicts such romantic fantasies by bluntly declaring the vulgar competitive reality of existence: "Whar thar ain't enuf feed, big childer roots little childer outen the troff, an' gobbils up thar part" (174). Self-interest and inequalities of power are the only reality; any other explanation of life is hogwash.

4. Robert Levine offers a compelling argument that the American romance is distinguished by the figure and theme of conspiracy, demonstrating how the form is grounded in a certain kind of "us/them" conflict in which the genuine identity and resemblance of those constituting the "us" becomes critical and is defined against the alien and covert forces of the "them" (e.g., the puritans against "popery" or Euro-Americans against Indians) (4–5, 7).

5. In her preface, Sedgwick makes clear her desire to combat prejudice against the Indian:

> The liberal philanthropist will not be offended by a representation which supposes that the elements of virtue and intellect are not withheld from any branch of the human family; and the enlightened and accurate observer of human nature, will admit that the difference of character among the various races of the earth, arises mainly from difference of condition.    (*Hope Leslie* 6)

However, though she wants to work against such prejudice, Sedgwick seems far from certain that the Indian could ever be fully incorporated in the body politic.

6. The frankly anti-sentimental cast of this racial invective is captured in Teddy Roosevelt's condemnation of Helen Hunt Jackson's documentary protest of the treatment of the American Indian, *A Century of Dishonor* (1881), as irresponsible, sentimental drivel "capable of doing great harm" in the hands of a "large class of maudlin fanatics" (68–69, 81–82).

7. In "What to the Slave is the Fourth of July," Douglass expressly frames his view of the Constitution in the kind of cosmopolitan and fluid terms that Kennedy dreads:

> No nation can now shut itself up from the surrounding world, and trot round in the same old path of its fathers without interference . . . Long established customs of hurtful character could formerly fence themselves in, and do their evil work with social impunity . . . [A] change has now come over the affairs of mankind. Walled cities and empires have become unfashionable. The arm of commerce has borne away the gates of the strong city. Intelligence is penetrating the darkest corners of the globe . . . Wind, steam, and lightning are its chartered agents. Oceans no longer divide, but link nations together. From Boston to London is now a holiday excursion. Space is comparatively annihilated. Thoughts expressed on one side of the Atlantic are distinctly heard on the other. (386)

8. Noting that the three novelists I have selected as exemplifying the philosophical romance are male, some readers may well be curious to examine the implications of this subcategory of romance in terms of gender. This is a topic of considerable interest – the historic conditions and contextual factors apparently suggesting different types of fictional production to male and female authors. For want of space, I have to leave a fulsome exploration of this topic to others, yet I cannot leave it without observing that philosophy looms large in the novels of such nineteenth-century women authors as Charlotte Brontë, George Eliot, Elizabeth Stoddard, Harriet Beecher Stowe, and others. Also, it strikes me that the philosophical romances of Poe, Hawthorne, and Melville variously seek to defy gender expectations, in part through feminized protagonists (one thinks of Melville's figuring of Ishmael as bride and Queequeg as groom in *Moby-Dick*) and in part through their suggestion that philosophical speculation has an androgynous aspect or mood. In the preface to *The Scarlet Letter*, Hawthorne expressly distinguishes his literary vocation from the masculine world of commerce and politics, and his philosophical romance ostensibly is inspired by the discovery of a bit of feminine dress, a scrap of embroidered fabric (104, 107).

9. While, like many others, I see a striking connection between the philosophical speculations of Emerson and the philosophical fictions of Melville, Poe, and Hawthorne, I should note in passing that these figures were hardly identical in their philosophical or literary views (Hawthorne's doubts about transcendentalism are apparent in *The Blithesdale Romance* and elsewhere, and Emerson famously dismissed Poe as the "jingle man"). Melville expressed his ambivalence about Emerson in a letter to his friend, Evert Duyckinck,

> Nay, I do not oscillate in Emerson's rainbow . . . Yet I think Emerson is more than a brilliant fellow. Be his stuff begged, borrowed or stolen, or of his own domestic manufacture he is an uncommon man . . . I love all those who dive. Any fish can swim near the surface, but it takes a great whale to go down five stairs or more . . . I'm not talking of Emerson now – but of the whole corps of thought-divers, that have been diving and coming up again with blood-shot eyes since the world began. (Leyda 292)

While Melville appears to be uncertain whether Emerson dives deep enough, even the implicit criticism (more explicitly stated elsewhere) suggests Melville's recognition of the connection in their speculative ventures.

10. Recent criticism has done much to excavate Poe's distaste for the institution of slavery, his distrust of abolitionism, and his fear of the racial other (Jones 239–40).
11. While many Americans, such as Margaret Fuller and Hawthorne's wife Sophia, were sympathetic to the republican revolutions sweeping Europe in 1848, as Larry Reynolds has pointed out, Hawthorne seems to have been somewhat more ambivalent – attracted yet skeptical ("Scarlet Letter"). Aptly locating the signs of revolutionary concern in *The Scarlet Letter*, Reynolds ultimately finds a greater, more complete skepticism about revolution in Hawthorne's novel than I do.
12. In "Egotism, or the Bosom Serpent," Hawthorne uses the comparison of man and snake to blur the boundaries between the human and the bestial.
13. I am indebted to Sharon Cameron's *The Corporeal Self* and *Impersonality* for the application of this philosophical distinction to Melville and Hawthorne.
14. Deadwood Dick's real name is Edward Harris. Two rich and apparently respectable characters, Alexander Filmore and his son Clarence, are responsible for the deaths of Edward's parents and the theft of his inheritance. Edward's transformation into Deadwood Dick and Dick's life of crime represent a reaction against the depredations of the upper classes. Similarly, in *The Life and Adventures of Joaquín Murieta*, the good-natured Joaquín Murieta is turned into a ferocious bandit bent on vengeance by the rape of his beloved Rosita at the hands of Anglo miners. Richard Slotkin has described how the Hawkeye figure of Cooper's historical romances mutates in the "cheap literature" from the 1840s to the latter decades of the century to become an outlaw:

> After 1875 . . . many of the most popular new dime-novel series abandoned Indian-war settings in favor of conflicts between "outlaws" and "detectives," and the struggle between classes. The hero of these postwar dime novels is no longer the protector or vindicator of the "genteel" values of order and respectability, as Hawkeye and his dime-novel successors had been. In fact, some of the most popular of these heroes are criminals drawn to banditry by a mixture of social injustice and an innate propensity or "gift" for antisocial behavior. (*Gunfighter* 127)

Deadwood Dick and the earlier figure of Joaquín Murieta are outlaw/heroes of the type Eric Hobsbawm describes in his book *Bandits*. They are "social bandits" pursued by the government as criminals but considered by many to be heroes (13). Social bandits have no revolutionary agenda, but they do avenge certain injustices committed against the weak and vulnerable, sometimes with a collateral influence on larger social or political movements.

## 2 The sentimental novel

1. Lori Merish sees the era's sentimentalism as tied to "construction of the feminine consumer as a new civic identity for women" (6). For Merish, nineteenth-century invocations of sentiment worked to depoliticize class and race relations by assuming

a generalized moral and national identity which erases the differences and divergent interests running through the society (13). Lora Romero challenges this type of starkly oppositional treatment, contending that sentimental fiction may be "radical on some issues (market capitalism, for example) and reactionary on others (gender or race, for instance)." Some may be "conservative without being . . . enslaving" or "oppositional without being liberating" (4).

2. As Philip Fisher puts it, "Compassion is . . . the primary emotional goal of sentimental narration. Compassion exists in relation to suffering and makes of suffering the primary subject matter, perhaps the exclusive subject matter, of sentimental narrative" (105).

3. The sentimental novel's emphasis on domesticity can be read as part of a widespread attempt to invest women and the home with a moral primacy as compensation for the declining economic importance of the home in a world where husbands and wives no longer jointly work family-owned farms but in which the men go off to work leaving the women and children at home alone (Romero 24).

4. In *Public Sentiments*, Glenn Hendler rightly cautions that eighteenth- and nineteenth-century notions of sentiment should not be thought of as "the sorts of unique, individualized, interior emotions they are in our more psychologized culture" (2). Yet while such emotions were not thought of in the same private or psychologized fashion as they are in our culture, Stowe and others clearly had some notion that the individual's internal emotional experience was critical to a one-to-one relation between the individual and God. Hence, a leap of some distance had to be made in conceiving of the individual's conversion experience as a model for the conversion of an entire society.

5. James M. Cox, for instance, has argued that Stowe wrote "against the law" out of what he calls her "essentially sentimental determination to choose the religion of love over the religion of judgment" (455). Taking at face value Stowe's characterizations of sentiment as a feminine alternative to the masculine realms of law and commerce, such accounts see Stowe as separating love from law, heart from head. In "The Ecstasies of Sentimental Wounding in *Uncle Tom's Cabin*," Marianne Noble pursues this line, arguing that Stowe's project is to get the head out of the way so that the heart can act (298–99, 304). This reading, however, strikes me as a simplification of Stowe's approach which ultimately recommends grounding rational process on one's emotional registrations of right and wrong. We can see this process at work in the debate between Senator and Mrs. Bird over the legitimacy of the Fugitive Slave Act and in the discussion between George Harris and Mr. Wilson on the propriety of George's escape from slavery. In both instances, sympathetic feelings and rational discussion combine to form a new consensus between people formerly at odds on the issue.

6. The symbolic significance of the various domestic spaces of the novel is well mapped by Gillian Brown's *Domestic Individualism* (13–38).

7. In her analysis of Harriet Jacobs's strategies of sympathy in *Incidents in the Life of a Slave Girl*, Dana Nelson observes that the goal of "[s]ympathy" is to "*bridge*

the gap of difference . . . Yet it neither can nor should *collapse* the differences that it bridges" (144). Critics such as Saidiya Hartman and Laura Wexler object that the project of sympathetic bridging or identification is impossible or inevitably oppressive (reinstating the unequal power relations with the sympathizer standing over, figuratively speaking, the sympathized). While sympathy can be oppressive, it seems less than helpful and not particularly believable to suggest or imply that it is inevitably so. Sympathy between friends who conceive of each other as equals (and who occupy similar stations in life) would not necessarily entail oppression. Hence, the problem is not necessarily about sympathy at all, but probably has more to do with inequality (e.g., the sympathy of the lord for the peasant, the slave holder for the slave, the millionaire for the beggar).

8. In discussing this passage with students and colleagues, I have often found that they are put off by the "Village of the Damned" quality of the Quaker community. Its odd absence of dispute makes it somehow frightening or disturbing.

9. It should be noted that while Stowe is uncompromisingly critical of the displacement of moral feeling by profit motive whether it occurs in slavery or capitalism, she clearly does not condemn the mechanism of contract as inherently coercive. Whether deluded or not, Stowe's views differ significantly from those of more recent commentators, such as Michel Foucault, Louis Althusser, and Carole Pateman, who are variously skeptical of the distinction between coercion and consent. Under the influence of Michel Foucault's view of all law as coercive, for instance, one may feel that the notion of a consensual legal mechanism is a contradiction in terms. See, for example, the image of law presented in the famous opening pages of Foucault's *Discipline and Punish* (see, also, Althusser 156–57, 167–68; Pateman 8).

10. As Eric Sundquist has pointed out, Stowe's advocacy of sentiment went "beyond the restricted 'women's sphere' of feminine involvement with the politics of slavery advocated by Catharine Beecher" ("Slavery" 18). Indeed, Stowe's jurisprudence of feeling transgressed Catharine Beecher's deference to the principles of "social rectitude" embodied in law and custom:

> In Catharine's earlier writings the law of God was roughly congruent with the laws of man. There was no inherent conflict between human institutions and heavenly proscriptions. Yet now in the 1850s Catharine saw a clear difference and possible conflict between heavenly and earthly justice and between religious benevolence and social rectitude. In all cases she maintained that the best rule for men to follow was a worldly rather than a heavenly one. (Sklar 247)

11. The importance of basic norms of proper deportment for black nationalists, such as Sutton Griggs, suggests a general acceptance among African Americans of the late nineteenth century that conventions of social interaction are an indispensable part of creating any polity, whether separatist or integrationist (Moses 178–81).

12. For contemporary readers, Phelps's religious message of compassion embodied in Sip Garth (the innately sensitive factory worker) and Perley Kelso (the mill owner's sympathetic daughter) may well seem distinctly inadequate as an answer to the

harrowingly grim existence of the New England mill workers and the economic forces at play in their oppression.

## 3    The realist novel

1. Like Michael Davitt Bell and June Howard, I am suspicious of paradigmatic distinctions between realism and naturalism. For one thing, as Bell points out, the realist practices of such definitional figures as Twain, Howells, and James are marked by stark and substantial differences (1).
2. In *Private Fleming at Chancellorsville*, Perry Lentz analyzes the parallels between Crane's war story and the Battle of Chancellorsville.
3. Richard Brodhead helpfully sums up some of the defining traits of this regional or local-color fiction:

   > It requires a setting outside the world of modern development, a zone of backwardness where locally variant folkways still prevail. Its characters are ethnologically colorful, personifications of the different humanity produced in such non-modern cultural settings. Above all, this fiction features an extensive written simulation of regional vernacular, a conspicuous effort to catch the nuances of local speech.  (115–16)

4. Booker T. Washington's famous example of the brick manufacture at Tuskeegee illustrates his version of freedom through economic contract – "We had something which they wanted [good bricks at a fair price]; they had something which we wanted [money]. This, in a large measure, helped to lay the foundation for the pleasant relations that have continued to exist between us and the white people in that section, and which now extend throughout the South" (153). Amy Dru Stanley provides a cogent and well-researched account of the centrality of contract for post-emancipation feminist reformers (4–17, 177–86).
5. Of course, women, Native Americans, African Americans, and many others reading this passage might well and with good reason ridicule Sumner's facile dispatching of the status-based models of citizenship then and now. But such inconsistencies between practice and principle provide the cultural leverage on which reform movements depend.
6. See, for example, Chief Justice Marshall's comments in *Ogden* v. *Saunders:* "If, on tracing the right to contract, and the obligations created by contract, to their source, we find them to exist anterior to, and independent of society, we may reasonably conclude that those original and pre-existing principles are, like many other natural rights brought with man into society; and, although they may be controlled, are not given by human legislation" (345).
7. Chesnutt's fiction is replete with suggestions of the shift from status to contract. For instance, the first short story in *The Conjure Woman*, "The Goophered Grapevine," begins and ends in the establishment of a new contractual relation between John, the Ohio businessman transplanted to North Carolina, and Uncle Julius, the narrator of the dialect tales.

8. Like Stowe, Howells had a keen sense of the novelist's moral responsibility. As Michael Davitt Bell points out, for Howells,

> the task of literature is defined almost wholly in moral terms; the proper role of the writer . . . is understood almost entirely in terms of his *responsibility* to society . . . The second essential component of Howellsian realism grows directly out of the first: the realist exercises social responsibility, first of all, by discrediting what is *irresponsible* – the "romantic," the "literary," the "artificial," the merely "artistic." (47–48)

9. As Ross Posnock points out, James described himself to his brother, William, as practicing pragmatism unconsciously. In this pragmatist vein, James conceives of contemplation as action, abolishing "at a stroke . . . classical epistemology's spectator theory of knowledge, which posits a static mind passively receiving sense data" (85).

10. June Howard rightly contends, I think, that naturalism presents brutal characters whose lives are shaped by forces beyond their control from the point of view of middle-class readers who are largely exempt from the deterministic factors hemming in the characters in naturalist fiction.

11. When Myra Bradwell complained that Illinois's refusal to admit her to the State Bar because she was a married woman violated the Fourteenth Amendment's equal protection clause, Justice Joseph P. Bradley referred to history and nature – both of which demonstrated the "wide difference in the respective spheres and destinies of man and woman." Bradley sees the professional woman as threatening to disrupt the "harmony" of the "family institution" (*Bradwell* 131, 136).

12. James Caron rightly notes that the grotesqueness of McTeague's physique is an emblem of the comic explosion of force one can also find in the old southwest humorists, a humor based on the recognition that the finer attributes of life do not govern life.

13. In *Hard Facts*, Philip Fisher makes a different but related point. He describes how "[w]ithin the city" described by Dreiser, "all things become commodities – all objects, all other persons . . . They are commodities not so much because they are desired and sold, but because our relation to them has shifted from caring for things that one has (whether given or bought) to buying things one hasn't" (134). He juxtaposes an ostensibly more authentic, more traditional relation between owner and thing in which the person values the thing because it has been absorbed into the owner's life (e.g., a tool one has used for years) with the more superficial purchase of the consumer driven by marketing and the fleeting appetite aroused in large part by the feeling that consumable things offer the buyer some vicarious allure or "sex-appeal." For my purposes, Fisher's analysis is very helpful in its recognition that we want things because we don't have them: absence is critical to the consumer's desire. Hence the rapidity with which our desire for such objects fades on possession.

14. Carrie's rocking chair is, as Robert Penn Warren noted, the embodiment of motion without progress.

15. Walter Benn Michaels has argued that the logic of the market dominates Dreiser's novel, but this seems to me less a testament to the irresistibility of the economic paradigm of the moment than a conscious attempt on Dreiser's part to argue that our desires are driven by the same principles of human nature whether in commercial consumption or pursuit of sexual and romantic gratification (29–58). Amy Kaplan sees Dreiser's portrayals of materialist desire as connected to a longing for meaning and agency that commodities can trigger but which cannot be slaked by consumerism: "The consumption of commodities in Sister Carrie functions in the novel to compensate for social powerlessness" (140–60).

16. In *A Sense of Things*, Bill Brown describes how, at the end of the nineteenth century, "the invention, production, distribution, and consumption of things rather suddenly came to define" American culture (137). In a replay of Jackson Lears's observation of anti-modernist and modernist trends in turn-of-the-century culture, Brown notes that certain writers and intellectuals were critical of the era's consumerism and growing obsession with things as both a sign and source of their society's alienation from traditional sources of meaning, while others found in the thing the possibility of a new form of connection between the subject and the material world.

17. James criticizes Howells for his distaste for excess. Life, says James, "is a mixture of many things: she by no means eschews the strange, and often risks combinations and effects that make one rub one's eyes." Adoring "the real, the natural, the colloquial, the moderate, the optimistic, the domestic, and the democratic," Howells looks "askance at exceptions and perversities and superiorities, as surprising and incongruous phenomena in general," and he doesn't, James complains here, want to rub his eyes or make us rub ours, which a certain degree of strangeness, opacity, or difficulty would make us do (Anesko 253).

18. Looking back at novels in the sentimental tradition, such as Harriet Beecher Stowe's *Uncle Tom's Cabin* or T. S. Arthur's *Ten Nights in a Bar-Room*, or novels caught between sentimental and realist modes, such as Rebecca Harding Davis's *Life in the Iron-Mills* or Elizabeth Stuart Phelps's *The Silent Partner*, one finds many scenes meant to shock the reader, such as Uncle Tom's martyrdom. To some extent, such scenes probably do reflect their authors' and readers' taste for overwhelming sensation, but the effect of this sensation cannot be said, I think, to disorient the reader or encourage skepticism. The moral thrust of scenes is never really in doubt. The slave holders and mill owners are cruel despots who should be deposed, and recognizing this truth is itself an important step in the direction of reform.

# Works cited

Alger, Horatio. *"Ragged Dick" and "Mark, The Match Boy."* New York: Touchstone, 1998.

Althusser, Louis. "Ideology and Ideological State Apparatuses (Notes towards an Investigation)." *"Lenin and Philosophy" and Other Essays.* New York: Monthly Review, 1971.

Anesko, Michael. *Letters, Fictions, Lives: Henry James and William Dean Howells.* New York: Oxford University Press, 1997.

Arthur, T. S. *Ten Nights in a Bar-Room and What I Saw There.* Cambridge MA: Harvard University Press, 1964.

Bakhtin, Mikhail M. *The Dialogic Imagination: Four Essays.* Austin: University of Texas Press, 1981.

Baym, Nina. "Concepts of Romance in Hawthorne's America." *Nineteenth-Century Fiction* 38 (1984): 426–43.

   *Woman's Fiction: A Guide to Novels by and about Women in America, 1820–70.* Urbana: University of Illinois Press, 1993.

Bell, Michael Davitt. *The Problem of American Realism: Studies in the Cultural History of an Idea.* Chicago: University of Chicago Press, 1993.

Benjamin, Walter. "The Storyteller: Reflections on the Works of Nikolai Leskov." *Illuminations.* New York: Schocken, 1969.

Bennett, Emerson. *The Prairie Flower; or, Adventures in the Far West.* Upper Saddle River: Gregg, 1970.

Bingham, John. *Congressional Globe.* 36th Congress, 2nd Session (23 January 1861). Appendix.

Bird, Robert Montgomery. *Nick of the Woods, or The Jibbenainosay. A Tale of Kentucky.* New Haven: College and University Press, 1967.

Brackenridge, Hugh Henry. *Modern Chivalry.* New York: American Book, 1937.

*Bradwell* v. *State of Illinois,* 83 US 130 (1873).

Brodhead, Richard H. *Cultures of Letters: Scenes of Reading and Writing in Nineteenth-Century America.* Chicago: University of Chicago Press, 1993.

Brown, Bill. *A Sense of Things: The Object Matter of American Literature.* Chicago: University of Chicago Press, 2003.

Brown, Charles Brockden. *Edgar Huntly; Or, Memoirs of a Sleep-Walker.* New York: Penguin, 1988.

*Wieland; Or The Transformation. An American Tale.* New York: Harcourt, 1926.

Brown, Gillian. *Domestic Individualism: Imagining Self in Nineteenth-Century America.* Berkeley: University of California Press, 1990.

Brown, William Hill. *The Power of Sympathy.* New York: Penguin, 1996.

Brown, William Wells. *Clotel; or, The President's Daughter: A Narrative of Slave Life in the United States.* Boston: Bedford, 2000.

*The Black Man, His Antecedents, His Genius, and His Achievements.* Miami: Mnemosyne, 1969.

Butcher, Phillip. *George Washington Cable.* New York: Twayne, 1962.

Butler, James. *Fortune's Foot-Ball: or, the Adventures of Mercutio. Founded on Matters of Fact. A Novel, in Two Volumes.* Harrisburgh: Wyeth, 1797.

Cable, George Washington. *John March, Southerner.* New York: Scribner's, 1898.

*The Grandissimes: A Story of Creole Life.* New York: Sagamore, 1957.

Cain, William E. "Presence and Power in *McTeague.*" *American Realism: New Essays.* Ed. Eric J. Sundquist. Baltimore: Johns Hopkins University Press, 1982. 199–214.

Cameron, Sharon. *Impersonality: Seven Essays.* Chicago: University of Chicago Press, 2007.

*The Corporeal Self.* Baltimore: Johns Hopkins University Press, 1981.

Cardwell, Guy A. *Twins of Genius.* East Lansing: Michigan State University Press, 1953.

Caron, James L. "Grotesque Naturalism: The Significance of the Comic in *McTeague.*" *Texas Studies in Literature and Language* 31 (Summer 1989): 288–317.

Carton, Evan. *The Rhetoric of American Romance: Dialectic and Identity in Emerson, Dickinson, Poe, and Hawthorne.* Baltimore: Johns Hopkins University Press, 1985.

Chase, Richard. *The American Novel and Its Tradition.* Garden City NY: Doubleday, 1957.

Chesnutt, Charles. "The Goophered Grapevine." *The Collected Stories of Charles W. Chesnutt.* New York: Mentor, 1992.

*The Marrow of Tradition.* Ann Arbor: University of Michigan Press, 1969.

Child, Lydia Maria. *A Romance of the Republic.* Lexington: University of Kentucky Press, 1997.

*Hobomok and Other Writings on Indians.* New Brunswick: Rutgers University Press, 1986.

Chopin, Kate. *At Fault.* New York: Penguin, 2002.

*The Awakening.* New York: Norton, 1976.

Coleridge, Samuel Taylor. *Biographia Literaria. Samuel Taylor Coleridge: The Oxford Authors.* New York: Oxford University Press, 1985.

Cooper, James Fenimore. *The Last of the Mohicans.* New York: Penguin, 1986.

*The Spy; A Tale of the Neutral Ground.* New York: Penguin, 1997.

Cox, James M. "Harriet Beecher Stowe: From Sectionalism to Regionalism." *Nineteenth-Century Fiction* 38 (1984): 444–66.

Crane, Gregg D. *Race, Citizenship, and Law in American Literature.* Cambridge: Cambridge University Press, 2002.

Crane, Stephen. *Maggie: A Girl of the Streets (A Story of New York).* Boston: Bedford, 1999.

*"The Red Badge of Courage" and Other Writings.* Boston: Houghton Mifflin, 1960.

Cummins, Maria. *The Lamplighter.* New York: Odyssey Press, 1968.

Davidson, Cathy N. *Revolution and the Word: The Rise of the Novel in America.* New York: Oxford University Press, 1986.

Davis, Rebecca Harding. *Life in the Iron-Mills.* Boston: Bedford, 1998.

De Forest, John W. *Miss Ravenel's Conversion from Secession to Loyalty.* New York: Penguin, 2000.

Dekker, George. *The American Historical Romance.* Cambridge: Cambridge University Press, 1987.

Delbanco, Andrew. *Melville: His World and Work.* New York: Knopf, 2005.

Denning, Michael. *Mechanic Accents: Dime Novels and Working-Class Culture in America.* London: Verso, 1987.

Doody, Margaret Anne. *The True Story of the Novel.* New Brunswick: Rutgers University Press, 1996.

Douglas, Ann. *The Feminization of American Culture.* New York: Avon, 1978.

Douglass, Frederick. *The Heroic Slave.* Boston: Jewett, 1853.

"The Slumbering Volcano." *The Frederick Douglass Papers: Series One – Speeches, Debates, and Interviews.* Ed. John Blassingame. Vol. II. New Haven: Yale University Press, 1982.

"What to the Slave is the Fourth of July." *The Frederick Douglass Papers: Series One – Speeches, Debates, and Interviews.* Ed. John Blassingame. Vol. II. New Haven: Yale University Press, 1982.

*Dred Scott* v. *Sandford,* 60 US 393 (1857).

Dreiser, Theodore. *Sister Carrie.* New York: Norton, 1991.

"True Art Speaks Plainly." *Booklover's Magazine* 1 (February 1903): 129.

Drinnon, Richard. *Facing West: The Metaphysics of Indian-Hating and Empire Building.* Norman: University of Oklahoma Press, 1997.

duCille, Ann. *The Coupling Convention: Sex, Text, and Tradition in Black Women's Fiction.* New York: Oxford University Press, 1993.

Edwards, Jonathan. *A Treatise concerning Religious Affections. In Three Parts. Part I. Concerning the Nature of the Affections, and Their Importance in Religion.* London: Booksellers, 1796.

Eggleston, Edward. *The Hoosier School-Master: A Story of Backwoods Life in Indiana.* New York: Grosset and Dunlap, 1913.

Eigner, Edward. *The Metaphysical Novel in England and America: Dickens, Bulwer, Hawthorne, Melville.* Berkeley: University of California Press, 1978.

Eliot, George. *Middlemarch.* New York: Modern Library, 2000.

Ellis, Edward S. *Seth Jones. Reading the West: An Anthology of Dime Westerns.* Ed. Bill Brown. Boston: Bedford, 1997.

Ellison, Ralph. *Invisible Man.* New York: Vintage, 1989.

Emerson, Ralph Waldo. "Experience." *The Norton Anthology of American Literature.* Vol. B. New York: Norton, 2003.

"Montaigne, or the Skeptic." *Emerson's Prose and Poetry.* New York: Norton, 2001.

"The Poet." *Emerson's Prose and Poetry.* New York: Norton, 2001.

Fern, Fanny. *Ruth Hall: A Domestic Tale of the Present Time.* Ed. and intro. Susan Belasco Smith. New York: Penguin, 1997.

Fisher, Philip. *Hard Facts: Setting and Form in the American Novel.* New York: Oxford University Press, 1985.

Fitzhugh, George. *Cannibals All! Or, Slaves without Masters.* Richmond: Morris, 1857.

Fitzhugh, George. *Sociology for the South; or, The Failure of Free Society.* Richmond: Morris, 1854.

Fliegelman, Jay. *Prodigals and Pilgrims: The American Revolution against Patriarchal Authority, 1750–1850.* Cambridge: Cambridge University Press, 1982.

Foster, Hannah. *The Coquette.* New York: Penguin, 1996.

Foucault, Michel. *Discipline and Punish: The Birth of the Prison.* New York: Pantheon, 1977.

Frankfurt, Harry. *The Importance of What We Care About: Philosophical Essays.* Cambridge: Cambridge University Press, 1988.

Franklin, Benjamin. *The Autobiography of Benjamin Franklin.* New York: Dover, 1996.

Friedman, Lawrence M. *Crime and Punishment in American History.* New York: Basic, 1993.

Fussell, Edwin. *Frontier: American Literature and the American West.* Princeton: Princeton University Press, 1965.

Gardner, Jared. *Master Plots: Race and the Founding of an American Literature.* Baltimore: Johns Hopkins University Press, 1998.

Garland, Hamlin. "The Future of Fiction." *Arena* (April 1893): 513–24.

"Under the Lion's Paw." *Main-Travelled Roads.* Boston: Arena, 1891.

Gellner, Ernest. *Postmodernism, Reason, and Religion.* New York: Routledge, 1992.

Gilmore, Michael T. "The Book Marketplace I." *The Columbia History of the American Novel.* Ed. Emory Elliot. New York: Columbia University Press, 1991. 46–71.

Girard, René. *Deceit, Desire and the Novel.* Baltimore: Johns Hopkins University Press, 1965.

Gossett, Thomas F. *"Uncle Tom's Cabin" and American Culture.* Dallas: Southern Methodist University Press, 1985.

Harper, Frances E. W. *Iola Leroy; or, Shadows Uplifted.* Boston: Beacon, 1987.

Harris, George Washington. *Sut Lovingood's Yarns.* New Haven: Yale University Press, 1966.

Hartman, Saidiya. *Scenes of Subjection: Terror, Slavery, and Self-Making in Nineteenth-Century America.* New York: Oxford University Press, 1997.

Hawthorne, Nathaniel. "My Kinsman, Major Molineux." *The Norton Anthology of American Literature.* Vol. B. New York: Norton, 2003.
  *The Blithesdale Romance.* New York: Penguin, 1983.
  *The House of the Seven Gables.* New York: Modern Library, 2001.
  *The Scarlet Letter.* Boston: Houghton Mifflin, 2002.
Heimert, Alan. *Religion and the American Mind: From the Great Awakening to the Revolution.* Cambridge MA: Harvard University Press, 1966.
Hendler, Glenn. *Public Sentiments: Structures of Feeling in Nineteenth-Century American Literature.* Chapel Hill: University of North Carolina Press, 2001.
Hentz, Caroline Lee, *The Planter's Northern Bride.* Chapel Hill: University of North Carolina Press, 1970.
Hobsbawm, Eric J. *Bandits.* New York: Delacorte, 1969.
Hooper, Johnson Jones. *Some Adventures of Captain Simon Suggs, Late of the Tallapoosa Volunteers.* Nashville: J. S. Sanders, 1993.
Horsman, Reginald. *Race and Manifest Destiny.* Cambridge MA: Harvard University Press, 1981.
Howard, June. *Form and History in American Literary Naturalism.* Chapel Hill: University of North Carolina Press, 1985.
Howells, William Dean. *A Hazard of New Fortunes.* New York: Meridian, 1994.
  *A Modern Instance.* New York: Penguin, 1984.
  "Introduction." *Dona Perfecta* by Benito Perez Galdos. New York: Harper, 1895.
  *The Rise of Silas Lapham.* Boston: Houghton Mifflin, 1957.
Imlay, Gilbert. *The Emigrants.* New York: Penguin, 1998.
Irving, Washington. "Rip Van Winkle." *The Norton Anthology of American Literature.* Vol. B. New York: Norton, 2003.
  "The Legend of Sleepy Hollow." *The Norton Anthology of American Literature.* Vol. B. New York: Norton, 2003.
Jackson, Helen Hunt. *Ramona.* New York: Signet, 1988.
James, Henry. *The American Scene.* New York: Penguin, 1994.
  *The Art of the Novel.* New York: Scribner's, 1962.
  *The Portrait of a Lady.* New York: Norton, 1975.
  "William Dean Howells." *Harper's Weekly* 30 (19 June 1886).
James, William. *A Pluralistic Universe. William James: Writings, 1902–1910.* New York: Library of America, 1987.
  *Pragmatism and Other Writings.* New York: Penguin, 2000.
  *The Present Dilemma in Philosophy. William James: Writings, 1902–1910.* New York: Library of America, 1987.
Jefferson, Thomas. *Notes on the State of Virginia.* Chapel Hill: University of North Carolina Press, 1982.
Jewett, Sarah Orne. *A Country Doctor.* New York: Meridian, 1986.
  *The Country of Pointed Firs and Other Stories.* New York: Doubleday, 1956.
Jones, Paul Christian. "The Danger of Sympathy: Edgar Allan Poe's 'Hop Frog' and the Abolitionist Rhetoric of Pathos." *Journal of American Studies* 35 (2001): 239–54.

Kaplan, Amy. *The Social Construction of American Realism.* Chicago: University of Chicago Press, 1989.

Kennedy, John Pendleton. *Swallow Barn; or, Sojourn in the Old Dominion.* Philadelphia: Lippincott, 1860.

Kern, Stephen. *A Cultural History of Causality: Science, Murder Novels, and Systems of Thought.* Princeton: Princeton University Press, 2004.

Kettner, James H. *The Development of American Citizenship, 1608–1870.* Chapel Hill: University of North Carolina Press, 1978.

Kirkland, Caroline. *A New Home, Who'll Follow? Or, Glimpses of Western Life.* New Brunswick: Rutgers University Press, 1990.

Kloppenberg, James T. *Uncertain Victory: Social Democracy and Progressivism in European and American Thought – 1870–1920.* New York: Oxford University Press, 1986.

Kolodny, Annette. *The Land before Her: Fantasy and Experience of the American Frontiers, 1630–1860.* Chapel Hill: University of North Carolina Press, 1984.

Lears, T. J. Jackson. *No Place of Grace: Antimodernism and the Transformation of American Culture, 1880–1920.* New York: Pantheon, 1981.

Lentz, Perry. *Private Fleming at Chancellorsville: "The Red Badge of Courage" and the Civil War.* Missoula: University of Missouri Press, 2006.

Levine, George. *The Realistic Imagination: English Fiction from Frankenstein to Lady Chatterley.* Chicago: University of Chicago Press, 1981.

Levine, Robert S. *Conspiracy and Romance: Studies in Brockden Brown, Cooper, Hawthorne, and Melville.* Cambridge: Cambridge University Press, 1989.

Leyda, Jay. *The Melville Log: A Documentary Life of Herman Melville, 1819–1891.* New York: Harcourt Brace, 1951.

Lincoln, Abraham. "Speech at Peoria, Illinois, Oct 16, 1854." *Collected Works of Abraham Lincoln.* Vol. II. New Brunswick: Rutgers University Press, 1990.

Lippard, George. *Blanche of Brandywine or, September the Eleventh, 1777; A Romance of the Revolution.* Philadelphia: Peterson, 1846.

*The Ladye Annabel; or, The Doom of the Poisoner.* Philadelphia: Berford, 1844.

*The Quaker City; or, The Monks of Monk Hall. A Romance of Philadelphia Life, Mystery, and Crime.* Amherst: University of Massachusetts Press, 1995.

Longstreet, Augustus B. *Georgia Scenes, Characters, Incidents &c. in the First Half Century of the Republic.* Savannah: Library of Georgia, 1992.

Looby, Christopher. *Voicing America: Language, Literary Form and the Origins of the United States.* Chicago: University of Chicago Press, 1996.

Lukács, Georg. *The Theory of the Novel.* Cambridge MA: MIT, 1990.

Madison, James, Alexander Hamilton, and John Jay. *The Federalist Papers.* New York: Penguin, 1987.

Maine, Henry. *Ancient Law: Its Connection with the Early History of Society and Its Relation to Modern Ideas.* London: J. Murray, 1930.

Martin, Terence. *Parables of Possibility: The American Need for Beginnings.* New York: Columbia University Press, 1995.

Marx, Leo. *The Machine in the Garden: Technology and the Pastoral Ideal in America*. New York: Oxford University Press, 1964.

McKeon, Michael. *The Origins of the English Novel, 1600–1740*. Baltimore: Johns Hopkins University Press, 2002.

Melville, Herman, "Bartleby, the Scrivener." *"Bartleby" and "Benito Cereno."* New York: Dover, 1990.

"Benito Cereno." *"Bartleby" and "Benito Cereno"*. New York: Dover, 1990.

*Moby-Dick; or, The Whale*. New York: Signet, 1961.

*Pierre; or, The Ambiguities*. New York: Library of America, 1984.

*The Confidence-Man: His Masquerade*. New York: Signet, 1964.

"The Tartarus of Maids." *The Norton Anthology of American Literature*. Vol. B. New York: Norton, 2003.

Merish, Lori. *Sentimental Materialism: Gender, Commodity Culture, and Nineteenth-Century American Literature*. Durham: Duke University Press, 2000.

Michaels, Walter Benn. *The Gold Standard and the Logic of Naturalism*. Berkeley: University of California Press, 1987.

Mill, John Stuart. *Autobiography*. Hazleton: Penn State University Press, 2004.

Mitchell, Isaac. *The Asylum; or, Alonzo and Melissa*. Poughkeepsie: Nelson, 1811.

Montaigne, Michel Eyquem de. "Of Experience." *The Complete Essays of Montaigne*. Stanford: Stanford University Press, 1958.

Moses, Wilson. *The Golden Age of Black Nationalism, 1850–1925*. Hamden: Archon, 1978.

Muthu, Sankar. *Enlightenment against Empire*. Princeton: Princeton University Press, 2003.

Nelson, Dana D. *The Word in Black and White: Reading "Race" in American Literature, 1638–1867*. New York: Oxford University Press, 1993.

Noble, Marianne. "The Ecstasies of Sentimental Wounding in *Uncle Tom's Cabin*." *Yale Journal of Criticism* 10.2 (1997): 295–320.

Norris, Frank. *McTeague*. New York: Penguin, 1982.

*Ogden* v. *Saunders*. 25 US 213 (1827).

Otis, James. *The Rights of British Colonies Asserted*. London: J. Williams, 1766.

Page, Thomas Nelson. *In Ole Virginia*. New York: Scribner's, 1895.

Pateman, Carole. *The Sexual Contract*. Stanford: Stanford University Press, 1988.

Pattee, Fred Lewis. "Introduction." *Wieland; Or The Transformation. An American Tale*. New York: Harcourt, 1926.

Phelps, Elizabeth Stuart. *The Silent Partner*. New York: Feminist, 1983.

Poe, Edgar Allan. "The Imp of the Perverse." *The Norton Anthology of American Literature*. Vol. B. New York: Norton, 2003.

*The Narrative of Arthur Gordon Pym of Nantucket*. New York: Penguin, 1999.

"Twice-Told Tales." *Edgar Allan Poe: Essays and Reviews*. New York: Library of America, 1984.

Poirier, Richard. *A World Elsewhere: The Place of Style in American Literature*. New York: Oxford University Press, 1966.

Porte, Joel. *The Romance in America: Studies in Cooper, Poe, Hawthorne, Melville, and James.* Middletown: Wesleyan University Press, 1969.

Porter, Carolyn. *Seeing and Being: The Plight of the Participant Observer in Emerson, James, Adams, and Faulkner.* Middletown: Wesleyan University Press, 1981.

Posnock, Ross. *The Trial of Curiosity: Henry James, William James, and the Challenge of Modernity.* New York: Oxford University Press, 1991.

Reynolds, David S. *Faith in Fiction: The Emergence of Religious Literature in America.* Cambridge MA: Harvard University Press, 1981.

Reynolds, David S., ed. *George Lippard, Prophet of Protest: Writings of an American Radical, 1822–1854.* New York: P. Lang, 1986.

Reynolds, J. N. "Mocha Dick: or the White Whale of the Pacific: A Leaf from a Manuscript Journal." *The Knickerbocker, or New-York Monthly Magazine* 13.5 (May 1839): 377–92.

Reynolds, Larry J. "*The Scarlet Letter* and Revolutions Abroad." *American Literature* 57 (1985): 44–67.

Richmond *Enquirer*, 23 January 1857.

Ridge, John Rollin (Yellow Bird). *The Life and Adventures of Joaquín Murieta, the Celebrated California Bandit.* San Francisco: Cooke, 1955.

Riis, Jacob A. *How the Other Half Lives: Studies among the Tenements of New York.* New York: Dover, 1971.

Ringe, Donald A. *American Gothic: Imagination and Reason in Nineteenth-Century Fiction.* Lexington: University Press of Kentucky, 1982.

Romero, Lora. *Home Fronts: Domesticity and Its Critics in the Antebellum United States.* Durham: Duke University Press, 1997.

Roosevelt, Theodore. *The Winning of the West.* Vol. I. New York: Putnam, 1926.

Rowson, Susanna. *Charlotte Temple and Lucy Temple.* New York: Penguin, 1991.

Rubin, Jr., Louis D. *The Edge of the Swam: A Study in the Literature and Society of the Old South.* Baton Rouge: Louisiana State University Press, 1989.

Ruiz de Burton, María Amparo. *The Squatter and the Don.* Houston: Arte Público, 1992.

  *Who Would Have Thought It?* Houston: Arte Público, 1995.

Rush, Rebecca. *Kelroy.* New York: Oxford University Press, 1992.

Ruttenburg, Nancy. *Democratic Personality: Popular Voice and the Trial of American Authorship.* Stanford: Stanford University Press, 1998.

Schuyler, George. "The Negro-Art Hokum." *Nation* 122 (16 June 1926): 662–63.

Sedgwick, Catharine Maria. *Hope Leslie; Or, Early Times in the Massachusetts.* New Brunswick: Rutgers University Press, 1999.

Simms, William Gilmore. *The Yemassee: A Romance of Carolina.* 2 vols. New York: Harpers, 1844.

  *Woodcraft* (originally published under title *The Sword and the Distaff*). Philadelphia: Lippincott, 1852.

Simpson, Lewis P. *The Dispossessed Garden: Pastoral and History in Southern Literature.* Athens: University of Georgia Press, 1975.

Sinclair, Upton. *The Jungle*. New York: Signet, 1960.

Sklar, Kathryn Kish. *Catharine Beecher: A Study in American Domesticity*. New Haven: Yale University Press, 1973.

Slotkin, Richard. *Gunfighter Nation: The Myth of the Frontier in Twentieth-Century America*. New York: Atheneum, 1992.

    *Regeneration through Violence: The Mythology of the American Frontier, 1600–1860*. Middletown: Wesleyan University Press, 1973.

Smith, Henry Nash. *Virgin Land: The American West as Symbol and Myth*. Cambridge MA: Harvard University Press, 1950.

Smith, Rogers. *Civic Ideals: Conflicting Visions of Citizenship in U.S. History*. New Haven: Yale University Press, 1997.

Southworth, E. D. E. N. *The Hidden Hand; Or, Capitola the Madcap*. New Brunswick: Rutgers University Press, 1988.

Spengeman, William C. *The Adventurous Muse: The Poetics of American Fiction, 1789–1900*. New Haven: Yale University Press, 1977.

Stanley, Amy Dru. *From Bondage to Contract: Wage Labor, Marriage, and the Market in the Age of Slave Emancipation*. Cambridge: Cambridge University Press, 1998.

Stephens, Ann. *Malaeska: The Indian Wife of the White Hunter. Reading the West: An Anthology of Dime Westerns*. Ed. Bill Brown. Boston: Bedford, 1997.

Stoddard, Elizabeth. *The Morgesons*. New York: Penguin, 1997.

Stowe, Harriet Beecher. *Men of Our Times; or, Leading Patriots of the Day*. Hartford: Hartford, 1868.

    *Uncle Tom's Cabin*. New York: Norton, 1994.

Streeby, Shelley. *American Sensations: Class, Empire, and the Production of Popular Culture*. Berkeley: University of California Press, 2002.

Sue, Eugène. *The Mysteries of Paris*. New York: Fertig, 1987.

Sumner, Charles. "Freedom National, Slavery Sectional." *The Works of Charles Sumner*. Vol. III. Boston: Lee and Shepard, 1872.

    "The Antislavery Enterprise: Its Necessity, Practicability, and Dignity." *The Works of Charles Sumner*. Vol. IV. Boston: Lee and Shepard, 1872.

Sumner, William Graham. *What the Social Classes Owe to Each Other*. New York: Arno, 1972.

Sundquist, Eric J. "Slavery, Revolution, and the American Renaissance." *The American Renaissance Reconsidered*. Ed. Walter Benn Michaels and Donald E. Pease. Baltimore: Johns Hopkins University Press, 1985. 1–33.

    *To Wake the Nations: Race in the Making of American Literature*. Cambridge MA: Harvard University Press, 1993.

Sutherland, Gillian. *Faith, Duty, and the Power of Mind: The Cloughs and Their Circle, 1820–1960*. Cambridge: Cambridge University Press, 2006.

Tate, Claudia. *Domestic Allegories of Political Desire: The Black Heroine's Text at the Turn of the Century*. New York: Oxford University Press, 1992.

Tenney, Tabitha. *Female Quixotism: Exhibited in the Romantic Opinions and Extravagant Adventures of Dorcasina Sheldon*. New York: Oxford University Press, 1992.

Thayer, H. S. *Meaning and Action: A Critical History of Pragmatism*. Indianapolis: Bobbs, 1981.

Thomas, Brook. *American Literary Realism and the Failed Promise of Contract*. Berkeley: University of California Press, 1997.

Thompson, George. *Venus in Boston, and Other Tales of Nineteenth-Century City Life*. Amherst: University of Massachusetts Press, 2002.

Tzvetan, Todorov. *Mikhail Bakhtin: The Dialogic Principle*. Minneapolis: University of Minnesota Press, 1984.

Tompkins, Jane. *Sensational Designs: The Cultural Work of American Fiction, 1790–1860*. New York: Oxford University Press, 1985.

Tourgee, Albion. *A Fool's Errand: A Novel of the South during Reconstruction*. New York: Cosimo, 2005.

Twain, Mark. *A Connecticut Yankee in King Arthur's Court*. New York: Bantam, 1981.

  *Adventures of Huckleberry Finn*. New York: Norton, 1977.

  "Fenimore Cooper's Literary Offenses." *North American Review* 156 (July 1895): 1–12.

  *Pudd'nhead Wilson*. New York: Penguin, 1987.

Tynan, Daniel J. "J. N. Reynolds's *Voyage of the Potomac*: Another Source for *The Narrative of Arthur Gordon Pym*." *Poe Studies* 4.2 (December 1971): 35–37.

Warner, Susan. *The Wide, Wide World*. New York: Feminist, 1987.

Warren, Robert Penn. *Homage to Theodore Dreiser*. New York: Random House, 1971.

Washington, Booker T. *Up from Slavery: An Autobiography*. New York: Carol, 1989.

Watt, Ian. *The Rise of the Novel*. Berkeley: University of California Press, 1957.

Webb, Frank J. *The Garies and Their Friends*. Baltimore: Johns Hopkins University Press, 1997.

Webber, Charles W. *Old Hicks the Guide; or, Adventures in the Camanche Country in Search of a Gold Mine*. Upper Saddle River: Gregg, 1970.

Weinstein, Cindy. *Family, Kinship, and Sympathy in Nineteenth-Century American Literature*. Cambridge: Cambridge University Press, 2004.

  "The Slave Narrative and Sentimental Literature." *The Cambridge Companion to the African American Slave Narrative*. Ed. Audrey Fisch. Cambridge: Cambridge University Press, 2007. 115–36.

Wexler, Laura. *Tender Violence: Domestic Visions in an Age of U.S. Imperialism*. Chapel Hill: University of North Carolina Press, 2000.

Wheeler, Edward L. *Deadwood Dick, The Prince of the Road; or, The Black Rider of the Black Hills*. *Reading the West: An Anthology of Dime Westerns*. Ed. Bill Brown. Boston: Bedford, 1997.

Whitman, Walt. *Leaves of Grass*. New York: Norton, 1973.

Williston, Samuel. "Freedom of Contract." *Cornell Law Quarterly* 6 (1921): 365–79.

Wills, Garry. *Inventing America: Jefferson's Declaration of Independence.* New York: Vintage, 1979.

Wilson, Harriet. *Our Nig.* Boston: Rand and Avery, 1859.

Wood, Gordon S. *The Radicalism of the American Revolution.* New York: Vintage, 1993.

Woodward, C. Vann. *The Burden of Southern History.* Baton Rouge: Louisiana State University Press, 1993.

Ziff, Larzer. *Writing in the New Nation: Prose, Print, and Politics in the Early United States.* New Haven: Yale University Press, 1991.

# Index